# THE FEATHER QUEST

## OTHER BOOKS BY PETE DUNNE

*Hawks in Flight*

*The Wind Masters*

*Tales of a Low-Rent Birder*

*More Tales of a Low-Rent Birder*

*Before the Echo*

*Small-Headed Flycatcher*

# THE FEATHER

A MARINER BOOK

Houghton Mifflin Company

BOSTON · NEW YORK

# QUEST

## A NORTH AMERICAN BIRDER'S YEAR

### Pete Dunne

WITH A NEW INTRODUCTION
BY THE AUTHOR

*Foreword by Roger Tory Peterson*

First Mariner Books edition 1999

Introduction copyright © 1999 by Pete Dunne
Copyright © 1992 by Pete Dunne
Foreword copyright © 1992 by Roger Tory Peterson

For information about permission to reproduce selections from this book,
write to Permissions, Houghton Mifflin Company, 215 Park Avenue South,
New York, New York 10003.

First published by Dutton, an imprint of New American Library,
a division of Penguin Books USA Inc.

*Library of Congress Cataloging-in-Publication Data*
Dunne, Pete, date.
    The feather quest : a North American birder's year / Pete Dunne ; foreword by Roger
Tory Peterson ; with a new introduction by the author.
        p. cm.
    Originally published: New York, N.Y., U.S.A. : Dutton, c1992. With new introd.
    Includes bibliographical references.
    ISBN 0-395-92790-0
    1. Bird watching—United States.   2. Birds—United States.
3. Bird watching—Canada.   4. Birds—Canada.   I. Title.
[QL682.d86    1999]
598'.07'23473–dc21            99-22725
                        CIP

Printed in the United States of America

QUM 10 9 8 7 6 5 4 3 2

o parents

*(who have the wisdom to guide and the confidence not to lead)*

# CONTENTS

# ACKNOWLEDGMENTS

HE NAMES OF THOSE WHO PROVIDED AID, COMfort and companionship during our travels or who assisted in their accounting reads like a partial *Who's Who of North American Birding*. Linda and I extend grateful acknowledgment and thanks to some very special people (and apologize in advance to any whose names have been omitted).

To: Gerald Adams, Otto Ademec and Rene Miller, Skip Ambrose, Mickey Baker, Louis Banker, Benton Basham, Rick Blom, Rick Bonnie, Roger and Jan Boyd and all the members of the Baldwin City Bird Club, Christi Carmichel, Bonnie Cartier, Chita Cassibry, Michael Carlson, Sue Clark, Mort Cooper, Jim Danzenbaker, Michael Danzenbaker, Dale Delaney, Charlie Delmas, Gale and Pat DeWind, Gladys Donahue-Schumacher, Bill Drew and other stalwart members of the Brookline Bird Club, Gerald and Irene Dunne, Kim Eckert, John Economidy, Victor Emanuel, Davis Finch, Andy Farnsworth, Gene and Ruth Goellner, Rosemary Gaymer, Red and Louise Gambill, Bill and Laura Lee Graber, David and Linda Hedges, Joe Himmel, Tom Hince, Cynthia House, Greg Jackson, Christine Kapsa, Kenn Kaufman, Jeff Kingery, Dave Kreuper, Howard Langridge, Ann LeDuc, Paul Lehman, and Shawneen Finnegan, Jean Lloyd, Eileen Lotz, Ed Manners, Phil Mattocks, Guy McKaskie, Greg Mensik, Gerry and Jerry Morgan, Robert Morse, Jody and Skip Mott, Bill Murphy, Roger and Ginny Peterson, Tom Pincelli, Galen Pittman, Jan and Pres Ripley, Charliene Roemer, B. J. and Sharon Rose, Gary Rosenberg, Bob Shawler, Debra Shearwater, Akimi Shono, David Sibley, Ted Simons, Harriet Smith, P. William and Susan Smith, "Smitty" of Scheelite Canyon, Bill Snyder, Walter and Sally Spofford, Judy Toups, Peter Whelan, Hal Wierenga, Charlie Wonderly.

Most favored acknowledgment status is hereby granted to:

Ann and Bob Ellis, Linda's parents, who pretty nearly subsidized our two-month California campaign.

Peggy Wang for her cartographic skills.

Larry Balch, Roger Boyd, Jim Brett, Bob and Lisa Dittrick, Kim Eckert, Victor Emanuel, Don Freiday, Shawneen Finnegan, Red and Louise Gambill, Tom Hince, Pete Isleib, Kenn Kaufman, Lynn Kaufman, John Kricher, Roger Peterson, Ginny Peterson, Tom Pincelli, Mary Lou Schadt, Debra Shearwater, and Judy Toups, whose 1990 holidays were interrupted by the appearance of unsolicited, unwanted, and barely readable manuscripts that begged to be reviewed.

To Bill Boyle, whose careful review of the entire manuscript saved me from considerable embarrassment.

To Dr. Paul Kerlinger for making me look as if I know a good deal more about the mechanics of songbird migration than I really do.

To Fletcher Roberts, Editor, New Jersey Sunday Section of *The New York Times,* who never knew where I was, or whether I would make a deadline.

To Dorothy Clair, EDITOR, whose peculiar cross it is to be burdened with my "raw material." No editor in the history of writing had deleted more superfluous commas with more cheerful equanimity.

To Tom Gilmore and the entire staff of the New Jersey Audubon Society, who had to assume added duties while one of their cohorts just up and went birding. I salute them, the finest environmental force ever assembled beneath an organizational banner.

Finally, a special note to readers: although *The Feather Quest* chronicles Linda's and my travels during 1989, two places—Attu and the Arctic National

Wildlife Refuge, both in Alaska—were visited in 1990, then integrated into the itinerary and text. You will understand that this was done out of logistical necessity. Spring is a short season, crowded with events, and as much as birders (and writers and photographers) might like, we cannot be everywhere at once.

## by Roger Tory Peterson

ETE DUNNE WAS JUST A TODDLER SCARCELY OFF formula, and Linda was not even born, when my British colleague, James Fisher, and I set out in 1953 on our grand tour around North America in search of birds. Over the years, at least half a dozen friends and acquaintances were inspired by *Wild America*, the book that chronicles our adventure, and set out to savor the birds of the continent for themselves.

Some, like Stuart Keith, Kenn Kaufman, and Ted Parker, were motivated by the listing game, to see if they could top the number of birds seen by James and me. Pete and Linda took a different tack. Their quest was not to capture a record but to gather an impression of a continent filled with riches. With this objective and with fresh eyes, they traveled to many of the birding hot spots visited by James and me.

As I have said before (in fact, as I say to Pete and Linda in the pages of this book), the observation of birds can be many things, depending on who you are and what you are. It can be a science, as it is with the members of the American Ornithologists' Union, the Wilson Ornithological Club, and the Cooper Ornithological Society, many of whom hold academic positions in museums or universities and who go deeply into the whys and wherefores of avian biology. Bird watching can also be an art—a visual thing—as it is for those who paint, or who practice a serious level of bird photography. I do both. My painting, for which I was trained academically, is hard work; it doesn't just flow from the tip of the brush. Photography is my therapy. There is a sporting immediacy to it, but it can also be an art form if it goes beyond simple "point and shoot" photography.

Birding can be a game or a sport, as it is with the listers, who prefer to be called "birders" rather than bird watchers. This large and growing crowd of binocular addicts is highly competitive, ranging from beginners to "hard-core" types who aspire to see over 700 species of birds north of the Mexican border. James Fisher and I tallied just over this number on our epic journey (although we did dip across the border into Mexico—something that would, now, be considered technically out-of-bounds).

The great majority of bird watchers are not goaded by the competitive drive of the listers. They watch birds simply for pleasure, mostly within the confines of the backyard or garden. They probably own a field guide to the birds—perhaps one of my own Eastern or Western guides. They may not own a pair of binoculars or be able to identify more than fifty or a hundred species of birds. No matter, bird watching is a recreation enjoyed by many millions; one that brings people to an awareness of the natural world and may lead eventually to environmental concern and even activism.

One of the best birders in Texas, a parish priest who you will meet in the pages of this book, says that watching birds can even be a religious experience. I can see that. Birds are unique in the animal world for having feathered wings, like angels. As another devout friend puts it, "They are God's messengers."

In sum, and in truth, birds can be anything or everything depending on the person. As James Fisher commented, they can even be a bore if you are a bore.

Pete Dunne's delight seems to be the challenge of identifying birds, and not just by the obvious field marks, but by their *gestalt*—the *jizz* (general impression and shape)—and actions by which they can be named on the far horizon long before the confirming field marks are obvious. And while this book, this feather quest, does look far, clear to birding's future in fact, it also looks close, at people—those who share our passionate obsession, and a few who do not. Being of Irish persuasion Pete has a way with words; a "wordsmith" we might call him. This book is full of lively dialogue with Linda, with friends, and whomever they meet as they explore the continent.

One of birding's greatest challenges is the Big Day or Century Run, where the idea is to spot as many birds as possible in a twenty-four-hour period. Later Big Days were transformed into "bird-a-thons" and are widely used as a vehicle for raising funds for conservation. It was Pete Dunne who took things a step further when he organized the first "World Series of Birding" in 1984. Thirteen teams competed *against each other* within the state of New Jersey. Our team (The Guerrilla Birding Team) won with a total of 201.

In chapter nine Pete takes his Guerrilla team to 210, a new record, but this time I was with them only in spirit. My advanced years can no longer take the physical strain. But read about it, and read about the Christmas count, too. Read about the great birding hot spots such as Cape May, the Everglades, the Gulf States, the Lower Rio Grande, Southeastern Arizona, the West Coast and Alaska—so many of the hops, skips and jumps that Fisher and I took, but with such a difference! Things have evolved. Not so much the birds, but the people who watch them, and their interactions.

Recently in an interview I was asked, "What good are birds?" Taken aback, I blurted, "They are alive, aren't they?" My interviewer expected me to go into the usual palaver about their beneficial habits—eating insects and all that. True, they are valuable as a "litmus of the environment," but need we always justify our concern for them in an egocentric way, arguing that whatever happens to them could eventually happen to us? Birds have rights of their own; they were here long before *homo sapiens.*

We react to birds, most of us, because they are such a vivid expression of life. They are as attractive as flowers and butterflies. But in addition they are agreeably vocal, each with a language of its own. They have wings and can come and go as they please. They have everything—or so it seems.

But we, the dominant primates, hold their survival in our hands. Some birds, like House Sparrows and Rock Doves, can live with us on our own terms. Others, more environmentally vulnerable, cannot. It is our moral duty, the humane thing, to save them from fading away. Extinction is forever. What would the world be without birds?

Think about that as you enjoy *The Feather Quest.*

—*Roger Tory Peterson*

# INTRODUCTION

*I*T HAS BEEN TEN YEARS SINCE LINDA AND I SET OUT ON the adventure recounted in this book. While much of the substance of the story remains as true today as it was then, some things have changed, of course.

First, and perhaps foremost, the popularity of birding has continued to grow. The waitress in Chapter 2 who thought birding seemed "kind of boring" may or may not still believe that. If she does, she is increasingly in the minority. Estimates are that between 1985 and 1995 the popularity of birding increased 150 percent, and this trend is expected to continue. In fact, it is projected that the popularity of "North America's second most popular outdoor activity" will continue to grow faster than the population well into the next century.

The economic ramifications of this change are profound; the last decade has been marked by a proliferation of stores that specialize in meeting the equipment and informational needs of birders and by an exponential increase in the number of birding festivals (now more than one hundred). It has been my privilege to address many of these, including festivals in England and Israel. Were Linda and I to embark on the Feather Quest today, be assured that a chapter focusing on the fun and excitement of birding festivals would be included.

I am happy to tell you that many of the personalities who engaged us during our travels are just as engaging today. If you travel to Bentsen–Rio Grande State

Park you will still be glad-handed by Winter Texans Red and Louise Gambill. Father Tom Pincelli is still much involved with birds and birding in the Rio Grande Valley, despite a change of parish. Judy Toups remains the grande dame of Mississippi coast birding. Larry Balch's Attour enterprise still anchors the literal and figurative fringe of North American birding. Debi Shearwater's Monterey pelagic trips remain a celebrated institution. And Ed Amerman, a genial member of our Churchill tour group (who at the age of eighty-five saw his 500th Life Bird), is now ten years and 114 Life Birds to the better. Congratulations, Ed.

You will be less pleased to know that Gerry's Woods, featured in Chapter 7, surrendered to development pressure and that increased birding activity has made for tighter regulations at some key birding areas. The Mexican Crow is no longer found at the Brownsville municipal dump. Like a fair number of other bird species, the Mexican Crow (*Corvus imparatus*) has been renamed. Starting in 1998, birders *just* north of the border in search of *C. imparatus* were on the lookout for the *Tamaulipas* Crow. But in this case, as in others where birds have been reclassified or renamed, I have chosen not to reflect the change in the text of the book. *The Feather Quest* is both a story and a historical document—a snapshot in time. It serves accuracy and history as it stands.

Sadly, some of the people who enliven the pages of the book no longer raise binoculars this side of the void. They include Louis Banker, whose generous heart finally gave out; Pete Isleib, commercial fisherman and Attu leader, who died in a tragic accident while refitting his fishing vessel; co-Attu leader Terry Savaloja, who succumbed to a rare disease contracted while birding in the tropics; and Walter, Arizona, of Portal (and Golden Eagle and hummingbird) fame.

The accounting of those whose names appear in this Afterlife List is, of course, headed by Dr. Roger Tory Peterson, who published his *Field Guide to the Birds* in 1934 and who began work on *A Field Guide to the Angels* July 28, 1996.

Although he was never specifically introduced to readers, Roger Dowding was the bush pilot who flew Linda and me into the Arctic National Wildlife Refuge. He died in 1996 while trying to extract a party that had been weathered in for three days after their scheduled pickup. He reached the limits of his incomparable skill and considerable luck on a mountainside deep in the Brooks Range.

In reading this book, you will not fail to note a strong conservation message; *The Feather Quest* definitely was intended to get people excited about watching birds as a first step toward fostering environmental awareness. You cannot be interested in birds without being protective of them. You cannot be protective of them and not be protective of the habitat that sustains them. If birding is a game, then the earth is its playing field, and the first rule in any game is "protect the playing field."

Some of the changes on the conservation front in the past ten years have been for the better, some for the worse. Many neotropical migrant species have continued their sad decline. Migratory fallouts at key migratory junctions, even at such heralded hot spots as Cape May, are a shadow of their former splendor.

On the other hand, Sharp-shinned Hawks, whose decline is discussed in Chapter 16, are much recovered in numbers. Kirtland's Warbler has responded positively to concerted management efforts. Waterfowl populations, which suffered a dramatic decline in the 1980s, rebounded in the rain-rich '90s. The California Condor Recovery Program, a work in progress when this book was written, has proven its merit. Young condors have been released in California and into the Grand Canyon, where their chances of establishing a viable population are deemed good.

Linda and I are ten years older, too, and well. Not long after the completion of the Feather Quest we moved to southern New Jersey, and soon thereafter I reassumed the post of director of the New Jersey Audubon Society's Cape May Bird Observatory, a position I hold today. Linda took a different tack. Having mastered outdoor photography, she put her camera aside. Went back to school. Became an emergency room nurse.

We continue to travel in search of birds as often as our time and budget allow. But no matter where we go or how often we go there, it never seems enough. On summer evenings, as we sit on the porch and watch fireflies take the field, or in winter when the flames recede into coals, our talk often turns to our year of the Feather Quest.

Wasn't it fun?

And wasn't it exciting?

And wouldn't you love to do it again?

The answer, of course, is yes. And who's to say? Perhaps some year she and I will put our workaday lives on temporary hold. Grab binoculars. Jump in a camper van. Set a new course on an old familiar road, one that leads by diverging and converging paths to the great birding locations of a continent and the lives of those who share our passion.

But until that time, this is the story of how it happened the last time.

*September 1998*

THE SOUND OF A WELL-SLAMMED SCREEN DOOR echoed through the neighborhood—the only sound on a day so dull that even the grass looked bored.

"Donna Jean McDowell! How many times do I have to tell you kids not to slam that door! You get back here this instant!"

But if Donna even heard her mother's familiar litany it didn't stop her. It was her birthday, and birthdays impart immunity from everyday standards. Pigtails flying, knees flashing through dungarees that had lost all dignity, one of history's great tomboys was already clearing her driveway and cornering hard en route to our house. From my spot on our front steps, I could see that she cradled something in her arms, something important—like a turtle or a kitten (probably a turtle; Donna was a real ace when it came to finding box turtles).

Like a deer, like a nine-year-old girl with a secret so delicious that it will die unless it is shared, Donna sprinted past the Le Feveres' mailbox, making the risky cut inside, running right across the lawn. Her pace never slackened until she reached the steps, panting through a smile so wide it almost doubled back on itself.

"LookwhatIgotformybirthday," she said, displaying her prizes. One hand held a pair of binoculars, the other a book—a book about birds.

There are events that shift the axis upon which lives turn. I didn't know it then, didn't know that these two items given to a childhood chum had the power to change a life. But they did. Mine. At the time, I just appreciated them for what they were. Not clothes. Not toys. But real *grown-up presents.* To a child, there is nothing in the world quite so important as growing up.

"Let's go on a bird hike," she invited.

"OK," I remember saying. "When?"

"Tomorrow," she fairly shouted. "Early."

"How early?" I wanted to know.

"*Real* early," she promised.

And it was, too.

# THE FEATHER QUEST

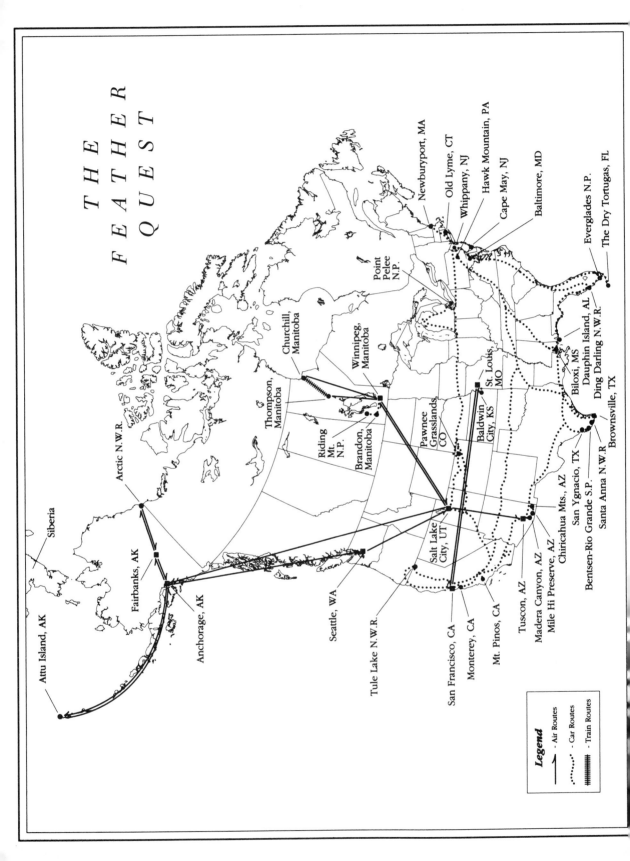

*T H E*
*F E A T H E R*
*Q U E S T*

Siberia

Attu Island, AK

Arctic N.W.R.

Fairbanks, AK

Anchorage, AK

Seattle, WA

Tule Lake N.W.R.

San Francisco, CA

Monterey, CA

Mt. Pinos, CA

Tuscon, AZ

Madera Canyon, AZ

Mile Hi Preserve, AZ

Chiricahua Mts., AZ

San Ygnacio, TX

Bentsen-Rio Grande S.P.

Santa Anna N.W.R

Brownsville, TX

Salt Lake City, UT

Pawnee Grasslands, CO

Baldwin City, KS

St. Louis, MO

Thompson, Manitoba

Riding Mt. N.P.

Brandon, Manitoba

Churchill, Manitoba

Winnipeg, Manitoba

Point Pelee N.P.

Newburyport, MA

Old Lyme, CT

Whippany, NJ

Hawk Mountain, PA

Cape May, NJ

Baltimore, MD

Everglades N.P.

The Dry Tortugas, FL

Biloxi, MS

Dauphin Island, AL

Ding Darling N.W.R.

**Legend**

⟋ - Air Routes

⋯⋯ - Car Routes

╫╫╫╫ - Train Routes

# 1 • WHIPPANY, NEW JERSEY:

## Birding with the Kid

HE DOOR CLOSED WITH A MUFFLED *CLICK*. WE paused, waiting for our eyes to adjust to sudden darkness, filtering the world through night-sharpened senses. From one of the houses lining the street, a dog barked, putting intruders on notice that its vigilance had not been compromised by a night of New Year's revelry. Somewhere to the east a rooster crowed.

Probably the last rooster in Whippany, I thought.

"Ready?" I asked.

"Yes," she said. The word appeared as a small white cloud.

Hand in hand, moving like hunted things, we crossed the patio and edged onto the withered grass. Silent as winter shadows, senses strained, we listened for the signal that would usher in the New Year and mark the first step of our adventure. It would happen soon, we knew. It might be any one of a dozen audio clues. But at precisely what moment and from which direction the signal would come, that was impossible to say. That was part of the game. There was nothing for us to do but listen and wait, while the cold probed for weak spots in our goose-down armor, while the night sky paled at the edges.

"Mockingbird," Linda chanted, the last syllable forming a smile that stayed on her face. The first bird of the New Year was hers.

Yes, I'd heard it, too—a scratchy rattle; a noise like a child dragging a stick over uneven pavement.

"Got it," I said, completing the litany.

"The Year of the Mockingbird," she observed.

"The Year of the Mockingbird," I agreed somewhat ruefully. "I was hoping for a Screech Owl myself."

"Could be worse," she cautioned. "Last year was the Year of the Starling . . ." Linda paused. "Did you hear the cardinal?" she added.

I turned my mind back, mentally recalling the sharp, metallic *pink* note that had sounded as Linda was speaking.

"I heard it," I affirmed. And I *had* heard it, subconsciously. A bird had called in the vicinity of the McDowells' yard, and somewhere in the deductive centers of my brain the sound had been linked to a name: *cardinal*. After thirty-two years, bird identification gets pretty easy; child's play.

But picking out birds by call or identifying them on sight is *not* that easy, not at first, anyway. If I needed to remind myself of this, all I had to do was look around at this suburban backyard thirty miles from Manhattan. This is where it had started for a suburban kid, nudged into a lifelong adventure by a birthday present given to a friend. In the process he discovered more challenge, wonder, and satisfaction than anyone could imagine from a suburban backyard.

"Junco," Linda asserted, pinning a name to a soft twitter coming from the bushes to the left, building up her lead.

"Crow . . ." I countered.

(I'll see your junco.)

". . . And Blue Jay."

(And raise you one.)

There are, in the optimistic estimate of market analysts, eighty million North Americans who are interested in watching birds. The U.S. Fish and Wildlife Service harbors a more conservative scope and view. They say sixty-one million—one in every four Americans. For most, birding's frontier begins and ends right in their backyards. These are people who have discovered the uncomplicated pleasure of watching the birds that share their world; people who can put a name to the birds of lawns and gardens as easily as they might a neighbor.

Every now and again, a Rumpelstiltskin appears at the bird feeder, or the birdbath, a bird that sheds all the common names experience can bring to bear. Goaded by curiosity or pique, the book with all the pictures is consulted until the mystery is solved. Sometimes the episode ends there. Sometimes it doesn't end until the paper work is completed—and a check mark falls next to Rumpelstiltskin's name, maybe even a date.

But there are about seven million Americans who have discovered that this window to the natural world doesn't end at the property line. It opens to the world, paves an avenue of adventure that runs out in every direction. This year, Linda and I would take that road—on a quest across North America. It would carry us to many wild and exciting places and into the lives of a wonderful host of characters—North America's birders.

The road would begin here, where all roads began for me, in my old backyard and in the woods behind my parents' house. And it would begin today, New Year's Day, 1989—an auspicious day and a timely moment for an accounting.

Why auspicious? Because in birding, as in the spirit of New Year's, January first makes all things new again. All the birds tallied last year went the way of the old year at midnight. This morning, Linda and I faced a clean slate and all birds, no matter how common, no matter how often they may have engaged our lives, became new again, became "Year Birds" as the expression goes.

It's just a game, of course, one of many, and it keeps birding fun.

Why timely? Because the century that saw a scientific endeavor (ornithology) transformed into an avocation enjoyed by millions (bird-watching) is ending—and with it, birding's golden age. All the wonder and discovery and bounty—and innocence (yes, particularly the innocence)—that characterized birding in the twentieth century will likely never be known again. The simple fact of the matter is that over much of the globe, birds are declining.

Does this mean an end to birding? No—in fact, just the opposite. Declining numbers put a premium on those that are left, strops a keener edge on people's desire to see them. But the golden age *is* ending. The time is not far off when young birders will listen open-mouthed to the elders rendering accounts of things beyond the reach of dreams—birds whose numbers darkened the skies; mornings in spring that were a mosaic of color and song. Things that in the last decade of the twentieth century, it is *still* possible to see.

If you hurry.

"Mourning Dove," Linda said, breaking into my thoughts, drawing me back to the challenge at hand. "On the wire," she directed.

Yes, I could see it—that is, I could see the silhouette of the bird. I wondered what our young guide would have to say about that—a Mourning Dove in January.

In our travels, we would enlist the skills and local knowledge of birders around the country. (Sharing is one of birding's most fundamental tenets.) The "expert" we were relying upon today was a young fellow . . . ten, maybe eleven. He used to live here about thirty years ago. Then, he grew up; moved away; became a director for the New Jersey Audubon Society—so he could only accompany us in spirit.

"Oh," you say, "he's just a make-believe guide."

Oh *no*! He is very real. As real as memory makes him.

"What was he like?"

Well, if you'll allow for a certain amount of bias, I can probably manage an accounting. He was tall (which is a good thing when you are in the fifth grade) and skinny (which is not). He wore T-shirts in the summer, flannel shirts in winter, jeans and sneakers all year long. The sneakers were usually wet. Often enough, the jeans were, too. Muddy and wet.

He collected baseball cards and pennants, displayed over a room that looked as if it had been pillaged. He hated school and spinach and was moderately well behaved (another way of saying clever enough not to get caught). If through some temporal alchemy he and I were ever to appear in a group photo, most people would note a strong family resemblance.

In the final analysis, the kid was pretty typical of kids that would someday be called Baby Boomers, except in one respect. From the age of seven, the kid had a passion for birds, and he spent every stolen moment watching them. He had a pair of binoculars that his father had brought back from "the war." He had a battered paperback book that contained illustrations and descriptions of 119 common birds. And he had a Nifty Notebook that he kept his records in—the time and place and date of the birds he saw, broken down by season.

This is why I wondered how he might regard a winter sighting of Mourning Dove. Because his notes for "Winter 1962" list twelve species: (Northern) Cardinal, English (House) Sparrow, (European) Starling, Black-capped Chickadee, Tufted Titmouse, Slate-colored (Dark-eyed) Junco, Brown-headed Cowbird, Hairy Woodpecker, Downy Woodpecker, American Tree Sparrow, Song Sparrow, and White-throated Sparrow. Mourning Dove probably would have impressed him. I thought of something else that might impress him, too.

"Let's see if we can get a rise out of the neighborhood Screech Owl before it gets too light," I said. Head drawn back, lips puckered, I gave a gargled whistle that rose and fell—a fair imitation of a screech owl whinny (and one that scores of owls have fallen for over time).

But the "house owl" must have been in a surly mood. It ignored the invitation to engage in a duet. My efforts only succeeded in touching off a canine chorus loud enough to trouble the dreams of even the most sodden New Year's survivor.

"Never used to be so many dogs in this neighborhood," I muttered.

"I think we better get out of here," was all Linda had to say.

I don't think the kid would have been very impressed.

We moved past the oaks where the White-breasted Nuthatch parried with gravity during the summer of 1960; past the limbs that the Baltimore Orioles used to favor with their pendulous nests. Behind the oaks was the thicket where every summer evening, the male Wood Thrush would lure the shadows out of hiding with his solo flute . . . until it was too dark to see a pop fly . . . until "dads" and "fathers" and "papas" would step onto their porches and whistle the kid-specific notes that sent batters, left fielders, and first basemen scurrying for home.

Overhead, visible now against a grainy winter sky, were the branches that had attracted wave after wave of migrating warblers in May 1964. The binoculars I had were good, but the magnification was insufficient. The books that served as field guides were inadequate and misleading. Given these handicaps and a vast amount of inexperience, there were names attached to some of those treetop birds that would *still* constitute state records for New Jersey—if only they had been correct.

But there was treasure gathered from those branches that has not turned into clay in my coffers over time—fire-throated Blackburnian Warblers, zebra-striped Black-and-whites, and jade-colored Tennessee Warblers. Migratory birds that twice each year, regular as the seasons, sweep across North America, putting themselves within the reach of even the most sedentary urban dweller.

To the chagrin of our guide, the trail wasn't where it used to be—in fact, we had to bushwhack through some hedge that wasn't indexed anywhere in memory, then fight our way through a wall of mature pines that had inexplicably sprung up where a bunch of stunted seedlings used to be. Happily, the cinder bed that marked the property's boundary and once served as a railroad right of way wasn't *too* overgrown.

We paused, considering our options, waiting for the several lights that had gone on in several neighbors' bathrooms to wink out. Only when the last dog had been silenced did we realize that the recalcitrant screech owl had finally spoken up. Its muffled whinny was emanating from a nearby tree cavity.

"It's about time," I complained, and for a moment I wished that our local guide could be with us in fact instead of fancy. Eastern Screech-Owl would have been a new bird for him—a "Life Bird," as it is known in the birding vernacular.

Screech owls are not particularly unusual. In fact, they are common woodland species over much of North America. On one auspicious Christmas Bird Count conducted in New Jersey, I whistled twenty-eight out of hiding —several were coaxed so close their wing tips brushed my face. But finding screech owls, like finding most birds, is a learned technique. There are tricks to the trade—tricks you either learn by doing or garner from others.

Braking with our heels, half-falling, we careened down the embankment, thrashing our way through a wall of branches. Leaves crunched beneath the frosted surface. Snow squeaked with cold. Branches stung our ears like hot whips, and toes ached and went numb.

"Didn't you believe in trails when you were a kid?" my wife scolded.

"That seems like a funny question for someone who used to be a back country ranger to ask."

"You don't get flayed crossing an ice field," she tutored.

"You don't get flayed teaching desert survival either, I suppose."

"That's different," she explained.

I turned, hoping to catch the smile that winked across my wife's face, and succeeded. Short and blonde, eyes the colors of van Gogh's palette, Linda looks like and is often accused of being a "California Girl," which is not far from accurate. Born in Pasadena, educated and groomed in the plastic heartland (whose coordinates as anyone, except, perhaps, a New Yorker, will tell you, lie somewhere near, if not right atop the center of the universe), Linda was well on her way to becoming an Olympic skier or concert flutist when the fast track hit a detour. Her parents bought into a cattle ranch in Alberta, Canada, opening up new horizons and career possibilities that would probably send your average Valley Gal Mom into group therapy. These included stints as a staffer with the U.S. Forest Service (1977), as a ranger in Alaska state parks (1979–1981), and as an instructor for the National Outdoor Leadership School (NOLS) (1982–1986), where her specialties included mountaineering, spelunking, ocean kayaking, and desert hiking.

Birding was just a hobby.

The woods opened up as we moved away from the edge. Red maples gave way to oaks; cat briers and blackberry bushes surrendered to dogwoods, hornbeam, and wild grape tangles. A band of Black-capped Chickadees and Tufted Titmice moved through the canopy like a hungry cloud—poking into crevices, searching for insect larvae with the intensity of engineers scanning a rocket booster for cracks or flaws.

"Hold up," I counseled. "Let's see if we can pull something out of this flock."

Winter birds are often flocking birds, a strategy for survival that serves them well. Many eyes see approaching danger better than a single pair of eyes; food discovered by one member of the band may be exploited by others.

Over much of North America, chickadees and titmice form the base of these flocks, and their lively banter makes finding them simple. Other birds sign on with these nomadic bands—hardy birds that thrive at winter's rim and half-hardy species that survive at winter's sufferance.

I tried the screech owl call again, flooding the glen with the warbled challenge. Several birds hesitated, considering the merits of engaging their ancient enemy in a diplomatic harangue. The owl had violated a temporal boundary and, in daylight, right and might were on the side of the flock. Now that we had their attention we tweaked their ire by pishing a hearty stream of invective their way, sending chickadees and titmice into a stuttering rage.

*Pishing*, incidentally, refers to onomatopoetic noises birders make that mimic scolding calls used by birds. If this isn't the definition you had in mind, then you were confusing pishing with something else.

The feathered frenzy swarmed around us, scolding, fretting, some closing to arm's length. White-breasted Nuthatches stalked us from tree trunks. A Downy Woodpecker flew in, rattling a challenge from the left; a squadron of Blue Jays hit the clearing with the coordination of a SWAT team, making the winter woodlands ring with their brassy cries.

"Golden-crowned Kinglet," Linda shouted over the din.

"Creeper," I called simultaneously.

We stared at each other. Brown Creeper and Golden-crowned Kinglets can sound maddeningly alike—a high thin call that barely brushes the upper registry of human hearing. As it was, we'd never know who was right, this time. There *was* a creeper, a furtive brown mouse of a bird working its way up a tree trunk. There was a kinglet too, a tiny, hyperkinetic bird with bright, black eyes and a yellow racing stripe down its crown. It was joined by another kinglet, and another, and then anoth . . .

"Ruby-crowned (Kinglet)!" I exclaimed. A bonus, a tough one, a different species and one that the cold temperatures should have put beyond our reach. The bird was sluggish, stiff with cold. It didn't have the energy to waste in this sort of melee, so we broke off the engagement and continued on. The flock, with the exception of one or two tenacious chickadees, went back to the process of surviving.

"Not a bad little pocket," I observed.

"A *good* pocket," Linda corrected. "Did you used to see kinglets back here when you were a kid?"

I had to think about that for a moment. "No, that came later. When I was in high school."

"Oh," she exclaimed. "Almost an adult!"

"Pretty close," I agreed, ignoring the sarcasm, and I wondered what the kid would have thought of that performance. The kid was more of the quiet stalker type; a Natty Bumpo with Audubon overtones. He didn't know any *real* birders; wouldn't meet any until he'd graduated from college. So he never learned any of the tricks of the birding trade, never heard of pishing.

But I think he would have been impressed. I think it would have made up for the screech owl.

We struck the walking path that circles the Brick Yard Ponds, but the kid ignored it, heading straight for the water's edge. The path, one of those wood-chip affairs favored by municipalities, was cut long after the kid had ceased to be a kid. It replaced the subtle track that circumnavigated the ponds, poking into coves and threading peninsulas, promising and often enough producing discovery around the next bend—sunning bass, painted turtles on logs, the moment frozen in time, when a blue-eyed boy and a golden-eyed heron stood, eye to eye, too startled even to blink.

We gave thought to following the kid and seeking out a trail that probably has greater substance in memory than in fact, but you can only follow a story line so far. We stuck to the yellow-chip road—through the oak and hickory woodlands, past brushy tangles that once harbored grouse, deer, and red fox, and might still. Past the sheltered cove where the phoebes always come first in the spring. Past the sharp, cut bank where a flock of Ring-necked Ducks once materialized out of the snow and landed a dozen feet away—the first Ring-necked Ducks I ever saw; the first and only time in my life I have seen the burnished band encircling the neck of the males that gives the bird its name.

The kid had wandered off as we'd rounded the pond. That's the trouble with memories. They require constant attention. I brought him back for the return trip because there were still some holes in our list. Three of the birds he'd tallied on the Winter 1962 list hadn't been found yet. I was going to hold him to them.

We followed a memory across the meadows where once a trail had been. A Song Sparrow hitched itself up on a milkweed stalk to see what all the commotion was about, and a couple of White-throated Sparrows fled at our approach. But American Tree Sparrows were inexplicably absent.

"Tree sparrows used to be everywhere around here," I said for Linda's benefit.

"Well, they are nowhere now," she said.

The kid was plainly perplexed, too. He wanted to head back to his parents' place. Tree sparrows used to be vermin there, used to just swarm over the birdseed he squandered his allowance on. But the feeders were empty now. My parents were moving; the house was sold. In a week, they'd be gone. They didn't start feeding this year, so as not to leave a lot of feathered minions in the lurch. No, my parents' backyard was not likely to produce tree sparrows today, whatever the precedent.

On the other hand, we'd run out of options.

"Want to head on back?" I asked Linda. "I'll bet Mom's got breakfast whipped into shape."

The kid ran ahead, probably bored with adult company.

"How long did you live here?" Linda asked suddenly.

" 'Til I got out of college," I replied.

She didn't ask why I left, because that's a silly question. I left for the same reason all people leave home. Because one day you realize that all the old paths have become too familiar. Because there is a world of discovery waiting and the first step toward the future is a step away from the past. So you leave. Go chasing rainbows, never thinking that maybe one end of a rainbow is just as good as another.

The kid was waiting for us in the backyard. He always was stubborn (and Linda might argue that very little has changed). A quick glance around showed that I'd been right about tree sparrows. The feeders were empty. Certifiably sparrow-free.

It had been a good morning, a good walk, and a fine way to usher in what would be a New Year of adventure and discovery. I felt bad about leaving on a sour note, but, hey, that's birding. You can't find 'em all.

But the kid wasn't ready to call it quits yet. Real stubborn, you know. I felt him tugging at my resolve, wanting me to go back on over to the corner and maybe try that pishing thing one more time. I didn't think it would do any good, but I suppose I owed him a favor or two.

"Let's try one more thing," I suggested to Linda. "That weedy patch over there used to be the Tree Sparrow Capital of Hanover Township."

We approached the corner, listened for a moment or two, and then I resorted to a little artificial stimulus. Sparrows are fairly secretive. More often than not, pishing makes them hunker down and freeze. But if you bring your index and middle fingers up to your lips, give them a high, sharp, smacking kiss—make a sharp *chip* note, it's not uncommon for even the most secretive sparrow to pop up.

"On the bush," Linda announced. One . . . two . . . no, *three* tree sparrows. *"All right!"* Linda likes tree sparrows. They remind her of Alberta and the ranch where she grew up.

We watched the birds. Admired the subtle interplay of rust and gray. Listened to their musical chatter. Watched them until the thought of breakfast began to intrude.

"Well," Linda invited, "what do you think?"

"I think the kid's got potential."

"What kid?" Linda said.

## 2 • NEWBURYPORT, MASSACHUSETTS:

## River and Roots

*ANN'S DINER*

HE SIGN PROPPED IN THE WINDOW SAID "OPEN." Yellow light poured from the windows, casting shadows that were swallowed by the dirt-studded snow. Careful as a harbor pilot docking an unfamiliar ship, allowing for windage and black ice, we slipped into a berth between flanking sedans—two corroded affairs that looked like they'd been worked over by a mob wielding crowbars, then laid down in salt. Our cranberry-colored camper fresh out of the showroom appeared magnificently out of place.

The diner verged on empty, which is not surprising. Outside it was very cold and very dark, and only one of these things was likely to show much improvement in the next couple of hours. New Englanders (at least New Englanders who are not birders) are sensible, God-fearing people. Sensible people don't try to push a day past its natural, God-given boundaries, and any chore so engaging that it cannot fit between sunrise and sunset is usually a chore that can wait until spring.

Slouched over a counter polished to a luster by half a trillion elbows was one of those young guys you always see in diners—fellows who are perpetually between jobs and who spend their time trying to engage waitresses in conversation. Wedged into a back booth were two weathered-looking gentlemen cloaked in denim so old it was white. Their association, whatever it might be, had long since transcended conversation. They sat quietly, staring at the coffee cups cradled in hands that were the size and texture of baseball gloves.

The only chatter came from the pair of waitresses who had commandeered a booth of their own. They spoke of head colds and hangovers and horoscopes and husbands. All the little building blocks of life.

Newburyport, Massachusetts, five minutes south and across the Merrimack River, is one of birding's oldest and most cherished shrines. A winter pilgrimage here is an annual tradition for almost any birder living within a day's drive. When winter closes over the Northern Hemisphere, northern birds are squeezed to the icy rim. New England lies well within winter's reach, but the Merrimack River is big enough and fast enough to shrug off ice. Hardy sea ducks, eiders, goldeneye and Oldsquaw, and the pale northern gulls gather here in numbers. Over the marshes and dunes of nearby Plum Island, hungry Rough-legged Hawks patrol the sky by day; Short-eared Owls haunt the marshes by night. The great Snowy Owl, annual here, does both.

Over the years, many thousands of birders have come this way, braving the cold for the birds that thrive in it. Accounted in their ranks are many of the Great Ones, birders who helped turn an elite and snobbish avocation into a national pastime. Allan and Helen Cruikshank probably stared out these same diner windows, keeping an eye on the cameras sitting in their car. Bob Smart, en route to "the bird of the century," might have slurped coffee in this very booth, and Jim Lane, the great pathfinder, probably munched a burger while contemplating the notes that would be translated into his famous bird-finding guides.

"You two wan' cahfee?" a voice hailed from across the room, a Massachusetts voice, the syllables walking a line between snarl and purr. Yes, we did.

"Cream, sugah?"

"No. Black's fine."

But these are names drawn from recent history, names that would constitute recent additions to the birders' hall of fame, might even be passed over by the judges until history has been better served. Because the history of birding in general and Massachusetts in particular goes back much farther, into another century. And Ann's Diner? How far back does this Salisbury diner figure into birding's past?

I looked around, studying the fixtures—the chrome and steel, marble and tile. Plastic was at a premium.

The coffee arrived, some in the cup, some not.

"Rady to ohda," we were told.

"When was the diner built?" I wanted to know.

Our waitress looked stunned. Apparently questions not relating to breakfast are procedural aberrations at Ann's.

"Nineteen fifty," she replied, recovering quickly, lifting her pad to bring matters back to the topic at hand.

"Oh," I intoned, somewhat disappointed. "Looks older than that. Two eggs up . . . and home fries," I added, ignoring Linda's warning gaze.

"Pancakes," Linda said, making the correct, low-cholesterol response.

Our waitress wrote as we spoke, ambled back toward the counter, then added:

"But thah was anothah beforh thisone; built in '42."

*Forty-two . . .* I mused. *That adds a few more players to the board. Ludlow Griscom? . . . maybe Witmer Stone? . . .*

But even these names hardly tap the depths, and they don't come close to touching bottom. The roots of North American birding go back very far and though they extend to every state in the union, the taproot lies buried in Massachusetts.

"I'll be back," Linda said, struggling through five layers of clothing to a standing position. "Know where the euphemism is in here?"

"Over that way," I observed, gesturing. "While you're back there, see if you can find any graffiti left by Edward Forbush or John James Audubon. Maybe somebody's scribbled directions to a Snowy Owl or something."

"Audubon died in 1851," Linda said. I interpreted this to mean that she didn't give the idea much credence.

But even if John James Audubon had been one of Anne's regulars, chances are that he wouldn't have been able to offer much assistance to questing birders anyway. The fact is, Audubon wasn't a birder, not in the sense birders think of themselves today. Audubon was an artist who searched for and painted the birds of a fresh new continent. Why? Because they were beautiful, they were animate, they were ripe for discovery. Some of those he found were birds that had never been described before. His tools were the brush and the shotgun; the birds that fill his famous portfolio were drawn from specimens, birds Audubon shot and painted. So it is likely that any directions that Audubon might have given to the location of a Snowy Owl probably would have led only to his game pouch.

Linda and breakfast arrived simultaneously.

"Any hints for visiting birders back there?" I asked.

"Nothing that specific," she said, cutting off conversation and giving her attention to her plate.

I stared down at the two eggs on my plate that stared accusingly back at me. An eyeball-to-albumen confrontation, and I blinked.

Why, you might ask, did Audubon, and Alexander Wilson, and the ornithologists who followed in their footsteps shoot birds? The answer is: they had to—that is, they had to shoot them if they wanted to get close enough to study them (which was, as it is today, pretty much the whole idea).

Birds are skittish creatures, suspicious of men and their motives, and these suspicions are not without merit. The history of birds and man has not been a particularly happy one from the bird's standpoint. In humanity's more cerebral moments, birds have been a source of inspiration and even worship. But even poets have to eat, so more often birds have served more practical and one-sided ends—food, fashion, decoration, sport, entertainment. Sometimes this meant internment: a canary in a cage, a hawk on a falconer's fist, a peacock in a garden. Most of the time it just meant a dead bird.

Birds are even less cerebral than most humans. They have a hard time distinguishing between poets who merely wish to appreciate them and pot hunters who want to eat them. So birds have adopted a blanket policy with regard to humans (and other dangerous creatures). When humans approach, birds retreat. Some do so by running to safety, some swim, most fly, and this is a considerable advantage over creatures who cannot. Shooting the bird, as Audubon and others discovered, negates this considerable advantage. In the hand, an artist or ornithologist could examine the bird at leisure.

I attacked the eggs like someone who had never heard of cholesterol. A yellow stain spread across the eastern half of the plate until it hit the mountain of hash browns.

The 1800s were a wonderful age of ornithological discovery in North America. Young scientists who made bird study the focus of their lives and gentlemen who made it their interest "collected" birds, their eggs, and their nests in every corner of the continent. Specimen by specimen, measurement by measurement, by description and by field notes, they built an understanding of North America's birds. The specimens filled drawers in museums. The insights and discoveries filled the pages of bulletins published by clubs like the prestigious Nuttall Ornithological Club in Cambridge, Massachusetts (the bulletin that metamorphosed into *The Auk*, journal of the American Ornithologists' Union).

A cold blast of air heralded the arrival of a new patron, a gunner wearing camouflage coveralls who ordered coffee to go and left. A duck hunter, I surmised, and a serious one to boot. Only someone who took his sport very seriously would venture out in weather like this. Hardy folk, these New Englanders.

In the free-for-all age before conservation, scientists were not the only ones "collecting" birds. Great numbers of birds were killed for sport and for market, and the myth of America's inexhaustible resources sustained the slaughter past the point of reason. Millions of shorebirds were killed during migration, packed in barrels and shipped to markets. Colonies of gulls and terns were ravaged by eggers. Fanned by Victorian fashion, the demand for plumes and bird skins led to an appalling slaughter of herons and egrets. Even songbirds like the Cedar Waxwing, Northern Flicker, and Northern Oriole were fair game for the millinery trade.

A dispirited gray dawn was beginning to swamp the lights cast from the diner window. A pair of crows flew by on crooked wings, and on a television antenna poised over a chimney, a starling muttered something incomprehensible and probably unprintable.

Another patron arrived, a tiny, bright-eyed man who entered through a side door, accompanied by morning sunlight. In measured steps, he strode to the center of the counter, charmed a smile from the face of our waitress, and took two things from her hands. A cup of coffee and a plastic bag that appeared to be filled with . . . bread? It occurred to me, after he'd gone, that I'd seen this man and this ritual enacted here before.

"The man who came in for coffee," I inquired when our waitress produced the check. "Is he a regular here?"

"Comes in every morning," she said, and once again the smile creased her face.

"What does he do with the bread?" I wanted to know.

"Feeds it to the geese," she confided with a diffident shrug.

As bird populations reeled from exploitation, concern among ornithologists and citizens awakened and flourished. John Burroughs, the eloquent and popular Hudson River writer, imbued society with a naturalist heart and soul. John Muir, the Rocky Mountain crusader, gave it spirit. A President named Teddy Roosevelt had both.

In 1883, the American Ornithologists' Union was founded—a society of scientists whose study was birds. Included within its agenda of scientific concerns was one not-strictly scientific subject: bird protection. In the same year, George Grinnell, editor of *Forest and Stream*, a sporting journal, initiated a new publication dedicated to saving the birds. He named the publication *Audubon Magazine*; distribution was free. But the magazine did not survive the decade. It was killed by success, overwhelmed by a readership that outstripped the finances and faculties of Grinnell and his staff.

But the arrow that struck at the heart of the slaughter was fired not by a scientist, a sportsman, or a nature writer. It was fired by a Boston matron, Mrs. Augustus Hemenway, who chanced one morning to read a graphic account of a heronry savaged by plume hunters. Shaken, propelled by the zeal of the newly converted, Mrs. Hemenway went to the social directory, culling the names of her fashionable, plume-wearing friends. The group, when it convened in Mrs. Hemenway's home on February 10, 1896, founded the Massachusetts Audubon Society, an organization committed to the protection of North America's native birds.

Other states followed, founding Audubon societies of their own. In 1901, the state societies met in New York and formed a federation that was the basis for a National Audubon Society. Some of the state organizations surrendered their autonomy to the new group; others, like Massachusetts Audubon, Connecticut Audubon, and New Jersey Audubon, maintained it.

Linda's plate was empty. Mine, too.

"Still want to go birding?" I asked, feigning indifference. "It's going to be awful cold on that river."

"You bet," she said. The sound of this archetypal western response in an old Massachusetts diner raised a smile and one or two heads.

Our waitress accepted the check and payment, cutting off our transaction with a brisk "Thank you." I'd wanted to ask about birders, to learn something of their patronage and her regard. But minding your own business is a New England specialty, and waitresses everywhere are adept at sensing and avoiding questions they don't care to field. Clearly, she'd grown wary of mine.

I recalled the waitress we'd had at dinner the night before, an ebullient young woman, evidently enjoying some university's midwinter break, who pegged us immediately for birders.

"Do you get many birders in here?" I inquired.

"Oh, sure," she observed brightly. "All the time. Lots of them."

But the words that stuck with me were offered as an afterthought that was wonderfully frank and right on the mark.

"It looks kind of boring to me," she added musingly. "But then, I never tried it."

Our waitress turned back to the booth and her friend. Back to head colds and hangovers and horoscopes and husbands. All the little trappings of life.

## BELOW THE IRON BRIDGE

The Merrimack tumbles south out of New Hampshire, a merry little river whose waters riffle and dance. Crossing into Massachusetts, the river turns

---

contrary, meandering north, then east, then north again, braking hard against every river's fate. But by the time Merrimack reaches the U.S. Route One bridge, all resistance has left it. Broad and accepting, swollen by the tide, the water flows past Newburyport's boat docks, its factory walls, and the gabled houses that mount the hillsides. Beyond the town it broadens into a bay flanked by marshes. Then, pinched between flanking breakwaters, it becomes, for a short span, a river once more, flowing quick and strong until losing itself in the cold green anonymity of the sea.

The birds are tied to the river, and the types of birds that are found along its course change as the river changes. Above the town, where the current still masters the tide, Common Mergansers and flocks of goldeneye—hardy diving ducks—gather and feed. Sometimes, when the winter sun breaks through the overcast, the males brace their bills against the sky, catching sunlight on feathers that gleam like green velvet, trying to catch a lady's eye. But in January the hens pay them no mind. Real courtship is still weeks away, and eyes are better occupied keeping watch on the Bald Eagles that patrol the river.

Where the river reaches the municipal boat launch, off Merimac Street, the Common Mergansers have been supplanted by brine-loving Red-breasted Mergansers, and past the bridge, where Merimac becomes Water Street, where the river opens into a bay, armadas of tiny Bufflehead maneuver over Joppa Flats. Oldsquaw, garbed in jester's finery, play hide-and-seek with hopeful observers, and delicate Bonaparte's Gulls hurry by, en route to someplace else.

Occasionally, visiting birders are startled to find themselves the object of scrutiny, pinned by the somber gaze of a harbor seal. But the seals, like the loons, like the grebes, like rafts of eider duck who rise and fall with the swells, seem to prefer the mouth of the harbor where the Atlantic Ocean and Merrimack River meet and become one.

"I've got one," Linda exclaimed. "On the left side of the flock, facing right."

"Male or female?" I demanded.

"Male," she affirmed.

I swung the spotting scope around, taking it off the pair of Bald Eagles quartering down river, bringing it to bear on the distant flock of goldeneye. Eagles are plentiful along the Merrimack in winter, and lots of other rivers, too. But Barrow's Goldeneye! *That* is a Newburyport specialty.

From this distance, with the unaided eye, the tiny white flecks bobbing in the current could easily have passed for chunks of ice. Filtered through a spotting scope fitted with a 20x eyepiece, the specks were transformed into a flock of diving ducks. Their shape, color, markings—their *field marks*—made them goldeneye, Common Goldeneye. All except one, the one that Linda had found "on the left." That one, according to Linda, was a Barrow's Goldeneye.

Both Audubon and Alexander Wilson, one of Audubon's contemporaries, tried using optics, telescopes, but their quality was inferior. Throughout the nineteenth century, the shotgun continued to be the accepted tool of the serious ornithologist.

Shortly after the Civil War, however, optics began to improve and proliferate. Telescopes gave way to field glasses—weak, 2x affairs that halved the distance between an observer and a bird, or 4x glasses that quartered it but often at the price of distortion. But the device made it possible to perceive and appreciate birds in a new way—as living creatures—and it neatly sidestepped the embarrassing contradiction between protecting birds and shooting birds inherent in ornithological tradition. The field glass was the catalyst that took bird study out of the hands of ornithologists and put it within reach of everyone.

Through the looking glass, more and more women found their avenue into bird study, and the male-dominated avocation was suddenly tempered by a new wave of interest and expression and consciousness. By the early years of the twentieth century, field-glass ornithologists using new prism binoculars were able to study living birds at a distance almost as well as a shotgun ornithologist could study a dead one in the hand.

There was, however, a problem. The diagnostic points that ornithologists had developed to distinguish birds in the hand—colors, bill shape, bill length, position of a bird's toes—were often indiscernible through binoculars in the field. There was another problem: a reluctance on the part of traditional ornithologists to lay down their weapons and accept the seriousness and legitimacy of sight identification.

There is a poignant story involving a boy named Ludlow Griscom, who grew up to be a famous ornithologist, and an elderly companion, a member of the prestigious Linnaean Ornithological Society of New York. The story is almost allegorical in its portrayal of the conflict between the field glass and shotgun schools of ornithology, and I like to think that it is true.

One day, Ludlow and the venerable ornithologist stopped at a home in Connecticut to secure permission to shoot whatever manner of birds were migrating through—the accepted ornithological practice of the time. Young Ludlow had the temerity to suggest that he could identify the birds without having to shoot them. To prove his point, he placed his field glasses on a treetop warbler and pronounced it to be a female Cape May Warbler. Skeptical, the ornithologist raised his shotgun and fired. *Mirabile dictu*, the bird was a female Cape May Warbler. The experiment continued, and Ludlow's identifications were correct time and time again.

The problem was, of course, that the only way to *prove* the accuracy of young Ludlow's identification was to shoot the bird. The problem has never been fully resolved.

I moved the spotting scope through the ranks of waterfowl, looking for the one that was like yet unlike all the others. The penchant that diving ducks have for diving made it challenging. The sun that lacquered the river with a protective layer of glare made it difficult. The east wind that was cutting pieces off my exposed face in frozen chunks and making the spotting scope dance like a seismograph in freefall brought the whole venture close to a fool's errand.

A drake popped to the surface, water flowing from its back like mercury, a drake Common Goldeneye. Another popped into view . . . another, a female this time . . . then anoth . . .

"I got it," I tried to shout through jaws whose synovial fluid had gelled. Then I settled down to admire my prize.

What made *this* duck different from any one of the other birds bobbing in an ice-choked river? What distinguishes a Barrow's Goldeneye from a

Common Goldeneye? For that matter what distinguishes a Common Goldeneye from a Common Loon? *That* depends upon who you ask.

Pose the question to a museum ornithologist and he will advise you that the bills of loons are sharply pointed, lacking toothlike projections, whereas the bills of waterfowl are more or less flattened, ducklike, with toothlike projections or ridges along the sides.

Pose the question to a birder and she will tell you about "field marks," the "trademarks of nature" that distinguish one bird from the next.

On my desk is a book entitled *A Field Guide to the Birds*. It was written and illustrated by a young man in his early twenties named Roger Tory Peterson. In 1934, the Houghton-Mifflin Company of Boston took a chance and published the unassuming little miracle.

There was, even in 1934, no shortage of books dealing with birds. Audubon and Wilson both had had their efforts set and bound. Ornithologists like John Krider had published descriptions of the birds "killed and prepared" by themselves. Neltje Blanchan and others had charmed the nature-lover set with books like *Bird Neighbors*. In 1904, Frank Chapman of the Museum of Natural History made a sporting effort to make the identification techniques used by ornithologists useful in the field with his *Birds of Eastern North America*, but though the book tugged at the ornithological halter, it could not break it.

Then in 1906, Chester A. Reed, of Worcester, Massachusetts, walked the rim of a breakthrough. He published the *Bird Guide*, a notepad-size booklet that gave descriptive accounts of eastern (and later western) birds, backed up by color illustrations, one bird to a page. A few of the accounts fell short of useful, but where the guide really fell short was the illustrations. The subjects were nicely painted, the backdrops natural. But the details Reed depicted were still the details visible on birds seen at arm's length; the details of a bird held in the hand.

What young Roger Tory Peterson did was simple, as most leaps of genius are. He took the bird out of the hand and put it in the bush. What he depicted, and what he described in text, was what observers using the low-power optics of the day *actually saw* from a distance in the field.

At a distance, individual feathers disappear. Shades disappear. Contrasts become more pronounced. Lines tighten. As a final refinement Peterson added tiny arrows to draw a viewer's attention quickly to a bird's distinguishing characteristics. Peterson's system was a system of simplification.

In 1904 Frank Chapman described a certain common species this way: "Ad. male—top and sides of head black, a white spot above the eye; rest of the upper parts grayish slate-color; margins of wings slightly lighter; tail black, outer feathers with white spots at their tips; throat white, spotted with black; rest of underparts rufous (tipped with white in the fall, becoming white on the middle of the lower belly)."

Give up?

Try Peterson's description as provided in the pages of his second edition: "One of the most familiar of all birds; easily recognized by its gray back and *brick-red* breast. In the male, the head and tail are blackish; in the female, paler. The bill is yellow."

In other words, a robin.

Chapman's description of the ducks playing in the current of the Merrimack might have been cause for consternation as well: "Ad. male—Head and throat dark, glossy *green*, a circular white patch at the base of the bill measuring, along the bill, less than *half an inch* in height; neck all around, breast, belly, exposed part of wing-coverts, speculum, and most of the scapulars white; rest of plumage black."

Peterson makes it simple: "Male—A white-looking duck with a black back and a puffy green-glossed head (black at a distance). A large round white spot between the eye and the bill is the best identification mark."

Both Chapman and Peterson called the bird the American Goldeneye; its name has been changed to Common Goldeneye.

And Barrow's Goldeneye? What distinguishes Barrow's from Common? Ah, well. That gets trickier.

Chapman advises that the head of a male Barrow's has a purplish sheen, that a Common shows green. But in the field, at anything approaching a distance and in poor lighting, this distinction serves for nothing. The heads of Barrow's *and* Common Goldeneye appear equally black. But as the treasured Peterson sitting on my desk advises, the thing to do is to look at "the *crescent*-shaped white patch in front of the eye. (American [sic] Golden-eye has a *round* white spot.)" Barrow's Goldeneye also shows a greater amount of black on the sides of the body (including a dark, crooked finger pointing toward the water). And the head of Barrow's has a "very different shape— a more abrupt forehead and a low rounded crown."

"Try to see *all* these characters before you put this rare bird on your list," counsels the young master, who at eighty-two is now the grand master of birding. And I did see them, filtered through glass and the eyes that Peterson gave us.

Throughout this century, the quality of optics has improved. Sharper, more powerful optics offer greater detail, and a number of fine field guides have been published, codifying all that has been learned about the field identification of birds.

Even Peterson's field guide, now in its fourth edition, bears little resemblance to the original. The plates now are more nearly bird portraits than stylized depictions, but in one key respect, the guide remains unchanged. It still depicts precisely what birders see in the field through optics.


## THE SEAWALL

Newburyport sleeps late in winter. The shops open late or not at all. Newburyport is not a bad place to be a homeowner who admires tranquillity, or a cop on the force.

On Water Street, on your way out of the center of town, en route to Plum Island, you pass a seawall, a raised concrete lip whose workaday purpose is keeping the bay at bay. But if Newburyport, Massachusetts, may be fairly called one of birding's shrines, then the seawall is its inner sanctum. In March 1975, birding reached its high-water mark as thousands of birders flooded the town. They came spontaneously, from across the country, to bear witness to a miracle—the appearance of a lipstick-colored gull that had absolutely no sane right to be there. "The Bird of the Century," as some have called it.

In the process, birders discovered something that took them completely by surprise. They discovered that they were many.

They have never forgotten that lesson.

There was only space for half a dozen cars in the seawall lot, but it didn't matter. Now, at midweek, Linda and I had the place to ourselves.

The tide was falling when we arrived, but bird activity was running high. Flocks of sea ducks, goldeneye, Bufflehead, and Oldsquaw, fought stubbornly against the rush of water, dodging slushy patches of ice that scraped and hissed. Large "white-headed gulls," mostly Herring, Great Black-backeds, and Ring-billed, patrolled the skies, searching for anything that might tempt a gull's palate—and this covers pretty much anything you might care to think of and lots of things you wouldn't. But farther out, resting on a slushy bar or fluttering low over the dark, oily surface, were delicate Bonaparte's Gulls, "black-headed gulls" (black-headed with a small *b*), their wings flashing silver and white. Now and again, one would pick something off the surface; occasionally one would settle on the water, spinning like a chip in the flood. But mostly, they just flew, back and forth, a hundred yards from the seawall, searching the water below them.

The gulls were the key. Just as with foraging flocks of titmice and chickadees, if you want to find uncommon seabirds, search through the ranks of common ones. Among the everyday white-headed gulls are two more Newburyport prizes. The pale Iceland Gulls with charcoal-smudged wing tips and the burly Glaucous Gull.

Bonaparte's Gulls play the role of Judas goat, too. The trick is to search through the melee of silver for the flash of a shadow—the darker underwing of the Common Black-headed Gull, a close cousin; or maybe a diminutive Little Gull (whose underwing is darker still). My "Life" Black-headed and Little Gulls had been seen from this seawall in 1976, one year too late for "The Bird of the Century."

"What's out there today?" a voice hailed. We turned, expecting another birder, but discovered instead a resident couple bundled like Russians, out for a morning walk.

"Just the usual good birds," I replied.

"No Ross's Gulls?" they inquired, through scarves that hid their grins.

"No," we affirmed. Ross's Gulls were at a premium today.

Oh, the residents of Newburyport remember the Ross's Gull all right. It's just possible that if we had found a Ross's Gull, the secret might have died with us right on the spot. There's no telling what a more insular resident might resort to in order to avoid a repeat of the siege of '75.

It started on March 2, when Walter Ellison, a card-carrying member of the Brookline (Massachusetts) Bird Club, and Paul Miliotis, a self-taught naturalist, spotted a peculiar-looking bird flying among the Bonaparte's. Its wedge-shaped tail, gray underwings, white head, delicate black bill, and large dark eyes were evident to those with discerning eyes and easily distinguished it from the accompanying entourage of Bonaparte's Gulls. But the thing that really set this bird apart was color. All the other birds in the flock were gray and white. The underparts on this thing were *pink*.

There is a bird that matches this description perfectly. Its name is Ross's Gull. The problem was not so much one of identification as mastering near-terminal levels of disbelief. Ross's Gulls, in 1975, were only known to nest along the banks of several rivers in Siberia. The feathered phantoms spend the rest of their lives flying around the edge of the Arctic ice sheet, searching for open water. What Ellison and Miliotis had just done was the equivalent of reaching into their pockets for change and coming out with the Hope Diamond.

The bird had never been reported in the continental United States. Only a handful of records existed for Canada. In fact, the only place where the bird was more or less "regular" was Point Barrow, Alaska, where, in October, flocks of Ross's Gulls, heading east across the Beaufort Sea, occasionally brush this northern tip of land. But Point Barrow was a long, long way from Newburyport, Massachusetts, and beyond the budget of most North American birders.

Newburyport, on the other hand, was *well* within reach, and through birding's amazing grapevine, via phones that rang deep into the night, North America's birding community was made aware that America's first extra-

Arctic Ross's Gull had been discovered, naturally, in Massachusetts, and, of course, in Newburyport. Within twenty-four hours not one state or province could claim ignorance of the bird.

And the rush was on. According to the pages of *American Birds*, between March 2 and May 6 as many as ten thousand birders may have jammed into sleepy Newburyport. Reliable estimates placed the number of those toting optics on March 8 and 9, the first weekend following the bird's discovery, at two thousand (not including the press). Among their ranks were birders like Roger Peterson, who accounted it as his 668th North American species. Newburyport was a circus. It was a treasure hunt. It was a cause célèbre. It was an operation on par with a military invasion—with one crucial difference. There was nobody in command. There were just a host of birders in crowded station wagons and airport rentals driven by two primary objectives—to find a place to park and *to get the bird.*

Actually, it is neither accurate nor fair to suggest that the deployment of birders was without direction or guidance. There was someone calling the shots, or maybe it's more accurate to say *something.* At the wave of a wing, the "pink seagull" could send hundreds of birders charging off in any one of several directions—to the seawall, the yacht club, the clam shack, or across the harbor to Salisbury Beach (a one-mile flight for the bird, a six-mile drive by car). But then, even the *rumor* of a sighting could do this, and sometimes even rumor was hard to come by.

Pete Bacinski, an investment consultant from Lyndhurst, New Jersey, recalls his day of quest. Arriving at the west end of the seawall, jammed end to end and shoulder to shoulder with birders and scopes, he asked about "the bird" and was told that it had been seen earlier that morning but not since.

Undaunted, he ambled down to middike and was told that "the bird had been there moments earlier but was gone now."

When he got to the east end of the seawall, he found those assembled studying "the bird."

Most birders had a tougher time of it. The Ross's Gull, despite its out-landish color, was not a gimme—an easy-to-spot bird—by any means. The Merrimack is not small, the bird was, *and* it ranged widely. The puckish little gull was given to periodic disappearances. At one point in late March, it absented itself for a knuckle-biting ten-day stretch, only to reappear.

Stories surrounding the Ross's Gull are legion, and matters of legend now. But the story that best illustrates the allure of the prize and the lengths birders will go to claim it is the story of one birder who drove to Newburyport on the eve of his daughter's wedding. Despite his best intentions, despite the iron-clad promises levied to a fretful spouse, he returned late.

Before his wife could utter one wrathful word, the resourceful birder made a preemptive offer.

"Wait," he commanded. "Before you file for divorce, there is something I want to tell you."

Taken aback by an unexpected frontal assault, the wife hesitated long enough to hear him out.

"I just want you to know," he continued quickly, "that I just saved us the cost of this wedding by going to see this bird now. Because that's what it would have cost for me to fly to Point Barrow to see it."

His case might have been stronger had the bird not remained until May sixth. But you never know how long a good bird will linger.

## 3 • FLORIDA:

# In the Wader Pool
# (Getting Our Feet Wet)

## THUNDERHEADS AND DUST

LOOKING BACK NOW, TWO MEMORIES OF FLORIDA STAND above and apart from all others. One is the clouds, the great flat-bottomed clouds that anchor themselves to the horizon. Pale as coral, soaring to heights that even the great black-and-white storks reach only in their dreams, they gather each afternoon to cast clay-colored shadows across the land. The other thing I recall is the dust—the fine talc of pulverized limestone that during the dry season covers everything in Florida like a shroud.

Men and machines cut deep into the limestone beds to make way for retirement communities, shopping centers, and highways. Armadas of recreation vehicles keep the dust circulating until it finds some surface to cling to. Property owners suck water from the earth to fill their pools and freshen their lawns and wash the dust away. Then the sun steals the water, drawing it aloft to join the clouds.

Every year, the water in Florida's aquifers retreats deeper in limestone wells. Every year, the land seems drier, the building grows more ferocious, and the dust falls thicker. Every afternoon, the great flat-bottomed clouds gather on the horizon to cast their shadows across the land.

Sometimes, in the evening, the clouds and dust conspire to make wonderful sunsets. People who sit on patios and people who walk beaches with drinks in their hands admire the sunset and their fortune until long after the sun has gone. Until the color has left the sky and the clouds have turned to clay.

Until the last of the great soaring birds have gone to their dreams.

## DING DARLING AND MARY LOU

"If everyone can come over here, we can get STARted," a voice chanted lyrically. Within seconds, what had been a directionless mob milling around in a parking lot coalesced into a mob with a common point of reference.

The voice belonged to a cheerful woman in her very early sixties, who surveyed us with undisguised pleasure. She said her name was Mary Lou Schadt, that she was on the board of the Sanibel-Captiva Audubon Society and a volunteer at the refuge, and that she would be our field trip leader "and . . . and . . . that it is a *pleasure* to welcome you here."

First we would see a short film program about the refuge, then return to our cars, form a caravan, and drive the auto loop, stopping here and there to enjoy the many winter birds in Ding Darling National Wildlife Refuge. Any questions?

All in all, the performance was fairly typical, a ritual enacted across the country every day of the week—the ritual of "the birding field trip." This one happened to be organized by a chapter of the National Audubon Society, but it might just as easily have been the Cleveland Museum or Point Reyes Bird Observatory. This field trip happened to be in a National Wildlife Refuge. Next week's trip might target a park, a reservoir, a Nature Conservancy sanctuary, or some privately owned swamp whose existence is known only to the owner (and North America's birding community).

While Mary Lou laid out the game plan, I studied the group with an appraising, professional eye. The crowd was "older," but then this *was* Florida. Age goes with the turf. Most in the group did not seem to be Audubon members or even Sanibel Island residents. Their cars boasted plates from seven states, and those wearing Florida tags bore the brands of Avis, Alamo, and Hertz. Most didn't even appear to be *real* birders, not yet. Birders have a look, a style, an attentiveness to things around them. There were too many golf shoes in this lot; too many brightly colored windbreakers; too many people listening attentively to instructions that were universally routine. No, Mary Lou had drawn a group of entry-level birders, low on birding experience, high on enthusiasm.

The coin of tribute in birding's realm is not skill, it is shared interest. With it, an individual buys passage into the ranks of North American birders. Skill is just something birders acquire over time. But the interest, and the pleasure people derive from watching birds, ah, well, those things are constants; those things are a priority. Those are the qualities that distinguish birders from society's rank and file.

A head count brought today's number of inductees to thirty-two.

Attesting to the level of birding experience, there were nineteen binoculars in the group—about thirteen short. *Real* birders don't share binoculars. Included in the optical arsenal was an eclectic assortment of zoom binoculars, minis, and a few from bargain basement bins. One woman brandished a pair of opera glasses, a relic right out of the stone-knife and bearskin age of birding. Some Guadalcanal veteran hoisted a pair of old navy Bausch and Lomb 7x50s that are probably still being carried on some ship's inventory. A younger couple drawn from the kiwi-and-croissant band of the human spectrum were armed with a Nikon glass that *Consumer Reports* had sanctified with a nod.

With the exception of Mary Lou's, there wasn't a spotting scope in the lot.

The shortcomings of our optical arsenal made me cringe. Clearly, some people were heading for a very frustrating morning. A few might even begin and end their birding careers on the very same day.

At a word from Mary Lou, we filed into the auditorium for a program in which the wading birds of coastal Florida held sway: herons and egrets; spoonbills and Wood Storks; larger than life, pretty as pictures. By the time the program was finished, the group was suffering near-terminal levels of anticipation. Mary Lou couldn't have asked for a more eager band of acolytes.

The string of cars angled down the wildlife drive, past stands of red mangrove, a tree of the tidal zone whose elevated root system resembles an arboreal flow chart. Tiny Blue-gray Gnatcatchers raised wheezy voices from the roadside tangle. Belted Kingfishers, blue projectiles cloaked in feathers, rattled their annoyance and fled. Take away the mangrove, take away the showpiece visitor center, and Ding Darling is much like national wildlife refuges all over the country—an expanse of wetlands with a corner set aside for public enjoyment.

Ding—actually Jay Norwood Darling—was a Pulitzer Prize-winning cartoonist who had a daytime job as head of the U.S. Biological Survey, forerunner of today's U.S. Fish and Wildlife Service. He was also instrumental in the establishment of the National Refuge System, which now administers hundreds of thousands of acres of habitat to preserve America's wildlife, particularly waterfowl.

The mangroves gave way to a large impoundment pool on the left and broad tidal flats on the right. Mary Lou drew to a stop, and down the row of cars brake lights flashed with frightening inconsistency. By some miracle, not a bumper got thumped. Caravanning, like field identification, is an acquired art.

The first stop was a treasure trove of birds—birds of every shape and hue, uncut, big as life, some standing, some swimming, some soaring overhead. It was Disneyland with feathers. It was a *National Geographic* special in three dimensions. It was, in a word, Florida.

Mary Lou, standing somewhere in the ranks assembled around her, was shouting out bird names and directions.

"Perched on the log over there, holding its wings out to dry, is a . . ." (bird whose name was drowned out by shouts of "Where? Where?").

"What did she call that?" a gentleman whispered to his wife.

"A Double-chested something or other," she mumbled.

"And look! Swimming right next to the pelican with its back to us is a small bird that looks like a duck. A Pied-billed Grebe."

"Want to see the piebald grebe?" the binocular-toting half of the yuppie couple asked the erudite half.

"Yeah. Here. Take the book. See if you can find it in there. It's not listed under ducks."

No, it's not. Not all ducklike birds are ducks. Grebes, as they soon discovered, are listed under grebes.

But the birds that held center stage, the birds that drew all eyes and more than their share of held breaths, were the great wading birds of Florida, the birds that had been the object of slaughter and that had inspired the Audubon movement.

Right in front of the group, an intercept line of White Ibis, forceps in feathers, waded across the shallows, oblivious to their open-mouthed admirers. Foraging behind was a troop of spoonbills, decked out in rose-colored raiment, and Wood Storks, somber as pallbearers, who strode along, methodically kicking food into their mouths. Crouched in the shadows was a Tricolored Heron, a rakishly plumed swordsman among water birds. Not far away, a Green-backed Heron was poised, cocked and ready, a dart gun in feathers, waiting for any fish foolish enough to cross its sights.

Mary Lou called them out as if she were introducing dear old friends to a recent acquaintance.

On the other side of the road was a Little Blue Heron, a bird the color of gunmetal with a bill that swayed like the head of a cobra. Farther out, off by themselves, were the Reddish Egrets, mad linebackers of the flats, running back and forth, throwing up their wings, thrashing and splashing, making sunlight ripple.

But the birds whose elegance surpassed them all were the egrets. The petite Snowy Egret, the bird with the yellow slippers; and the Great Egret, the stately white stalker. These were the birds whose poise and plumage drew all eyes first . . . and last.

Wading birds are perfect subjects for beginning birders. They are big. They are beautiful. Best of all, they stand still—long enough for unskilled hands to bring binoculars to bear; long enough for field guides to be consulted and identifications backed up with certainty. Unless pressed too close, the birds will stand there as long as you do (which, for beginning birders, is a long time).

The woman with the opera glasses was having obvious and predictable difficulty. Even at the ranges we were dealing with, her low-powered heirlooms were more hindrance than help.

"Here," I suggested, offering my pair of 7x42 Zeiss. "Try looking through these."

A little self-consciously, she brought the binoculars to bear on the closest group of birds, the White Ibis. Her mouth opened, forming a word that I suspect would have been "Oh . . ." but she simply forgot to say it. At forty feet, at 7x, the image of the ivory-colored birds with their hot-pink bills stitching the water must have been stunning.

"Thank you," she said, returning them to my hands. "They're wonderful."

"There's a big difference between 7x and 2x," I admitted.

Two-power optics halve the distance between the viewer and the object; 7x makes things appear *seven times closer*. But a satisfactory image is not just a matter of magnification. Optical quality has a great deal to do with image quality. There are 7x binoculars that offer images that are incredibly sharp and wonderfully bright. There are 7x binoculars that are garbage, that should be made illegal.

"How much are they, if you don't mind my asking?" she asked.

"About eight hundred dollars," I said, apologizing with a smile.

Her face assumed that dazed, flat expression you see on accident victims, and her mouth drew that silent *O* that I'd seen before.

"OK," Mary Lou chanted. "Let's move on to the next spot."

On my way back to the car it occurred to me that maybe the *O* wasn't an "Oh" at all. Maybe she had been saying "Ow."

The next stop offered fewer herons and egrets but greater numbers of waterfowl. Sleek Red-breasted Mergansers that dove and disappeared; unspectacular Mottled Ducks whose specialty seemed to be sleeping. But most of the "good stuff," the colorful stuff like drake American Wigeon and Northern Pintails and their complement of hens, were out in the center of the pool, out of harm's way—all except one . . .

"Blue-winged Teal," Mary Lou shouted, pointing to a drake a stone's throw away. Teal are small, finely proportioned ducks. This species boasts an exaggerated bill, a blue racing stripe down the side (actually, along the folded wing), and . . .

"A white crescent," Mary Lou directed her troop. "Look for a bold white crescent just behind the bill; like a big white quarter moon. That's the best field mark on the male."

And they did look, too. They *looked* and they *saw* and they *appreciated* in a way that few experienced birders ever would. They did so because they were beginners, and a world of beauty and discovery was unfolding before their eyes. For many, this was the first time they had ever set eyes on the bird who wore the crescent moon on his face. And for some, it might be the last—the last time they would really see and really appreciate the incredible rose-and-green blush on the bird's head; the last time they would marvel at the patterned flanks that look as though they were carved out of bird's-eye maple. The next time they saw this bird, it might be just a dark shape on the horizon identified by "a crescent moon on its face."

Of course, a few couldn't see colors or patterns even now, not with the optical junk they'd brought into the field with them.

"Excuse me," I said to a gentleman who was clearly having difficulty, "could I see your binoculars for a second?"

A little reluctantly, he handed them over. They were one of the models with the teeter-totter focus mechanism that first-time binocular buyers seem drawn to. They *are* easy to focus, and that's a bonus. But they aren't very durable, and this pair looked like it had some miles on it. I brought them up to my eyes and discovered immediately what the gentleman's problem was. The shattered image caused by binoculars desperately out of alignment almost brought me to my knees. The barrels of a binocular are supposed to draw a bead on the same spot. God only knew where these things were pointing. Clearly, they'd been dropped once too often.

"Would you mind taking a look at mine?" a woman standing nearby asked.

Her problem was a simple one, but a common one, too.

"This setting on the right ocular lens," I asked, "the small ones you look through, do you always leave it all the way to the right like this?"

She smiled and shrugged.

"That's an adjustment knob," I explained. "It is used to compensate for the small differences between the right eye and the left eye. You set the adjustment once. Then you never need to touch it again. All focusing should be done with the center focus wheel."

"By the way," I added, noting that she was an eyeglass wearer. "Do you leave your glasses on when you look through binoculars, or take them off?"

She left them on. "Is that all right?" she wanted to know.

"That's fine," I said. "But you're much better off rolling the rubber eyecups down. That lets you bring the binoculars closer to your eyes, giving you a larger field of view. It makes it easier to find things."

Word spread quickly that there was a binocular "expert" in the group, and in short order I was besieged with questions about makes and models. Linda, who has seen it all before, just shook her head and went birding.

It was warmer now. The birders had shed their jackets; the birds had retired to the shade. The intrepid Mary Lou produced treasured glimpses of Anhingas, their wings spread in benediction, and an Osprey that flew in carrying a fish, then circled the group, whistling its defiance at the adult Bald Eagle cruising high overhead. She labored valiantly to pull a Eurasian Wigeon from the ranks of American Wigeon, mostly for my benefit (and hers). But it wasn't to be, and it didn't matter, anyway. For thirty-two birders who had crossed a threshold and whose minds were already spinning with half-remembered names and visions that ran together in a blur, Eurasian Wigeon is just another name, another bird. The special birds can wait until the time when they are special.

We got back to the lot and the cars disgorged their passengers. Good-byes were said; thank yous directed toward Mary Lou. Then the group dispersed, some heading for the exit and wherever their schedule carried them, some beating a path to the visitor center.

But two, at least, got back in their cars and started around again—visitors from northern parts going back for another look at the great wading birds of Florida. Maybe to get some pictures of the duck that wears the crescent moon on its face.

## LOUIS

He was standing in the middle of the crowd that he had drawn, an older man with the reflexes of a child and the aura of a prophet. One hand held a book, a field guide to the birds, that he referred to often. His words held those around him like a spell. At first, I'd taken him for an Everglades seasonal naturalist, then the leader of some bird club's outing. But he was neither. He was just a birder, one whose enthusiasm made him blind to any barriers standing between a stranger and a friendship. One who offered his knowledge and skills to others because they were his to give.

He gave his name as Louis Banker.

I watched for a time, marveling at his energy and how his enthusiasm affected the crowd that had gathered along the banks of Mrazek Pond in Everglades National Park. Birders, armed with binoculars, asked him the short, easy questions:

"Where can I find an ani?"

"Is the Bahama Swallow still being seen near Homestead?"

He answered them with the adroitness of a talk show host.

"Ani? Go to the EcoPond. Back side of the island. Here, I'll draw you a map.

"Bahama Swallow? Yes, seen yesterday. I called the hotline at breakfast. Just park near the on ramp and scan through the swallows nesting under the overpass. You can't miss it."

Tourists, armed with video cameras, asked him the long, hard ones:

"I'd like to buy my wife a bird book. Can you recommend a good one?"

"Say, maybe you can help me. We just saw this bird with long, skinny legs and a long, thin beak . . ."

And he handled these, too.

Louis Banker. Age? Who knows. Profession? Birder. In a recent former life, he was a high school debate coach. Then one day a doctor told him that his test results were bad, that the stress would kill him, that he had to get out before his heart gave out.

Then this rare human being did a very rare thing. He listened. He retired. And he took up birding.

"All I want to do is see five hundred species and then I'll be happy." That's what Louis Banker thought. That was the goal he set for himself.

But he saw five hundred . . . and he didn't stop.

OK, then, six hundred. That's all I want before my ticker stops.

Neither his ambition nor his ticker stopped at six hundred, or seven hundred either.

"Mr. Banker," I said, addressing the ebullient wizard. "My wife and I are looking for a Mangrove Cuckoo. I know that they're hard to find this time of year," I added apologetically.

He smiled, smiled as Oedipus might have smiled after he'd heard the Sphinx out; smiled the way the master magician smiles when his hand closes over the ears of the rabbit and the crowd still holds its breath.

"I saw one yesterday," he confided, "along the Bear Lake Trail. Come on. I'll take you there."

And he did.

There's nothing particularly unique about Louis Banker. The ethic of sharing runs strong among birders because birds are things that can be shared. But few, even among the ranks of birders, can match the level of friendliness housed in this man. Throughout our travels, strangers would ask us, "Have you met Louis Banker?" We'd smile from the memory and say yes. Then they would smile from their own memory and the smiles would vault the barrier that stands between strangers and friends. They would recount for us their own encounter with the remarkable man who pulled miracles from his hat, whose trademark was a smile.

# 4 • EVERGLADES NATIONAL PARK, FLORIDA:

## Going to Snake Bight

*I*T WAS LIGHT ENOUGH TO DISTINGUISH SHAPES, STILL too dark to see colors, and we were late. Two vehicles had already claimed spots near the trailhead, a rental and a van, both bearing Florida plates. We pulled up behind the van, exhumed our spotting scopes, donned binoculars and day packs, and headed for the trail, headed for Snake Bight.

There was a padlocked chain across the entrance—a barrier against unauthorized vehicles and a final warning to innocents who don't know what they are getting into. It's not much of a barrier—only knee-high, easily vaulted, and to the best of my knowledge it has never stopped a birder. But this time I hesitated, the chain drawing me up midstride, one foot planted in front, one behind.

"Did you remember water?" I asked, turning, looking back.

"Yes," Linda sighed.

"Gnat thwarter? Film? Forty-power eyepiece?"

"Yes."

It was a two-mile walk out to the flats, and that's too far to be casual about backtracking for missing gear. I paused, trying to think of anything we might have left out of our kit.

"Do you want to bring a field guide?"

Not far away, a cardinal began singing a lusty challenge, heralding the changing season. A catbird mewed a question, and overhead, a series of *chip* notes betrayed and identified a flock of Yellow-rumped Warblers to anyone with ears to hear.

"No," Linda replied, after a pause so slight that it barely deserves to be called hesitation. "We won't need one."

We stepped across the barrier with no more words between us, hurrying down the dark tunnel cut through living trees, hurrying toward Snake Bight.

The road is an old one, packed and polished by many feet—birders' feet. Tourists don't walk the Snake Bight Trail. They catch the ten o'clock tram, staring in fascinated horror at the sweating figures loaded down with optics, who mock them with smiles. A few birders might sneer.

The road is a long one, too, particularly if it is hot (which it usually is) or if there is some blisteringly rare bird waiting at the end (which is often the case). But passage will be hurried whatever the weather or fortune. The mosquitoes will see to that. Like smoke from a grass fire, they rise from the evil canal flanking the road. They come whining out of the tangled mangroves, making any who pass this way pay a price in blood.

Where does the road go? Just where the name implies—to Snake Bight! A sweeping bulge in Florida Bay rich in tidal flats and tidal birds. *Bight* refers to the cut of the shoreline, not to the implanted fangs of a viper. It's the mosquitoes who put the "bite" in Snake Bight (and it's strictly an insider's joke to refer to the road as "The Mosquito Bite Trail").

The trees locking their limbs overhead are tropical beyond the measure of this latitude. The elevated roadbed supports gumbo-limbo trees identified by their red peeling bark (the trait that gives the tree its colloquial name—the "tourist tree"). There are Jamaica dogwoods, cabbage palms, strangler figs, and cocklespur—a vine with thorns and flowers whose scent makes the air reek with the smell of cut peaches and hum with the wings of bees.

White-crowned Pigeons explode from the canopy, but binoculars hang limp from our straps. Waterthrushes *tack, tack, tack* monotonously from behind the wall of mangrove roots, and the songs of dueling Prairie Warblers drag their way up the scale. All go unheeded. Even the sly taunt of a Man-

grove Cuckoo doesn't break our stride for long. We hurry on, heads down, all but oblivious to the birds around us.

For Linda and me, the Ding Darling days of birding are over. The wonder that marked our early discovery-filled years has been supplanted by experience. Every identification made has been quietly woven into the net of our birder skills—the net that birders use to seine the world around them.

At first our nets were small and the mesh wide. They caught only the large and obvious birds. Experience increased the dimensions and tightened the mesh, catching birds that are harder to find or more difficult to identify, the birds that inexperienced birders miss. The nets knit of skill make it unnecessary to puzzle over common, everyday birds that fall into the net, and these may be jettisoned out of hand, leaving the net free to catch "better" birds.

*This* is the break point, the point where *bird-watching* ends and *birding* begins. From this junction on, the focus on birds becomes more a test of skills and less an esthetic pursuit. Each warbled taunt from the foliage, each wheeling silhouette against a cloud, is a challenge, a glove thrown, a target for a birder's net. Each bird correctly identified by sight or sound becomes a token of a birder's growing skill (and another strand in the net).

There is a price, of course. As skills grow, the sense of wonder that supports beginning birders diminishes. What replaces it is discovery. Wonder is something a child can hold in its hand, a feather or a bird fallen from the nest. Discovery is a prize garnered by ambition and skill. It is not as great as wonder. But it is very close, and it is also very addictive. Once a birder has a taste for it, there is only one thing that can satisfy the craving. And that is *more*.

More birds. More challenges to test growing skills. More discoveries to satisfy a growing need. The drive for more means that every cast of a birder's net must always be thrown with greater skill (or it gathers no new discoveries). When all the birds of a backyard or a county or a state have been gathered, it means that the net must be thrown into new seas (or the birds it gathers are always the same). For some birders, whose skills are very great and whose net has been cast in every imaginable sea, *every* throw becomes a cast for birds that lie at the limit of possibility, becomes a throw for the horizon.

For Linda and me, the horizon lies beyond the birds that level their challenges from the trees beside the Snake Bight Trail. We have no time to pursue these common birds for no greater gain than pleasure—not with Snake Bight so near. Because although Snake Bight is not necessarily birding's horizon, *sometimes*, if you are lucky, you can see it from there.

The trees fall away. The shrill whine of mosquitoes retreat into the shadows. The smell of brine makes nostrils tighten, and the blaze of sunlight turns eyes to slits. Before us is a platform, upon it several figures. In front of them, reaching all the way to the horizon, is Snake Bight.

Our approach was telegraphed to the birders on the observation deck through the walkway boards. They turned, looking us over quickly, then turned back to the birds that held their attention and would soon draw ours. We didn't recognize them; none of them recognized us.

We gained the deck, moved to a vacant corner, and began to set up our spotting scopes in silence, taking the measure of our fellow watchers. One guy was tall, built like a linebacker, and branded by an aura of friendliness that was impossible to conceal. A fellow I took to be his companion was slighter, slimmer. The third gentleman, standing at the corner that offered the best angle, was older than the other two, tanned and tennis-fit. His eye was fused to the eyepiece of a Questar telescope, which is sort of the Rolex of optics. I figured him for the Alpha male and linked him to the BULBUL van we'd seen in the parking lot. No words were traded between them, and there was nothing awkward about the silence.

"They all know each other, then," I surmised, objectively understanding, subjectively feeling the silence that bound them together and shut us out. We were the newcomers, strangers. It was up to us to make the overture, to invite their approval (and maybe to test the assailability of their privacy).

"Anything good out there?" I inquired, placing just the right inflection on the key word *good.*

*(Translation: I'm new here, not savvy to any hot birds in the area, but not looking for trash, either. I challenge you to name a bird that meets my idea of "good.")*

A neophyte would have given himself away by asking whether there were any "interesting" birds. He might have betrayed his generalized interest by asking whether any birds were "around" instead of directing his interest "out there," on the flats. Shorebirds take time to master. They aren't a game for beginners.

It was the linebacker who responded. "Nothing unusual. We just got here ourselves." A tricky bit of subtlety, that.

*(Translation: There's birds out there, Mr. Unknown Birder. But let's see you put names to them. P.S. If you do come up with something special, we're covered for not having discovered it first because we haven't had time to go through them thoroughly.)*

The Alpha male's attention never wavered from the spotting scope. The guy was serious, whoever he was; serious and probably good.

That ended conversation. It was clear that our credentials were still being checked out. I started setting up my spotting scope, letting each section of each tripod leg fall with a loud, unmuffled snap.

*Take note of this tripod, fellas. See, we know good equipment.* The message had already been conveyed via the quality binoculars slung around our necks. This was just insurance.

A small sandpiper flew over calling loudly enough to be heard over the din of the feeding flocks. Breeep? it said. The rising inflection at the end made it sound like a question.

"Least [Sandpiper]," I announced casually.

*(Translation: See. I know shorebird calls.)* That one, anyway.

This display elicited nothing, neither approval or disapproval, and this could mean one of two things. It *could* mean that these guys weren't savvy to shorebird calls and that I'd just scored big-time. But it could also mean that they were *quite* savvy to shorebird calls. Their silence was just a way of saying: *That's small potatoes, friend. You're going to have to do better than that if you want to make the grade in this company.*

Evidence suggested the latter.

I planted the tripod carefully, trying not to jar the platform. It doesn't take much to bounce the image in a Questar, and there's no fortune to be had in getting the Alpha male riled. Binoculars up, Linda and I started sweeping the horizon, seeing what we were up against, trying to figure out how to bird this course.

The bay was a mosaic of salt-blistered mud flats and rippled sunlight. The smell swept in by an onshore breeze was sour and wholesome, a combination of baked coral, brine, and vegetation cooking in the sun. The tide was decidedly out.

In the distance were islands of trees and islands of birds that floated upon a rippling blue mirage. Some of the islands were tall and white and pelicans. Some were short and black and skimmers. A few were ragged and craggy and herons. Scattered far and wide across the flats were feeding shorebirds, several thousand of them—Western Sandpipers, Dunlin, dowitchers, yellowlegs, Semipalmated and Wilson's Plovers. The distance made identification difficult. The sun, which reduced all plumages to silhouettes, made it almost impossible. The guy with the Questar, I noted, had the barrel pointed in the direction of one of the more distant flocks.

"*Damned* good, if he can do something with *those* birds," I mused.

A commotion way down in the ranks of feeding birds caught and drew my attention. A large falcon, invisible to the naked eye, was moving across the flats putting birds to flight. Its size, the rippling cadence of its wing beat, and probability marked it for what it was.

"Peregrine," I shouted, feeling the heads of the others snap erect. "Just left of that mass of shorebirds out there," I directed. "Half a field over the horizon. Going right."

It wasn't an easy bird to find. Not at that distance; not with that sun; not with the cloud of shorebirds going every which way. But these guys were good. They got on the bird long before it claimed a perch overlooking the flats.

One by one, the binoculars came down. Glances were exchanged among the triumvirate, then the eyes turned on us and stayed.

"Good," the Alpha male observed, speaking for the first time. "Maybe he'll push some of those birds in here where we can do something with them."

"There's been an immature Peregrine hanging around," he added,

addressing us for the first time. "That must be him," he concluded, returning to his scope.

*(Translation: Hi. I'm the local expert. If it moves out here, you can count on me to know about it and this bird's already on the books.)*

But the message said something else, too. It said we'd made the grade.

There is no shelter at Snake Bight, no protection. There are no leaders to tell you what you are seeing or field guides to put names to frail silhouettes that swim in an ocean of sun glare. There is only you, your ambition, and whatever net of skills you bring to cast at the horizon. If you are lucky, there will be others there, too, who will throw their nets beside yours. And the horizon will not seem so formidable.

Spotting scopes rake the flats, searching through the shorebird masses, seeking anything to catch and hold a hunting eye, seeking the odd bird out. A bird standing off by itself is cause for scrutiny. A bird that stands just a little bit taller than those around or probes the flats with a different motion calls attention to itself.

The man mantling the Questar stands and stretches.

"Do you know about the Curlew Sandpiper?" he asks, putting a name to the bird that lay on his horizon.

No, I admitted, I hadn't heard. It was OK to admit this, now; now that we'd been accepted.

"Well, there's been one reported from here."

The operative word was *reported*. The bird had not been *seen*, which would have denoted acceptance and verification. The bird was only "reported." There was a margin of doubt.

"When?" I asked, declaring my neutrality by avoiding damaging verbs.

"Yesterday," he confirmed.

"Who was the observer?"

"I don't know. One of the Everglades people."

"Ah," I said. This explained the cautious margin. The observer was someone whose credentials were unknown.

"I was here yesterday afternoon," I offered. "I met three guys I know from the DVOC [Delaware Valley Ornithological Club] in Philadelphia. Good birders. They didn't mention a Curlew Sandpiper."

"The bird was seen in the morning," the Questar owner advised. "It came in on the rising tide."

"When's high today?" the linebacker wanted to know.

" 'Bout an hour. Howard Langridge," he said, offering his hand.

"Pete Dunne," I said, taking it. "My wife, Linda."

*Howard Langridge? Howard Langridge? . . . Ah, the Regional Editor for* American Birds. *Whew. The Alpha-Alpha male.*

"Pleased to meet you," he intoned.

"How good is Curlew Sandpiper down here?" I inquired.

"I need it for Florida," Howard allowed, confident that I had enough information to appreciate the enormity of this disclosure. "But I've seen it other places."

Curlew Sandpiper, a Eurasian species, was plainly a rare bird in Florida.

"They're fairly regular in New Jersey," I confided, "but not so regular that the DVOC crew wouldn't have mentioned seeing one."

I hesitated, holding back the disclosure that was aching to find release. There was a bird on our horizon, too. Not a Curlew Sandpiper. Something much rarer, much more elusive. A tall pink will-o-the-flats so rare that its status in North America is blurred by controversy and denial. Yesterday, from Snake Bight, the horizon had brushed my DVOC friends. The will-o-the-flats had taken earthly form, stalked the shallows, then retreated into the rippling glare.

It was a great prize, this bird from beyond the horizon. A prize worthy of any birder's net. It was the bird that Linda and I were casting for. This is why I hesitated to speak of it. Because sometimes, if you want something very badly and you say it, it will not happen.

You may tell me this is superstition. I tell you that just as will-o-the-wisps take on corporeal form as they draw near the horizon, superstition incorporates the properties of cause and effect.

"The DVOC crew *did* have something special," I blurted finally, unable

to restrain my tongue any longer. "They had a bunch of flamingos come in and land out toward the southeast. We got here about thirty minutes late."

The disclosure did its work, shutting down conversation; pulling linchpins on the fragile foundation of our credibility. It was Howard who recovered first.

"I haven't heard of flamingos out here for a while," he informed us. "How many were there?"

"About twenty, they said."

"Any immatures?"

"They didn't say."

The implications of the nearby Flamingo Campground notwithstanding, flamingos are irregular visitors in the Everglades. Wild birds from the Bahamas or the West Indies may sometimes wander into Florida. But most of the flamingos that turn up are regarded as escapees from assorted tourist parks and, as such, are not officially sanctified for birder consumption. But a flock the size of this one might well harbor wild birds among the suspect ranks. Whatever their official standing, a flock of flamingos would certainly be something to see, a vision right out of the pages of Audubon's portfolio.

The pink shadow passed and conversation picked up again. While we spoke, we scanned, searching the silhouette flocks, cursing the sun and begging the tide to push the birds our way. There was talk about Curlew Sandpipers, and whether their bills *really* are more curved than the bills of Dunlin—whether head shape wasn't a better way of telling them apart. There was news of the Bananaquit that had been discovered north of Fort Lauderdale and an update on the Cassin's Kingbird at Loxahatchee Refuge. Shop talk.

All this time, the scopes remained on the horizon.

The sun climbed and conversation moved on to equipment . . . then acquaintances . . . then back to birds, again. The tide came in and left and it did not bring a Curlew Sandpiper. The sun burned the blush off the morning and then it took the color out of the sky.

The scopes stayed pinned to the horizon.

It grew hotter. Now the distant flocks danced in an ocean of heat waves.

The sun made the mud shine like silver slime, engulfing the flocks in pools of mercury. The sun dried us. The wind dried us. Conversation dried us, too, until there was nothing left to talk about and conversation stopped.

Lunchtime came and went. Watches were consulted with epidemic frequency. Feet grew restless and minds were preyed upon by the thought of cold drinks sitting in the coolers back at the car. But nobody moved to leave. Nobody stopped looking.

You will want to ask me, maybe, what it is that makes people bind hours of their lives to the horizon like this. It isn't stubbornness, that much I can tell you. Stubbornness is the bulwark of pride, and people don't search horizons for pride. They look within themselves.

It isn't for lack of imagination. It doesn't take much imagination for thirsty people to conjure the notion of getting something to drink.

It's not for fun, either. There's nothing particularly fun about dehydrating on some salt-blasted mud flat.

The fact is, I don't know what makes birders scan a horizon for hours on end, any more than I understand why anyone would be driven to run a marathon or write a sonata. I don't know. We all just cast the nets we have at the horizons we see. Sometimes, if we wait long enough, if we cast far and skillfully enough (and if we are very, very lucky), *sometimes* we reap an answer.

The line of birds emerged from the liquid shimmer that encased the horizon, taking on substance and color as they rose. Then their wings failed them. They fell back into the molten light lying thick and heavy at the rim of conjecture and disappeared.

*It was them*, I thought, I knew, and even the empty horizon could not shake this conviction.

*They were big. They were pink. Their wings were flashing black, so they weren't spoonbills.*

It was them.

"I've got them," I shouted, and on command, the great flowing line rose above the shimmer again, a frail string of birds buffeted by heat waves, half held in the corporeal world only by the strength of my will.

"WHERE?" a chorus of voices demanded.

"On the horizon. Going left. No reference. They keep drifting in and out of the heat waves."

I felt several bodies run up behind me to line up their scopes along mine. The vibration shattered the fragile image, and when it returned, the birds were gone.

"They're down again," I counseled, hoping it was true. "I can't take my eyes off the spot or I'll lose them," I apologized for not surrendering the scope to another. "Just line up on where my scope is pointing."

Seconds passed. Too many seconds. What was wrong? Was that it, all the vision our skill could buy? Were they gone?

"They're up," somebody else shouted. I panned left and caught them again. Seventeen birds with hardly more substance than a dream, lining out across Florida Bay. I held onto them until their forms dissolved into the heat; until the rhythm of their wings melted into air. Until they passed, once more, and finally, beyond the horizon and the net of our skills.

Where discovery ends, and wonder begins.

## 5 • RIO GRANDE VALLEY, TEXAS:

## _The_ Valley

### THE THIN, GREEN LINE

HERE ARE TWO KINDS OF DESERTS IN SOUTH TEXAS, the natural kind and the unnatural kind. The natural desert is covered by chaparral and a host of spiny plants united by a common vendetta against all things that bleed. It's a harsh, dry land, cluttered with the debris cast off by human ambitions that came up short. It is also big, and before I forget to say it, beautiful in a desperate sort of way. If you have never driven Route 77 south of Corpus Christi and would like to gain some feel for the place, get in your car and seek out some vacant city lot, one where the weeds outnumber the jetsam. Choose a day that is so hot the tar runs in rivulets in the street and construction makes the air taste like baked flint. Roll your windows up. Turn the heater to high; the blower on full; now _stare_ at the lot . . . and imagine that its boundaries reach clear to the heat-warped horizon.

This is what much of South Texas is like.

The other Texas desert is the agricultural desert. Sometimes it is sterile and green. Between crops it is sterile and brown. The operative word is _sterile_. At no time does it support the wealth of birds and animals that a comparable riparian woodland would, although before they were cut, the forests of the lower Rio Grande Valley did support such wealth.

So, these are the deserts of South Texas, and there is little to distinguish them from the deserts of northern Mexico. There is, however, a line of demarcation—a verdant swath of green called the Rio Grande in the north, the Rio Bravo in the south. There the river dips deep into sovereign Mexico, scooping up birds of semitropical flavor, placing them within reach of North America's birders. Exotic birds with exotic-sounding names: Plain Chachalacas, Common Pauraque, Rose-throated Becard, Great Kiskadee, Altamira Oriole, birds that appear in places like Pennsylvania so infrequently that "never" seems an optimistic assessment.

It's true, of course, that any North American birder can just travel to Mexico to find these and other exotic birds in numbers. But this will not satisfy the American Birding Association, the body that defines the rules and regulations under which serious North American birders operate. For a bird to "count" on a birder's North American List, both the bird and birder must be in bounds. And "in bounds," according to the ABA referees, means that both bird and birder must be found on the American side of the Rio Grande.

So every year, from December through March, birders head for "The Valley," canvassing what's left of the riparian woodlands for exotic birds that are in bounds by a geographic whisker. Places like Palm Sanctuary, Santa Ana National Wildlife Refuge, the Santa Margarita Ranch, Salineno . . . and Bentsen-Rio Grande State Park—"the best bird birding spot in the Lower Valley" sayeth Jim Lane. Amen.

## BENTSEN STATE PARK—WHERE CHECK MARKS GROW ON TREES

If you pull into Bentsen late and sleep through the predawn chorus of pauraques and the wake-up calls of Great Kiskadees and Couch's Kingbirds, the Plain Chachalacas will rouse you for sure. This ground-hugging relative of the turkey is dressed like a shadow and moves like a pickpocket. At dawn, the raucous clamor could drive Saint Francis to an act of violence.

But birders are no more likely to sleep late on their first morning in Bentsen State Park than a child on Christmas morning. The 587-acre stand of subtropical vegetation is one great avian piñata; housed within its wood-land borders is more avian treasure than you can shake a stick at.

Linda and I beat the chachalacas up by an easy ten minutes, but we won no prize for early appearance. The trailer loop, the very heart of Bentsen, was already flush with birders. Most in the morning promenade were drawn from the ranks of RV owners, retirees from northern states spending a week or two savoring the pleasures of Bentsen. "Winter Texans" is the name given them by native Texans (one of the names, anyway).

Augmenting the ranks of RV birders were day-trippers, easily distinguished by their drove-all-night faces, doughnuts on the rental sedan's dashboard, and the powdered sugar around their mouths. Some are students or teachers on winter break, others businessmen who tacked a few days of vacation onto a business trip to Houston. Unlike the RV owners, their hours in Bentsen are precious and few—they are hit-and-run birders who must scoop up what treasure they can in a single morning, then surrender to the tyranny of tight schedules.

On the dashboards of their Alamo rentals (right next to the box of doughnuts) is their Bible—*A Birder's Guide to the Rio Grande Valley of Texas*, by Jim Lane. Planted firmly in their cerebral cortex is an avian hit list of the birds that Saint James, patron saint of the needy (bird) lister, says are to be found in Bentsen.

No ordinary birds, these. These are LIFE BIRDS! The birds that have, thus far, eluded their grasp; the ones that mock them by flaunting empty boxes next to their names on their Checklist of North American Birds. They gnaw at a birder's tranquility, these feathered recalcitrants. They are the impetus for all-night drives to places that even the Census Bureau hasn't heard of.

There is only one way for a questing birder to find peace. Each empty box must be etched with a check mark, the little building blocks of a birder's Life List. Each check is a step closer to one of birding's milestone plateaus—the 500 club, the 600 club . . . who knows—maybe someday even the 700 club. Seven hundred species of birds. All seen in North America. No, no birder sleeps late on his first morning in Bentsen State Park, where the wings of Mexican birds brush North American, where the check marks grow on trees.

The first half-dozen checks fall into their boxes easily. A White-tipped Dove strolls out of the shadows (*check*). Yellow flashes in the trees betray a Couch's Kingbird (*check*) . . . a Brown-crested Flycatcher (*check*) . . . a Great Kiskadee (*check*).

A green flash brings you face to face with a Green Jay, an impossible bird painted like a verdant clown. Then a rolling call draws eyes to the Golden-fronted Woodpecker, whose head is buried in an orange half affixed to a tree.

*Check/check.*

But these are just the everyday "good" birds of Bentsen. The next tier is more elusive. They include Tropical Parulas, with their maddeningly intermittent song. Northern Beardless Tyrannulets, a drab, cut-down flycatcher whose name is longer than the bird. The sometimes-there, sometimes-not Blue Bunting. *Then* there is Clay-colored Robin, phantom *turdis* of Bentsen. It lives in shadows. It appears moments after you have gone (to chase the tarannulet or the parula). It retreats back into the woods behind Campsite 12 mere *seconds* before you return.

The *Damn* Robin.

Some birders trust to their own skill and luck to locate those second-generation specialties, and many succeed. But if you are short on one and down on the other you might try orbiting around the clusters of birders distributed along the Bentsen loop. Good birds create congestion and a group of twenty people standing in the same place, looking straight up, is much easier to locate than a tyrannulet or a . . .

"BECARD?! Where?"

"Up there. Near the top. Look. It's moving."

"Oh . . . I got it. Oh, wow."

Or, you can hitch your fortunes to one of the two local stars, Red and Louise Gambill, Winter Texans who have donned the mantle of hosts to visiting birders.

"Clay-colored Robin? It was here just a minute ago," Red will announce

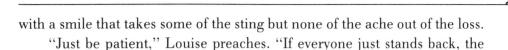

with a smile that takes some of the sting but none of the ache out of the loss.

"Just be patient," Louise preaches. "If everyone just stands back, the bird will probably come out again. It's just shy."

Many are the North America birders who have Louise's discerning ears and Red's sage wisdom to thank for their Life becard or Clay-colored Robin. They never seem to tire of walking visiting birders along the paths of the Rio Grande hiking trail in search of the Hook-billed Kite, a stealthy raptor with a bulbous bill and a golden eye. They can always be talked into heading down toward the Rio Grande for Green Kingfisher—an emerald dart with a penchant for being on the wrong side of the river. And when the rumors of some smoking-hot rarity drift north out of The Valley, America's birders call Red and Louise for confirmation (*before* calling their travel agent).

By midmorning (i.e., shortly after sunrise), all the easy birds have been found, and most of the semitough denizens of Bentsen as well. The clusters of birders that marked the location of the becard, the tyrannulet, the Tropical Parula have been reduced to anxious handfuls of birders-come-lately. Most in the morning promenade have gathered around the site where the Clay-colored Robin was last reported. They are elated by success. Their faces shine with it. Their voices are strained with it.

"It took me forever to find the becard and it was right there. Right there. But until it moved . . ."

"Oh, I got a quick glimpse of the tyrannulet. Not a portrait but good enough to tell."

But elation, like any emotional high, is difficult to sustain. New triumphs find comfortable niches and become old successes. The sun climbs and the heat leaches the songs out of the air. Minutes pass and the robin does not.

Watches are consulted. Miles to next destinations calculated. Singly or in small groups, the birders disband—the RV owners to breakfast, the day-trippers to their doughnuts and the tyranny of their schedules. Later, when the day's wages are calculated in the comfort of an RV or from a down-and-out motel room, empty boxes next to some very special names will be filled with very satisfying check marks (and a vendetta will be sworn against the phantom *turdis* of Bentsen).

When the time comes to look back at the highlights of a lifetime of birding, that morning at Bentsen will be accounted among the great ones. The morning check marks grew on trees. That's the good news.

The bad news is, you can never do it again. First mornings at Bentsen come once in a lifetime.


## TO HAVE AND HAVE NOT

We hurried down the entrance road, past the Santa Ana Refuge Visitor Center, past the dike that guarantees one hundred years of protection against flood, past the pond on the left where the Least Grebe alternately bobs and dives.

I was ahead, carrying the scope. Linda, lugging our magnum-size camera bag, trailed behind. I'm 6'2" and long-legged. Linda's 5'2" and not—not particularly long-legged and not particularly happy about being second in a two-horse race en route to a Life Bird.

"Slow down," she commanded. "Or take this bag and give me the scope."

"Sor-ry," I puffed, slowing to something under an Olympic half-miler's gait. Even at this more leisurely pace we came quickly to our destination, the "old refuge manager's residence."

The one-story ranch house is abandoned now, but the birds have not shifted allegiance. Great Kiskadees scolded and chattered from the ebony trees surrounding the house. Blue-gray Gnatcatchers spoke in lisping whispers. Smoke-colored chachalacas hidden among the branches made the air ring, and the Tropical Parula had departed so recently that even the limbs of the trees were ignorant. Each thought the next still held the bird.

Around the house is a fence, and the fence is clustered with flowers—long-stemmed orange blossoms that flourish beneath the trees. Somewhere around this flower garden was the bird we sought. Its name was "Buff-bellied Hummingbird."

"We had it earlier," a couple from Ohio confirmed, smiling that maddening smile that birders who have already seen the bird flash to birders who have not.

You know this smile. It's the smile that gets flashed at a party by some snippet who tells you a story about your husband that he's never told you. The smile that a younger coworker, two grades down, smiles when he lets slip information about a major restructuring in the department that you haven't heard about. *That* smile.

"Just be patient. *You're sure to see it!*" they added, binding us in a spell of failure by uttering this fatal curse.

We could have killed them. Strangled them with their binocular straps. Harpooned them with tripods thrown with lethal intent. Never, ever tell another birder that they are "sure to see" something. It is the kiss of death. It is an indiscretion beyond forgiveness.

"Thank you for the information," I heard myself saying.

"Has the Clay-colored Robin been seen?" Linda inquired sweetly, innocently, playing a hunch. *Why were the two of them sticking around if they'd already seen the bird?*

The smiles disappeared—crumbled, actually.

"No," the couple from Ohio who had already seen the Buff-bellied Hummingbird admitted. It hadn't.

"Oh, well," Linda offered, "the Bentsen bird has been very cooperative the last two mornings. Site 12."

"We're going there next," the couple from Ohio who had already seen the Buff-bellied Hummingbird (but not the Clay-colored Robin) said quickly. "Site 12?"

"Site 12," Linda confirmed. "Sometimes Site 16," she added. "Oh, well, thanks," the couple from Ohio who had not seen the Clay-colored Robin said, half-smiling, half-turning, starting to walk away. "Just be patient. You're *sure* to see that hummingbird," they reminded us.

"Occasionally Site 9," Linda replied, waving, pulling the teeth on their smile and neutralizing their spell.

"How'd you know they hadn't seen a Clay-colored Robin, yet?" I wanted to know.

"Just a guess," Linda replied.

As it was we were quite prepared to be patient for something as exquisite as a Buff-bellied Hummingbird; prepared to wait as long as might be necessary. There is no such thing as an ugly hummingbird, and, even among the ranks of hummers, the Buff-bellied is a prize, distinguished by its colors and its very restricted U.S. range.

As stakeouts go, hummingbirds give good odds. They are a tenacious lot, territorial to a fault. When a hummingbird commandeers a flower patch his allegiance is resolute, and this bird had been the master of this patch all winter. Even though the garden was a large one, even though the morning was warm, so the birds' visits would not be frequent, we felt confident about seeing our prize.

So we just settled in to the familiar rhythm of waiting, an art and a science that birders cultivate. While waiting, a part of your mind is always there, always alert for motion or sound. Set on hummingbird mode, eyes become calibrated to pick up any vertical movement among the flowers; ears are tuned to detect hummingbird *ticks* or *snits* and *snarls*. The rest of the mind is free to wander, to turn in upon itself, swim through the memories and musings that are the companions of those who spend lavish amounts of time in the field.

Not that our wait was a lonely one. We had each other, and soon enough we had more company. A couple from St. Cloud, a doctor from Florida, another couple from Walnut Creek, California. Disparate lives with a common interest, drawn together by a bird in a flower garden on the banks of the Rio Grande.

The wait was not even a long one, not as these things go. Less than half an hour—hardly any wait at all. People have spent days waiting for a Life Bird to show. No one saw the bird appear. But suddenly, there was a vibration among the flowers . . . and *there it was.*

The head flashed with turquoise hues, the tail shone like polished copper, the bill was orange unto red. The feathered figurine drank deeply from one flower, then the next, and so on down the line. When the gem had taken its fill, it took a perch just above the gate next to the house and began to preen. In the scope, at fifty feet and 20x, every iridescent feather glistened.

Looking at birds is a little like viewing art in a gallery. The difference is that birding adds an element of excitement that galleries lack, the excitement born of risk. Very few works of art, however skillfully crafted, can approach the splendor of a living bird. Mind, I did not say that Great Art is not alive. Art *is* alive—imbued with the life of the artist and sustained by the viewer (and this is what distinguishes Great Art from mere art). But birds are more than just alive. Birds are *omnisciently* alive. Wild birds are not caged for our pleasure. They are free and we see them at their sufferance —or we may not see them at all. That's the risk. That's the element of gain and loss that motivates human ambition.

It might be that even something as exquisite as a Buff-bellied Hummingbird cannot hold people's attention indefinitely. There are, after all, other birds to find and matters like lunch and rest rooms to consider. But we'll never know. The bird moved first, exercising its free will, breaking the spell that bound our group together. Smug and elated with success, we said our good-byes, sharing the smile that birders smile when they have just shared a good bird. Our *ad hoc* gallery disbanded, some going one way, some another. Linda and I started for the parking lot.

On the way we met another couple, a young couple, hurrying down the road. He was carrying a scope and leading. She was carrying a long-lens camera, struggling to keep up and doing very well. Our smiles must have been evident from a long way off.

"What have you seen?" the fellow shouted with one hundred feet still between us.

"We had the Buff-bellied Hummingbird," I assured, feeling the smile widen across my face.

"WHERE?" they demanded from a range of fifty feet.

"Working the orange flowers around the gate next to the old residence," Linda explained cheerfully.

"WHEN?" he shouted at our faces.

"About ten minutes ago," I confided, beaming.

Their faces took on a pained, stricken expression, but their pace never slackened.

I almost slipped and told them that they "wouldn't have any trouble seeing it." But stopped myself in time.

"It's been regular," I assured, choosing my words with care.

"THANKS!" he said to the empty trail ahead of him.

"Thanks," she said as she passed.

Linda and I smiled at each other. Not the smile that birders smile when they've seen a bird and you haven't. The kind of smile that couples smile when they share a thought that has no need for words.


## A TAPE

Trapped in a cone of amber light, the figure framed against the public phone appeared frail and small. Her face, partially obscured by shadows, was creased by weariness or worry.

If I were an artist, I thought, I'd do her in charcoal and call it "The last digit could be a 4 or a 9." I'd call it "Hello . . . Daddy?" I'd call it . . .

"Desperation!" Perfect! Only desperation could drive a person to a public phone during the hours that lie between the time the bars in McAllen close and the churches open; desperation (or the anticipation of a Good Bird—which is just a form of desperation).

As I watched, the figure placed the phone back on its receiver. Folded the paper she had been writing on into quarters. Pocketed it. And made her way toward the van.

"We should have called last night when it was warmer," Linda grumbled.

"I need coffee," I replied sympathetically.

"Head west on 83," she directed.

"Coffee," I said, nodding. "And gas," I amended uneasily.

Linda glanced at the dashboard to get a first-hand damage assessment. From her angle, the needle must have looked pretty darn in-the-red.

"Boy, we're having some fun now," Linda said, straightening, speaking to her reflection in the windshield.

We nosed out of Bentsen State Park, down Park Road 2062 en route to the freeway and another day of quest along the banks of the Rio Grande.

Some (a watching custom's agent, for instance) might wonder who

Linda could have phoned that would be receptive to a call at four o'clock in the morning—early even by birding standards. The answer is, Linda wasn't calling a "who." Linda was calling a "what." Linda was calling NARBA, the North American Rare Bird Alert, a hotline operated by the Houston Audubon Society that directs birders to rare, aspired-to birds all over North America. NARBA is the functional overlord to a feudal network of over ninety birding hotlines scattered across forty-two states and six Canadian provinces. Access to NARBA is restricted to card-carrying members who pay an annual tithe of twenty-five dollars for the privilege of having news of North America's blisteringly rare birds right at their fingertips.

Of course, the NARBA number doesn't change every year. Anyone who already has the number doesn't have to pay another dime to tap into its services. But birders are disgustingly honest. Most are perfectly willing to ante up annually to support a service that serves them. Regional and statewide hotlines, on the other hand, are free (as free as telephone rates make them). For anyone who cares to call, information and directions to a Bananaquit in Florida or starlings in Alaska are just a touch-tone away, dispensed in plain, birding English (except in Quebec).

Most bird alerts are sponsored by birding clubs or ornithological societies. Most are changed weekly or, if some extreme rarity turns up within the tape's geographic fiefdom, at need. All are simple extensions of birding's ethic of sharing.

The information Linda and I sought had to do with Red-billed Pigeons, a Rio Grande specialty with a knack for not being found. The birds *may* be seen along the Rio Grande hiking trail in Bentsen. More often, they are not. But, according to NARBA, some benighted soul had discovered a roost right alongside Highway 83 near Zapata, Texas—a mere two-hour drive from Bentsen. We were going to cash in on it.

Providing we could find some all-night convenience store with a gas pump. And coffee.

"It's got to be right here," I insisted, glancing at the odometer, pulling onto the shoulder, trying to pick a spot that was free of beer bottles and cactus and settling for one that just had cactus.

"There," Linda said, pointing up along the roadside, toward the black outline of a barbed wire fence . . . and the little bitty piece of surveyor's tape hanging from the top strand—the one the Hotline assured would be there. The one we had driven past twice.

"Now what?" I demanded, draining the last of my second twelve-ounce cup of coffee and wishing I'd gotten the sixteen-ounce instead.

"Get out and look north," Linda read. "The birds are in a wooded ravine, visible from fence and the tape," she added from memory.

We clambered out of the van, into a chill Texas dawn, and climbed toward the fence. Aside from the tape, there was nothing about the place to suggest that it held anything more interesting than a cactus. In fact, it looked pretty bleak—a harsh, scabby landscape whet by winter and unsheathed by spring.

Dawn was just getting serious. One of the rarely spoken advantages to being a birder are the number of sunrises you get to appreciate in the course of a lifetime. Most people come onto a day full blown—to a sun already high in the sky, a world already in motion, and the impossible task of catching up. They rarely see the tentative side of morning or appreciate the great struggle between light and darkness played out on a world stage. Some mornings come raging over the horizon, angry and red. Some are so subtle that the transformation of night and day seems like an afterthought. All are different and all are priceless.

Sometimes, as I stand, waiting for a dawn and some bird to appear, I recall a conversation with my friend and coworker Gordon Schultze, director of the New Jersey Audubon Society's Lorrimer Nature Center. The normally amiable director arrived one morning, and a dark cloud followed him through the door.

"What's the matter with you?" I demanded, jabbing at what I assumed was just a standard morning grump.

Gordon didn't reply right away. He just regarded me with the frightening steadiness an executioner might assume while taking the measure of a man approaching the gallows.

"I just realized, today," he replied, "that I've already seen more sunrises in my life than there are sunrises left for me to see."

There is no response to a truth so blatantly spoken, and I didn't try to find one. But I recall his words often; maybe because of them I count each sunrise the way a miser counts his gold.

This one leaned toward the tentative end of the scale. The sky was overcast, and colors could not be infused into the landscape no matter how much light was spent. It was windy, and the wind was cold. Behind us, the telltale tape fluttered, making impatient tapping sounds. There was rain, and it was not far off.

Chihuahuan Ravens navigated a gray horizon, and caracaras took up sentry duty atop telephone poles (the poles not already claimed by Harris's Hawks). From the far side of the road, a Black-throated Sparrow clambered atop a wasted bush and threw its song at the wind.

"There," Linda said, bringing her binoculars to bear.

Two dark, pigeonlike forms rose from a branchy ravine, lighting on the arm of a withered stump of a tree. They were too big and too burly for doves. In the absence of any other indigenous pigeon, they were, by default, they *had to be* Red-billeds.

But there is something about a Life Bird that demands more confirmation than this. In the case of birds that are named for some particular attribute—"Horned" Lark, "Ruby-crowned" Kinglet, "Red-billed" Pigeon—there is some maddening compulsion to actually see the distinguishing characteristic, even when better identifying characteristics exist.

The light was poor and the distance extreme, but through a Kowa TSN-4 spotting scope at 20x, what had been an all-dark pigeon became an all-dark pigeon with a dark red bill.

"Satisfied," I said.

"Satisfied," Linda affirmed. "And frozen."

"Where to, now?" I wanted to know.

"San Ygnacio," she said. "White-collared Seedeater," she translated in response to my look of puzzlement.

"Oh, San Ygnacio," I said, nodding. "Patron Saint of the White-collared Seedeater."

## A BOOK

It's likely that not a fraction of North American residents have ever heard of San Ygnacio, Texas. But of those who could place it on a map, perhaps ninety-nine percent know it as the "Seedeater Capital of North America." What significance this oddly prosperous riverside town might hold for the balance of society I cannot begin to imagine, and this is precisely what I would say under oath.

The Seedeater Capital of North America lies ten miles northwest of Zapata, which is fifteen miles up Highway 83 from Lopeno, which is not far from Falcon Dam. It is also forty miles south of Laredo, but Laredo is not particularly close to anything. Despite the allegiance of the post office, the town of San Ygnacio is eminently Mexican. The sun-bleached homes, the narrow streets, the town cemetery dressed in Easter finery—all are bound by cultural lines that go south, not north. Even the resident "English" (House) Sparrows have disposed of their Anglo heritage. Most go around trying to pass themselves off as White-collared Seedeaters, and not a few succeed.

If notoriety is accepted as the foundation of San Ygnacio's identity, then the town's patron saint is not the martyred bishop of Antioch but James A. Lane, whose bird-finding guides opened a continent of discovery to North American birders. For birders on the hunt for new birds to add to Life Lists, his Birder's Guides to: *Arizona, the Texas Coast, Colorado, Southern California, Florida, Churchill, North Dakota,* and *the Rio Grande Valley of Texas* are as indispensable as binoculars and a field guide.

The key to the guide's success is simple. Birds are predictable. They are predictable because they are biologically tied to certain schedules, certain places, certain habitats, even to certain plant communities (microhabitats). Find the proper habitat and you find the bird that calls it home. Or, looking at this another way, find a bird in a certain place, at a certain time, and you can dependably count on finding it, or another of the same species, in the same place, under similar circumstances, again.

Now, if you can write directions to the site and express all the temporal and behavioral modifiers in the form of instructions, then you can direct another person to the bird, too. This is precisely what Jim Lane did, and "precisely" is how he did it—step-by-step instructions right down, in many cases, to which bush to kick and which nesting cavity to peer into.

Others have written bird-finding guides. Before Lane there was Olin Sewall Pettingill, whose expansive two-volume *Guide to Bird Finding East [and West] of the Mississippi* was generous with its entries but leaner on detailed instructions of a bird-finding nature. After Lane, after the great mobile mob of birders that he helped create exhausted the reach of his assistance, a host of bird-finding guides came into being. Guides to bird finding in Utah, Tennessee, Seattle and King County, the Delaware Valley, and many other places both great and obscure. Some are good. Some are not so good. Few have the poignancy, the style, or the wit of the Lane Guides. Some say none.

Jim Lane, birding's great pathfinder, died in 1986, and books as specific as the Lane Guides need constant maintenance. The bushes to kick sometimes get cut. Nesting cavities are not forever. Harold Holt assumed the burden of Lane maintenance. It was one of his revisions that guided us to San Ygnacio.

"Now what?" I said into an upended can of soda.

"Now," Linda explained, "we look for the post office. Lane says the birds are usually found behind the post office and in the cemetery. There's supposed to be a dirt road south of town."

"Excuse me," I asked the proprietor of a convenience store, whose mind was on inventory and who had probably never knowingly set eyes on a White-collared Seedeater in his life. "Where's the post office?"

"Center of town," he said not too helpfully.

"Where's the center of town?" Linda asked.

" 'Bout half way between here and the other side."

"Thanks," we said, not certain we meant it.

We found the center of town (just where he said it would be) and the post office, and the road, and the river. We split up to cover more ground and discovered, independently, the same weedy lots, and the same dusty troop of House Sparrows. We did not find a seedeater, and this is about par.

There are accounts of people who have made as many as six trips to San Ygnacio in search of seedeaters who went away each time with nothing more tangible than disappointment.

What is a seedeater that it can command this kind of desperate loyalty? It is a drab, dirt-colored finch that would have to stretch to see the top of a saltshaker. Why would anyone go out of his way to see a diminutive, drab, dirt-colored finch? Because when you ink that check mark next to the bird's name in your field guide, it's just as big and beautiful as the check mark next to a Buff-bellied Hummingbird.

That's why.

"Seen any finchlike birds?" I asked my hot, tired, and approaching spouse.

"You bet," she replied not too enthusiastically. "Those," she said, pointing toward the resident flock of House Sparrows that were panting in the shade of a bush and not even trying to pass themselves off as seedeaters. Both of us were on the verge of calling it quits. Midday is the absolute nadir of bird activity, and seedeaters were clearly at a premium in San Ygnacio.

"Let's go down to the river," I suggested, trying to sound optimistic. "I don't know about seedeaters, but at least there might be some birds down there."

We ambled down the short, steep dirt avenue leading to the Rio Grande, stopping in front of a tall stand of river grass. Not very enthusiastically, I touched two fingers to my lips and started making a series of long, squealing sounds—the kind of sounds that a starling might make to protest the grip of a Cooper's Hawk. It's Pavlovian, actually. I "squeak" automatically at the sight of riverside grass (but thickets elicit the same response).

All of a sudden, there it was. A diminutive, dirt-colored bird with swollen bill keyed up atop a grassy stem twenty feet away. It must have been hidden among the reeds and hitched itself up along a stem to see what all the commotion was about. The buffy finch with the swollen bill remained for something short of a minute—and then dropped from sight.

White-collared Seedeater. Goal scored by Dunne and Dunne. (Jim Lane credited with an assist.)

"Pretty little thing," Linda observed generously.

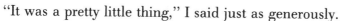

"It was a pretty little thing," I said just as generously.

We ambled up the road toward the van. The House Sparrows, sitting in their bush, paid us no mind.

Funny. They don't look a bit like seed eaters.

## AND THE KEYS TO THE CORVID

You can see it from the freeway—Our Lady of Guadalupe. The red tile roof supports a single domed bell tower. The walls are brick, the color desert-sand. The architecture of the church betrays a Spanish influence and recalls a time long, long ago. This is the church of Tom Pincelli, Father Tom Pincelli—the voice of the Rio Grande Valley Birding Hotline.

The road from Connecticut to Brownsville, Texas, is as complicated as a man's life or as simple as a vow. When Father Tom donned his collar and received the Roman Catholic Sacrament of Ordination, he also accepted (with humility) the wisdom of Rome and whatever assignment suited it. For a newly ordained priest and avid birder, it seemed nothing short of Divine Providence that the Rio Grande Valley should be his ultimate destination.

Father Tom is a slim, precise, energetic man in his forties. He looks like a cross between Tom Selleck and Groucho Marx (but favors Tom Selleck). He talks enthusiastically about birds, hunting, his parish, his work, social projects . . . in short, about everything. Father Tom is a man brimming with life and vitality. Preparing souls for the afterlife is just what he does.

"How did you get into birding?" I inquired, one of the stock questions governing such meetings.

"I used to take afternoon beach walks with a birding friend in Connecticut," he said, looking at the ceiling of his office. "He used to just point birds out. You know. 'There's a Willet . . . there's a Sanderling . . . there's a . . .'" He stops, shrugs. A shrug that says: "You know how it is."

Yes, I know how it is.

"And you were hooked," I said, to convey my understanding.

"I was hooked," he responded, completing the litany.

Being hooked, being the Texas Valley's most avid birder, doesn't absolve

Father Tom from the duties of his ordination, which are considerable and formidable. Brownsville, Texas, is a city populated largely by Mexican-Americans and Mexican-American aspirants. It is also a town caught in a web of tensions. Tensions between two cultures . . . tensions rising from a poor economy . . . tensions rising from rapid changes in a traditional family structure that merely begin with a new assertiveness on the part of women.

In a culture that has long looked to the Roman Catholic church for strength and guidance, it might be argued that preparing souls for the afterlife is only a small part of Father Tom's job. Most of his time is consumed by having to deal with the problems of the living. The busy parish priest has one day a week to take off his collar and don his binoculars. Thursday. If the Second Coming falls on a Thursday, Father Tom may not learn about it until late that night because come Thursday, he is as he put it "out the door and gone."

Gone. But not often alone. The voice of the Rio Grande Valley Hotline and nationally known authority on birds in The Valley is often called upon for assistance. It was Father Tom who showed Roger Tory Peterson his seven hundredth North American Life Bird—Clay-colored Robin. Linda and I were taking it on faith that his charity might extend to us as well.

"What do you have in mind?" he asked, getting down to business. "I'm going to be tied up this afternoon," he added both as an apology and a cap on his availability.

"Any chance you could take Linda and me to the dump for Mexican Crow? It would be a Lifer for me."

Father Tom didn't grimace, didn't even flinch—despite the fact that this was probably the billionth time that the request had been posed to him. The Brownsville dump is the only place in North America that Mexican Crow can be found with utter certainty. It is Father Tom's peculiar cross to be called upon to lead needy listers there.

"Sure," he said unhesitatingly. "Let's go."

Father Tom didn't need binoculars for this particular assignment any more than he needed a road map to what is, very possibly, the most public of public landfills in North America. He has done escort service there so many times he could probably claim residency. The gatekeeper took one look at the vehicle and its driver and waved us through. We didn't even have to lift our binoculars, the traditional passport for unescorted birders seeking access to the dump.

Under Father Tom's guidance we plowed a track through some freshly packed deposition. High atop the artificial mountain, beneath a cloud of Laughing Gulls, we could see our objective. Fresh garbage was being deposited by the truckload. The birds would almost certainly be there.

A light rain made the going torturous. Three times, the sedan lost traction and bogged. Three times some miracle pulled us back from despair.

Chihuahuan Ravens, surly as sentinels, stood beside the track and watched our progress with quiet detachment. Near the hilltop a solemn assemblage of Cattle Egrets huddled in the lee side of the trash pile, looking bored and wet. A newly arrived truck dumped its load, closing the mound in a cloud of gulls.

A small, trim corvid popped into view out the driver's side—a bird too small to be a raven, too stocky to be a Great-tailed Grackle. "There," Father Tom cried, pointing—but the angle didn't inspire confidence. "Wait," he cautioned. "Not sure," he mumbled.

The bird turned, rose, flew parallel to the car, dispelling all doubt.

"Sure," Father Tom said confidently. "That's one." And so it was. While we watched, the pint-sized crow with the glossy plumage sat down on a Clorox bottle and rasped a benediction.

"Want to see any more?" our guide asked wryly. We didn't particularly. The setting wasn't exactly inspirational and the thought of four wheels settling into several hundred feet of sodden garbage wasn't confidence-building.

Besides, we already had the bird—the only reason for sitting in a garbage dump two thousand miles from home. Without a good bird, a dump is just a dump, and what kind of fool wants to waste time standing around in a dump? Might as well stand around in a sewage treatment plant. Not that that doesn't happen, too.

# 6 • BALTIMORE, MARYLAND:

## The Pink Pukka

HE FOG THINNED, GOING FROM SOMETHING THAT was the color and consistency of Maalox to something with the physical properties of skim milk. And sure enough! The son-of-a-bitch with the New York plates passed me again! I had a glimpse of a sour little man with his face pressed against the windshield. Then the car sped by, drew up beside an eighteen-wheeler that materialized out of the fog . . . and slowed to a forty-mile-per-hour crawl. Boxing me in. If cars came equipped with heat-seeking missiles, I would have been one New York driver closer to making ace.

Even under normal circumstances, drivers who can't maintain a consistent speed on interstate highways make my teeth hurt, and this situation wasn't even within negotiating distance of normal. We had risen at two on a perfectly good Saturday morning in March. We had maneuvered a three-hour course around drunks, accidents, and the deer who like to stand on foggy roads. We were en route to the reincarnation of the "Bird of the Century," *and* we were a week late getting to it. Walter Mitty up ahead had been compromising my God-given, constitutional right to life, liberty, and the pursuit of a good bird ever since we'd crossed the Maryland line.

It was at this sublime moment that a sign about the size of Kansas materialized directly overhead announcing the exit for the Baltimore Beltway, I-695. *Our* exit.

I missed it.

For Linda and me, the chase had begun the previous Monday with a 7:00 A.M. phone call: Paul Kerlinger, director of the New Jersey Audubon Society's Cape May Bird Observatory, for Pete Dunne. "Hey," he wanted to know, "did you hear about the Ross's Gull?"

"The Cape Ann bird?" I asked, suspecting that it wasn't.

"No," he said, the Baltimore bird. "A Ross's was found on Saturday and seen again Sunday. I thought you'd want to know. I know how much you like gulls."

Actually, I like gulls about as much as I like shopping, and I like shopping less than self-immolation. But a *Ross's* Gull. That's different. That's *very* different.

"Ooooo," I said, making the correct reply. "What kind of plumage is it in?"

"Adult, winter," he intoned. "Don't ask me who found it," he added, anticipating my question. "I don't know. I got it from Sandy Sherman. She saw it yesterday. Hey. I'll see you. I got to make some calls. All the details are on the hotline." Paul hung up.

*A Ross's Gull*, I repeated in my mind, savoring the thought, reaching for my appointment calendar. *A Ross's Gull. Pink Pukka of the North. Wow!* In my mind I could conjure the creature—a feathered figurine, pale as ivory, with an eye so balefully black that a basset hound would die from envy. The bird was a prize. It was the kind of bird you could build a religion around. It was worth a chase; worth dropping everything and running out the door, binoculars in hand, right now . . . *except* . . .

"Damn," I muttered, staring down at a calendar burdened by five straight days of meetings, appointments, and deadlines. A presidential appointment secretary couldn't have knotted a tighter noose of commitments. "Damn."

*Shift some things*, an evil little voice inside my ear whispered, a voice I recalled from the thousand or so mornings that I hadn't completed my home-work assignments. It's the same voice that surfaces on that first day in March when temperatures reach the hormonal flash point. The voice that comes in on northwest winds on that morning in September when the cold front clears, coating the trees with migrating birds. It's the voice birders hear every time a hot bird hits town.

*Look*, the tempter tempted, *the afternoon's free tomorrow. Cancel the morning meeting with the video people. Reschedule it for next week.*

"I can't," I whimpered. "That meeting has been rescheduled twice already. Our backs are against the wall on this one."

*OK, OK*, the siren soothed, *don't panic. Thursday, then. What's another garden club luncheon, more or less, right? Skip the luncheon, run down, run back, and you can be here in time to meet your magazine crew at 5:00.*

"No," I moaned, "I'm covering that garden club for a friend and his wife's a member of that club."

Of course, the voice had anticipated all these objections. They were just a feint. They were just stepping stones on the way toward building a case for . . .

*Wednesday, then. There's no other alternative. It's got to be Wednesday. Just call in sick . . .*

"Just call in sick," I repeated.

*. . . and skip the staff meeting.*

"And skip the staff meeting," I said, nodding. So simple.

But I couldn't miss the staff meeting. Half the items on the agenda were mine. Half the reason for having these quarterly meetings was to help me organize New Jersey Audubon's magazine. I couldn't miss a staff meeting.

The phone rang again. It was Greg Hanisek, an editor with the *Easton Express*, birder and captain of the Bausch and Lomb World Series of Birding Team—the team that had won the event four years out of seven.

"Hey," he demanded, "have you heard about the Ross's Gull?"

"Yeah, thanks," I heard myself say. "Kerlinger called it in."

"You going down?" he probed; he prodded; he tempted.

*Am I going down?* I thought. The weather for midweek was supposed to be good. Sunny, warm for March. The ride would be an easy one. I looked down at the schedule and winced. I looked out the window and weighed the options.

I thought of Ross's Gull, fluttering like a white dream among wheeling flocks of Bonaparte's Gulls. I thought of all the hundreds of hours I'd given to New Jersey Audubon, all the late nights, all the early mornings.

*They owe it to you*, the voice whispered.

"They owe it to me," I said, forming the words with my mouth.

I thought of all the good birds I missed by waiting too long; all the twenty-four-hour wonders. I thought of Greg Hanisek's beaming face at the World Series of Birding brunch, could almost hear his voice: "It was cake. Three hours down; three hours back. The bird was right there. Too bad you missed it."

*YES* (I almost screamed into the phone). *Meet you at the sewage pools* (I wanted to say).

But I didn't. Because another thought occurred to me. The thought of Gordon Schultze, the director of Lorrimer Nature Center (and unofficial Eyore of New Jersey Audubon), looking at my empty chair at the meeting. How he would smile his impish smile and say: "So, Dunne's 'sick,' today, huh. That's too bad. I was going to ask whether he knew about the Ross's Gull down in Baltimore." I thought of how the puckish smile would stay on his face as the import of his words sunk in. I thought of how the eyes of my boss would widen in perception and about the little black mark that would fall in his mental ledger.

"You creep, Schultze," I muttered.

"What?" Greg said.

"Nothing," I choked. "I can't get down there until the weekend," I said.

"No?" Greg prodded.

*NO?* the voice screamed.

"No," I affirmed. "I'm just going to have to gamble on this one and hope it sticks."

That's how it began. That's how they *all* begin. A bird appears, shakes birding's grapevine, and word spreads like wildfire—from friend to companion to club member to acquaintance to friend.

"There's a Ross's Gull in Baltimore."

One person, birding in a corner of the universe, catches a star in his binoculars and kindles a flame.

"Uh, hello, Rick. This is Gene Scarpulla. Listen, please return my call when you get in because, well, I know this sounds crazy but I just had a bird at the Back River Sewage Treatment Facility that looks like . . ."

*"A Ross's Gull."*

And then Gene, and Rick, and a handful of close confederates assemble the next morning. And then . . . "LOOK! Holy Shit! It *is* a . . ."

*"Ross's Gull!" "Ross's Gull!" "Have you heard that there's a Ross's Gull."*

The name has wings. It sings across copper wires and bounces off satellites. It is printed on telephone-side note pads by the hands of spouses and children, who have been carefully trained to "take down the location, the name, and telephone number of the caller." It hides beneath the blinking lights on a thousand answering machines. And before nightfall, birding hotlines across the country have committed the details to tape.

"This is the voice of the Naturalist, a Service of the Audubon Naturalist Society . . ."

" 'Afternoon, everybody, this is NARBA, the National Rare Bird Alert, sponsored by the Houston Audubon Society. This is report 90-41 . . ."

An eager band of acolytes stands ready with paper and pencils in hand or tape recorders placed up to the receiver. The tapes convey the details:

The Time: "On Saturday, March 3 . . ."

The Place: ". . . at the Back River Sewage Treatment Plant in Northeast Baltimore . . ."

The Bird: *A Ross's Gull!*

On Monday, day three in the Ross's Gull Chronicles, all the hot local birders and the needy Bird Listers were on hand, hopped up on hope, picking through the flocks of Bonaparte's Gulls with surgical skill.

And the bird was found.

It was there again on Tuesday, picking its way across the sewage pools for a new wave of onlookers. Again on Wednesday . . . Thursday, the first Ross's Gull on the Atlantic Coast, south of Connecticut, the sixth record for the U.S. since the Newburyport bird appeared in 1975.

Before the appraising eyes of fifty and sixty birders at a time, the pearly prince of effluent fluttered and dipped into the suspect principal, extracting tiny unmentionables, tossing them down before approving eyes. In the evenings, the bird appeared on the TV screens of Baltimore residents, a tiny white gull with eyes like Bambi. What Baltimore Sewage Treatment Authority officials thought of their surprising notoriety they kept to themselves.

As the week progressed a pattern emerged. The bird usually appeared in the morning, as early as 6:45, as late as 9:20. But it was most regular between 7:45 and 8:15 in the vicinity of the round holding tanks. Those who came in the morning inevitably saw the bird. Those who missed the prescribed time also missed the gull.

On Thursday evening, both of Maryland's hotlines and the NARBA carried Ross's Gull reports. On Friday, the line into the Maryland hotline carrying daily updates was jammed with callers. Those who got through got the latest. The bird had been seen on Friday. Most callers got nothing but a busy signal. They just took their chances, setting out in a blind fog for an aspired rendezvous with a bird that might not even be there.

Linda and I were two of these.

The stream of screams, curses, threats, and denunciations rose so fast that they backed up in my throat. All that emerged was a strangled snarl whose timbre would have cut metal.

"What's the matter, hon?" Linda mumbled, stirring.

"THAT," I screamed, throwing the word at the bumper ahead of me. "That evil, squinting, Kallikak with the driving skill of a lobotomized toadstool who *made me miss my EXIT, THAT* (not the fog, not my inattention) is the problem."

"Oh," Linda said, snuggling deeper into the impromptu jacket pillow. "Take the next one," she suggested. Marriage imparts a certain immunity from irrational anger, and Linda is quick to invoke this right when the situation dictates.

"Would you mind handing me the directions to this bird, please," I said in the measured monotone that denotes real anger in a person.

"Sure, hon," Linda said, stirring. "Where are they?"

"On a piece of paper folded in that notebook," I said, pointing, exasperated beyond expression that a wife can't do something as simple as read her husband's mind.

But the directions weren't there.

"Are they in your pocket?" Linda prompted.

"No," I growled, peering into the gray soup for anything that looked like an exit.

"Do you remember any of it?" she inquired.

"Yes," I lied, braking and steering hard for a ramp that materialized next to the car.

"Do you want me to pull out a map?"

"No," I said, coming to a stop halfway through an intersection, then swinging back onto I-95 northbound. "This is a sewage treatment plant we're looking for," I chastised. "Not the Baltimore Aquarium."

"OK," she said cheerfully, snuggling back into place. "If I smell it I'll let you know."

If I hadn't been so furious, it might have occurred to me that there is something pretty comical about driving around in a blind fog, searching for a sewage treatment plant that stood a good chance of beating the Baltimore Aquarium for attendance on this Saturday in March. But I *was* furious. And it didn't occur to me. And frankly nothing seemed particularly funny at the moment.

Somehow we blundered onto the Beltway and managed to be in the proper lane whenever the highway branched into sudden, unannounced parts. A shadow of a road sign advised the imminence of "East Something-or-other." The *East* part sounded familiar. As memory served, the road we were looking for was East or Easter or Eastern.

"Did you get the name on that sign?" I demanded.

"East Boulevard," Linda announced.

"That's it," I decided—but it wasn't an *it*. It was a *them*. East Boulevard had two exits, one heading east; one west. We overshot the first exit, caught the second one by a miracle, and found ourselves heading down some fog-bound stretch of pavement without guidance or direction.

"This is ridiculous," I pronounced after a quarter-mile or so. "I have no idea where we are. I can't see where we're going. I can't begin to tell you where that is, anyway."

"Just keep going," Linda insisted, sitting upright, rolling down the window. "It's around here somewhere. Smell," she commanded.

Sure enough, the air bore unmistakable traces of treated sewage, a smell familiar to every committed birder in the world. Sewage treatment facilities serve as bird oases in urban deserts. In true desert climates, they may offer birds the only liquid substrate for hundreds of miles. Waterfowl, shorebirds, and gulls in particular are attracted to them, and places like the McAllen Sewage Ponds in Texas and the sewage pools of Eilat, Israel, rank among the great birding junctions of the planet, right up there with Auburn Cemetery in Cambridge.

We nosed along another couple hundred yards and, miraculously, an industrial-strength fence appeared on our right. The fence fell away to reveal a gate and a guardhouse and beyond it a newly routed wooded sign. It read: "Welcome Birders." Beyond it was another sign with a directional arrow. It said: "Ross's Gull."

It was early, still dark, but already the birders were beginning to gather. Five cars were lined up between the rows of large round tanks bearing the legend "Final Clarifiers." The bird, according to the tapes, was usually seen around these tanks.

"Clearly, a bird of refined taste," one of the members of the Delaware Valley Ornithological Club dead punned.

"As sewage treatment plants *go*," Armas Hill, voice of the Philadelphia hotline observed, "this one isn't bad." In fact, for a sewage treatment plant, it was stunning; an architectural cross between a Roman villa and Fort Knox; Monticello with the outside plumbing.

If you closed your eyes, concentrating on the sound of water rushing through the fog, you could imagine yourself . . . on the coast of Maine . . . at the rim of Niagara Falls . . . anywhere that land and water and the human soul meet. The one thing you couldn't block out was the smell—the inelegant tang of treated sewage.

"It smells like victory," John LaVia, one of DVOC's worthies observed, sniffing lustily. "I love the smell of sewage in the morning."

By dawn the crowd had grown to over a hundred and cars continued to file in at a rate of one a minute—cars bearing license plates from New York, Pennsylvania, Virginia, Delaware, North Carolina, Connecticut, and, of course, Maryland. A few birders from more distant parts had flown in and picked up rentals at the airport, but not many. Ross's Gull was more along the lines of a regional rarity, not in the league of a first North American Record. A first record for America would have depleted the stock of airport rentals all the way to Philadelphia.

There was excitement. There was anticipation. But the anxious intensity that surrounds a first record for North America was dampened. Many birders present already had Ross's Gull on their North American list—had seen it in Massachusetts in 1975, or in Churchill, Manitoba, where a small colony of Ross's Gulls were discovered nesting in 1980. A few might have seen the first winter plumage Ross's Gull that played hide-and-seek with birders in Massachusetts earlier in the winter.

But people don't drive predawn hours to stand in a sewage treatment plant just to pass the time. Ross's Gull was a prize, a first for the lower forty-eight for some. A Life Bird for many. A year bird and a state bird for all.

It was also the catalyst for a festival. Because every hot rarity signals an impromptu gathering of the clan, an excuse for birders to see friends and meet people of like mind. By 7:00 A.M., the Back River Sewage Treatment facility was nothing more than the backdrop for one grand birding block party with three hundred in attendance and more arriving all the time.

John LaVia and Bill Tannery, staked out near Final Clarifier Number 9, were part of the advance guard of what would be a big DVOC contingent. Bill was quietly intense, attentive to movement in the crowd or motion in the air. Bill needed Ross's Gull for a Life Bird. John was jocular and philosophical and not particularly concerned. He'd seen Ross's before.

"I maintain a very good sense of humor when it comes to other people's Life Birds," John explained.

"Shut up," Bill suggested.

Chandler Robbins, author of *A Field Guide to the Birds of North America* (or as it is better known, the Robbins Guide) was there with wife, Helen. Chan, too, needed Ross's for a Life Bird.

Bob Augustine, a photographer and rarity chaser of pathological proportions, was playing the crowd, showing off a newly minted portfolio of Ross's Gull photos taken early in the week—a cruel form of torture. Anita Covington, soon to be Mrs. Paul Guris, showed off her engagement ring while Brian Moscatello and Janet Sedicino nodded affirmations and confirmed that the baby was due "in September," just about the time Connecticut warblers start moving through in numb . . .

"Tito?"

"Pete! How are you?"

"Fine; real fine. Linda, this is Tito McLane. Remember my telling you about Mike Heller? The fellow who used to be the counter at Hawk Mountain. Tito is Mike's father-in-law. Tito, this is my wife, Linda."

One of the treatment plant workers moved shyly through the crowd, the only person in sight not wearing binoculars and one of the few not locked in conversation.

"Get a few birders through here this week?" I asked.

"Gobs and gobs and gobs of 'em," he replied without a ghost of a smile.

"What do you think about all this?" I invited, gesturing toward the impromptu block party.

"Oh," he said mildly, shyly, "I like to see people having fun."

"If you want to see some fun," I promised, "wait till you see what happens when this bird gets here."

The fellow looked quickly around at the hordes of people, measuring a response. "Mister," he said finally, honestly, "if that bird shows up, I'm getting out of here."

The danger wasn't as acute as his anxiety made it. If ill fortune found him positioned between the crowd and the bird, and if he chose, unwisely, to stand his ground, his chances of being knocked down were still probably less than fifty/fifty. But in his reply the fellow *had* put his finger on a very good point, a concern that was beginning to grow on other people's minds, too. The fellow had said *if*, not *when*. So far, the bird had not shown up . . . and it was getting late.

The 7:15 deadline had come and gone. Bonaparte's Gulls materialized out of the fog and settled into the tanks, dabbling for tasty tidbits. By 8:00 anxiety was beginning to undermine the festivities and gnaw at the social fabric. A sudden movement or a loudly spoken word would shut down conversation midsentence and bring heads up all around. A binocular trained too long on one bird would elicit a rash of scrutiny. The gull had never been this late before.

By 9:00, anxiety was beginning to be replaced by disappointment. What had been a block party now more closely resembled an accident scene. Nine-twenty, quitting time for Ross's Gull, passed without a trace of the bird. The animate pool of birders began coalescing into conversational clumps. Options were discussed. Theories postulated. Then, finally, in ones and twos and resigned threes, they began to settle out. By 9:30, ten minutes after the temporal limit for the bird's daily appearance, birder defection began en masse.

There is a delicious irony about birding in a sewage treatment facility, one relating to human filtration and its limits. Despite the utilitarian ambition of the Back River Sewage Treatment Plant, there wasn't any place in the whole aquatic labyrinth for needy birders to deposit processed coffee. And *most* of the three hundred-plus birders present had ingested great quantities of coffee during their predawn drives.

The bird's tardiness might have been the principal cause for mass defection. But it wasn't the only one.

"Do you think the bird is gone?" an Italian diplomat inquired, his eyebrows arched in a gesture that expressed both fatalism and hope.

"No," I said, "I think its feeding pattern may have been disrupted by the fog. People who have seen the bird this week tell me that the number of Bonaparte's Gulls is just a fraction of what is here normally. The bird is probably with the balance of the flock.

"The Massachusetts bird was seen off and on into May," I added. "It's probably still around. Why would it leave?" I invited, gesturing toward the surrounding facility. "This place has everything a gull could ask for."

He nodded, accepting the information. "Thank you," he said. "I will come back then." And he left.

The number of observers had fallen to half a hundred. Conversation lagged. Thoughts turned inward, toward options ahead, toward might-have-beens behind.

*You shouldn't have waited*, a familiar voice whispered in my ear.

I nodded, hoping to avoid the subject with quick surrender. But my conscience is more persistent than that.

*Hear the long-range forecast for next week*, it chatted, feigned, setting me up. *Supposed to be in the eighties . . . maybe nineties. Crazy for March.*

I nodded, again, knowing what was coming, not knowing any way of ducking the punch.

After a long, savoring pause, the voice continued.

*I guess that's that. Can't imagine an Arctic gull hanging around in weather like that, can you?*

"Maybe," I said. The Newburyport bird stayed until May.

*Can't imagine it*, the voice continued, ignoring me. *Too bad. Opportunities like this don't come often. Might as well leave. Lots to do. Deadlines and dinner engagements. Should have come earlier.*

"Might as well go," I said to Linda.

*Should have come earlier*, I thought to myself.

We said good-bye to the stalwart few. Wished John and Bill good luck. Waved to Tito.

Sometimes a three-hour drive goes quickly. The highway falls away and miles mount behind. There is no traffic after a successful chase. There are no lines at tollbooths, and attendants flash smiles. State troopers are always looking the other way and a car will run forever with the gas gauge on E (or at least until you get to the next service area—but probably forever).

But this drive wasn't one of them. Chases that fail always make the ride home seem twice as long. Engines develop funny noises, and if you want to listen to Pink Floyd, your spouse wants to hear Vivaldi. Tollbooths are jammed and attendants act as though they have never heard of receipts.

And you can't find your vehicle registration.

And you must have thrown the new auto insurance card out by mistake.

Later, after dinner, we called the hotline and managed to get through after a mere ten minutes. The tape contained "the report we have been waiting for all day."

The adult Ross's Gull finally showed at 4:15 around the square tanks. It stayed two minutes and left.

I hoped that Bill and John stayed.

I wished that next week's work schedule was lighter.

# 7 • *MISSISSIPPI, ALABAMA, FLORIDA:*

# *Gulf Coast Spring*

## *WHITE LIES, BLUE CANARIES*

*L*IES HAVE A WAY OF CATCHING UP WITH A WRITER, AND mine have finally caught up with me. Through the course of these pages I have held winter up to the eyes of readers and told them it was so. And so it was. The part I wanted them to see.

But what they did not see was how the icicles melted beneath the strong February sun in Newburyport or how pintail pressing north drove a wedge into winter, opening a way for spring. There was no passage describing how the pairs of Red-tailed Hawks sat side by side on Shenandoah Valley snags in March, or how the clouds of Broad-winged Hawks boiled out of Mexico.

I never spoke of these things. They did not fit with the story line.

But now you must see how this story has progressed past winter, how day by day the great planet has come around, inclined itself toward spring. You must see behind the pile of deceits and know that while Green Jays cavorted in Texas, the woodcock danced in New Hampshire, a flock of goldeneye tossed their heads in Wisconsin, and a Violet-green Swallow was seen in Oregon and later that day in Washington.

You must see these things, because if you do not you may come to believe that spring appears suddenly and full blown upon the continent. That one morning, people wake up and the trees are filled with color and sound.

That suburban lawns lie beneath hordes of "blue canaries," and branches bow beneath the weight of brightly colored warblers.

This would be a misconception. This would be a lie. This is not how spring comes to North America at all. This is only how spring appears along the Gulf Coast, in places like High Island, Texas; Dauphin Island, Alabama; and along the Mississippi coast.

That, at least, is not a lie.

## GERRY'S WOODS

It's a suburban neighborhood, prosperous and well tended. It might be anywhere. You would have to be pretty savvy about plant distribution and architectural idiosyncracies to place it in Biloxi, Mississippi.

We were heading for Gerry's Woods "to see what was around." We'd been chatting, drinking coffee, and someone suggested going down to Gerry's Woods, and everyone agreed that it sounded like a good idea so that's what we were doing. We, incidentally, consisted of Linda, me, Gerry Morgan, and, of course, Judy Toups.

Judy is a sixty-year-old self-confessed grandmother with arthritis in both shoulders and a voice that could make a drill sergeant envious. This may not sound flattering, but Judy is above flattery, except, perhaps, where her skills as a writer and a birder are concerned—and *these* are considerable. Judy Toups, wife of one, mother of six, and leader of the pack, practically invented birding along the coast of Mississippi. Through her columns, articles, birding courses and book, *Birds and Birding on the Mississippi Coast*, she has built a national reputation for herself and her favorite corner of the world.

Gerry Morgan, married to Jerry Morgan, is one of Judy's protégées. She is maybe fifty, looks thirty-five, and is quietly hated for this. The woods are named for her.

Gerry's Woods are two blocks from Gerry's house, a stand of pines with a brushy understory, fairly representative of woodlands in Harrison County, Mississippi. I don't know how big it is. Thirty acres, maybe forty. Gerry didn't know either, and neither does Judy. But both could recite its history—"owned by this family, sold to this woman, logged by this gentleman . . ."

That's a funny thing about Mississippi. Everyone seems to know the personal and business dealings of everyone else at least as far back as Appomattox. To a person who grew up in a state where people may not know the first names of their next-door neighbors, this seems odd, and only reflects poorly upon me.

Gerry, incidentally, doesn't own the woods. She merely birds it "pretty regularly." There are several reasons for this. It is nearby. It has a trail running through it. And it has birds. When a wave of migrants hits the coast, it has *lots* of birds. In spring "pretty regularly" means at least once a day.

We picked our way through piles of leaves deposited by sundry homeowners and moved down the trail, single file, eyes and ears alert. A long, slim form flew across the path, snaking through the trees, weaving through branches the way a superb skater moves through ranks of amateurs.

"Cuckoo," our quartet sang, but without harmony. There are two North American cuckoos. The group was split on the identity of this one.

"It landed," Gerry said, hurrying ahead for a better vantage.

"Can anyone see the tail?" Judy demanded, trying to work her binoculars around three opposing heads.

Nobody could. But through a hole in the foliage I could see the bill and a pale-rimmed eye taking the measure of us. "It's Yellow-billed," the more common of the two species, here, I confirmed. But the very next bird was also a cuckoo, slimmer, snakier, colder overall than the one before. This one was Black-billed Cuckoo.

"A year bird," Judy chortled happily. Judy holds the Mississippi record for most birds seen in one calendar year—304 species. She takes her "year list" seriously, and sighting the Black-billed Cuckoo had just brought her list up a notch.

Cuckoos were clearly "in." The day before, they had been absent, now they were in. Most nights deposit at least *some* new treasure under the trees. Every morning holds new promise from late March through early May—as long as spring lays hold of the Mississippi coast.

"You should have been here Thursday," Judy counseled, shaking her head, expressing both the wonder of it and the injustice of our inopportune arrival. "That was the day of the fallout. ThOUSAnds," of birds she pronounced, letting the syllables climb in measure of the flight. "Thou-sands," she repeated.

Yes, Thursday, by the estimates of all we spoke to, had been incredible, so many songbirds that bushes vibrated with motion. Friday had been merely "terrific" and Saturday "fair." Today, Sunday, was "leftovers." Embarrassing fare to serve up to guests by the reckoning of our hosts.

But in Linda's and my estimate, the fare was little short of a banquet. A feast for winter-weary eyes. There were birds *everywhere* in Gerry's Woods. In good numbers and good variety. Year birds for northern visitors.

In shadowed places, Wood Thrush paced in their halting fashion. Hooded Warblers, golden knights with black mail hoods, scolded from the bushes. A Kentucky Warbler, pished into a stuttering pique, came out scolding, and a Worm-eating Warbler tried to pass itself off as just another Red-eyed Vireo—without success. Gerry Morgan is too good a birder for that.

A red form flashed from underfoot, a sporting clay bird fired in some ethereal kiln, still glowing with heat. Only the bird's wings looked cool enough to touch—Summer Tanager. Some prefer the Scarlet Tanager, a bird that looks as if it were dressed for the hunt with its bright red coat and boot-black wings. Well, there were Scarlet Tanagers in Gerry's Woods, too—males and females, fresh from the tropics, deposited daily at the door, as long as supplies last, as long as tanagers are in season.

"Isn't this great?" Judy observed to nobody in particular. It was great. A great way to while away an afternoon with friends and savor a bit of spring.

Spring birding along the Gulf Coast differs from the sort of birding Linda and I enjoyed in the Rio Grande Valley. Winter birding in Texas might be likened to sitting beneath a faucet with your tongue hanging out, begging for each new drop to fall. Each new drop is greedily taken and savored, but it quickly disappears, leaving you still thirsty, still wanting; leaving your eyes fixed on the next drop.

Birding the Gulf Coast in April is like standing beneath a fountain. When conditions are right, you can drown in a sea of birds. A morning afield

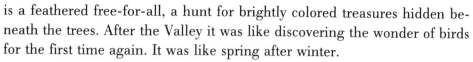

is a feathered free-for-all, a hunt for brightly colored treasures hidden beneath the trees. After the Valley it was like discovering the wonder of birds for the first time again. It was like spring after winter.

And it was, as Judy assessed, just "leftovers."

## WAITING FOR THE YUCATÁN EXPRESS

It's hot in the sun but cooler beneath the tree's limbs, spread out like the spokes of a great wheel, filling the clearing. They seem impossibly long and their girth would shame the trunks of most trees. But not this tree.

I look up, staring into the leafy maze, staring at the play of sunlight and shadows, feeling the good, rough comfort of the trunk behind my back.

"No," I think. Not this tree. Not this old tree.

"Good *ol'* tree," I say aloud, because there is no one to hear me, because I want to hear the sound of it sitting under the tree. It sounded fine and I said it again.

A very old tree. Even by the reckoning of the oyster shells piled around it, maybe beneath it. The uncollected garbage left over from ten thousand Indian beach parties.

The place isn't a beach anymore. It's a forest. Built on a garbage pit, a mollusk necropolis, paved in polished white food containers as impervious as plastic. Alabama birders call this place the Shell Mounds. A sign, nearby, just over the nearest pile of shells, tells of its historic significance.

The oak has a name, too. It's called the Bee Tree.

This morning, the Shell Mounds were crowded, packed. Birders from the Alabama Ornithological Society and birders from Mississippi scoured the grove, searching for warblers. This was the third weekend in April, migratory prime time, according to conventional wisdom. Dauphin Island was *the* place to be.

More convention.

There was little to find, not that that made much difference. A couple of warblers here. A vireo there. Shortage just makes the finding that much more exciting. The less you have, the more it's worth. Somebody wrote about it once. Some Englishman. Not Audubon. (Audubon was French.) Some economist. Something about the iron law of the market; something about supply and demand.

Well, the birds were in short supply. The demand had finally gone somewhere else—off to search the flats and beaches for migrating shorebirds during the heat of the day. Off to sit beside air conditioners in motel rooms.

But I'd decided to stay and wait. Just me and the tree. Waiting. Even though we'd just met.

They'll be arriving pretty soon, now. Very soon. Another hour I guess. No more. They are due in at four o'clock. Arriving on the nonstop. Pulling into the Shell Pile. Getting off at the Bee Tree. Here. Four o'clock. Sharp.

Arriving on the Yucatán Express.

*They lift off at dusk, clearing the canopy heading out, over the Gulf of Mexico, climbing gradually into a tropical sky. Yesterday's sky.*

*At two thousand feet, beneath planets and stars, they level off, fixing a course along coordinates locked in genetic flight plans, falling into the rhythm of flight. A series of flaps followed by a folded wing glide. For the next twenty-one hours, this will be the rhythm of their lives.*

I could have guessed that this was a bee tree without knowing the name. Three honeybees, their wings shattered by a life of service, have fallen in my lap since the tree and I became acquainted. Two made off under their own steam. One needed assistance. They aren't the only insects in the grove, not by half. Some small, brown ant is swarming, rising in the afternoon air. The ants' shed wings sparkle in the sunlight. They lie, like fish scales, like discarded oyster shells, on the ground, on my pants legs. Newly grounded ants sneak down shirt collars and up unguarded pants cuffs.

It's annoying. But not really annoying. I could leave, but I don't want to. What if the Yucatán Express arrives early? What if the wind was good and the birds are ahead of schedule? I don't want to miss it. Not now. Not after I've waited so long. Beneath the tree. Spent the whole afternoon sitting here. Waiting for the Yucatán Express.

*They are flying machines, these birds, honed by evolution to a perfection of flight unapproached by anything but human dreams. Muscle and bone, feathers and fat. Flight weight: sixteen grams, a weight that could be sent anywhere in the United States for one first-class postage stamp.*

*Three to four of those grams are fuel. Each gram good for 200–250 kilometers flying at peak efficiency, and they fly at peak efficiency. They must. The closest land is 860 kilometers, and most traveling on the Yucatán Express will fly farther than that—1,000 kilometers at least. Were it not for prevailing southerly tail winds, winds that double a warbler's 20–22-mile-per-hour flight speed, the birds could not bridge the gulf at all.*

They seem to have a penchant for naming trees, here on Dauphin Island. There's another tree nearby called the Goat Tree, another favorite birding spot. It's several trees, actually. All live oak. All low-limbed. Maybe only one is called the Goat Tree, but I don't know which. They all look pretty goaty to me. All shaggy and knobby and goat-stubborn.

I asked one birder I ran into about the place. How to find it. How it got its name. He said it came to be called Goat Tree because a man once saved his goats from flood tides by putting them up in the tree. The goats, once they'd gotten the knack of it, continued to climb.

I'm not sure I believe it. I'm not saying a goat can't climb a tree. I just doubt that a man could make one do it.

"What do you think, tree?" I said to my tree. "Do you think goats can climb trees?"

*At dawn the birds climb, ascend to 4,000 feet. Nobody really knows why. Maybe the colder temperatures help keep them from overheating. Maybe from nearly a mile up, the birds can better gauge the distance to their destination. After a night of flying, it would be good to see an end to it. I would want this if I were a bird.*

*The birds are also lighter now, having burned up most of their fuel. Lighter means slower and slower prolongs the ordeal.*

It should be very soon, now. They must be very close. The light is not so bright and the air seems not as warm. The Yucatán Express cannot be far. Less than twenty miles from shore. Ten!

Unless they hit a headwind. God help them if they hit a headwind.

I look up at my friend the tree. There are no birds yet. No movement along the limbs. No breeze stirring the leaves.

Somewhere above the grove Chimney Swifts are twittering. Purple Martins, too. But Chimney Swifts are crazy—they fly in the heat of the day. And Purple Martins are no better than Chimney Swifts. It's the ants, of course. Swarming overhead. Drawing a hungry crowd. "But if there're insects right over the grove," I think, "the air must be still." A wind would scatter the hatch if there was any wind.

But warblers? Warblers are nowhere. Not in the limbs of my tree. Not in the reach of my horizon, which is also the tree. My comfortable tree that is good to lean against while I'm waiting for the Yucatán Express.

*The fat larded beneath the skin is burned first, was burned last night. The birds grow slimmer, leaner, more aerodynamic as they fly. When the subcutaneous deposits are gone, they burn abdominal fat. When this is gone, they use their reserves—the fatty deposits around internal organs.*

*When the reserves are spent, the birds have one final recourse. They burn protein, the muscles that keep them aloft. It is an act of desperation; a muscular meltdown. But the situation is desperate. One way or another, when the engine starts consuming itself, the flight is almost over.*

There are still no birders. This morning, they massed here. Crowded the trails. Crowded the glen, though clearly there was no significant fallout. They could tell this just by looking. They could tell this by the number of birders departing early, or those departing told them. But many stayed anyway. Stubborn individuals who coalesced into tenacious clusters, who dwindled back to individuals, again, as the morning moved on, greeting each other with raised eyebrows and shrugged shoulders.

Since noon, there have been as many birders at the shell pile as Indians, as goats.

"OK, tree, you don't want to talk about goats. Let's talk about Indians. Made a hell of a mess, didn't they?"

But the birders will all be back, soon. Arriving as soon as the sun drops just a little more. Any birds that were here this morning will be here this afternoon. These will be augmented by the new arrivals due in at four, arriving on the Yucatán Express.

*It's the last leg of the journey that is most dangerous. The home stretch. That's where the winds can turn contrary, northerly, if a cold front penetrates the gulf. Instead of a friendly tailwind to see them home, the tired birds must face a headwind. And their progress is reduced to a crawl.*

*They have no choice in the matter. None at all. They cannot turn back. Their fuel is spent. They can only go on. Holding at 4,000 feet if they are able. Losing altitude if they must. Below is the gulf that swallows warblers whole, and the hunting falcons, Merlins and Peregrines who watch and wait from shoreline perches with hungry eyes.*

*They have no choice. They must go on. Reach the shore if they can. Reach the trees. The oaks standing above the sterile pines. The oaks, just ahead. Almost below. Still . . .*

*Just ahead.*

*A flutter of wings. A close-winged glide. A few more feet.*

*A flutter of wings. Close-winged glide. A few more feet. A few feet, closer to the tall beckoning oak, standing above the pines. On the island.*

*Just ahead.*

It should happen any time, now. It's cooling nicely. The birds already here should be getting active. Maybe I'll get up in a minute or two. Take a look around. See what's moving.

"What do you say, tree? See any warblers up there yet? Anybody crossing the finish line?"

I bring my eyes down, meeting the eyes of a woman who'd quietly entered the grove. I smile. Flash a goofy grin. What other kind of a grin would you give to a person who found you talking to trees?

"You might have warned me," I chastise the tree, after I'm certain she's gone. *Should have told her I was a Druid*, I thought, too late.

Another person wanders by, another birder, a guy I'd seen this morning. The Goat Tree man. I watch him bring his binoculars up and follow the line of his sight . . . to a small warbler or vireo foraging overhead.

"Bingo," I think. Yes, the local birders are pulling into the station. On this wind, on this date, the Express should be right on time. Set your watch by it. With the little hand on Four and the big hand going straight up and . . .

*Straight down. Like a stone. Like a meteor. Like Icarus. Just like the English physicist who used to sit beneath apple trees said. The birds drop in, a 4,000-foot free-fall, cheating the dark-eyed falcons. Just above the leaf tops, the feathered meteors open their wings, one last time, breaking their fall, settling into the protective canopy.*

*Sometimes you can even hear it. The sound of the Yucatán Express pulling into the station. Right on . . .*

"Time," I say; I stand, stretching to take some of the stiffness out of my shoulders; rubbing my back to erase the imprint of the tree.

"Enjoyed our conversation," I thought to the tree—but I could not say it, not with so many birders about, birders arriving by the minute. I went off in search of Linda to see how her photography had gone. Then, together, we'd join the others who have gathered. On this third Saturday in April. On Dauphin Island, Alabama. Eager to greet the disembarking passengers of the Yucatán Express.

## DRY TORTUGAS

The bird stood at the base of the small stone fountain that lies in the courtyard of the fort. Except for an occasional tremor, the bird stood absolutely still, a shrunken scarecrow of a bird the color of snow after a rain. People wearing binoculars moved around it, avoiding it with feet and eyes. Their interest was not on the bird, and the bird, for its part, seemed not to notice the people.

With its head drawn down, its eyes half closed, the pale scarecrow looked more than half asleep. But the truth was it was more than half dead. What little life remained was focused, wholly, upon the fountain and its brackish trickle of water.

When the hosts of eager birders had poured through the gates of the fort, several hundred Cattle Egrets had stood in the court yard, standing like onlookers at the scene of an accident. But over the course of the morning, those egrets that could had fled the island.

Only a handful remained.

The fort is Fort Jefferson. It straddles a coral island seventy miles west of Key West, Florida; one of seven reefs discovered by Ponce de León in 1513. *Las Tortugas*, he named them in recognition of the number of sea turtles he found there. Thirsty mariners, who later visited the coral clusters added the disgruntled modifier *dry*—the Dry Tortugas. To this day, anyone visiting the place must bring drinking water and provisions or do without.

With or without drinking water, the Tortugas are beautiful. In the morning, the new sun puts a shimmer on the water, and when the morning breeze comes up, it nudges the mirrored surface until it resembles the scaly sides of a tarpon. During an hour that passes quickly, the sea turns violet and turquoise, and where the coral rises to the surface to form the islands, it is baked brown at the edges.

The horizon, which seems not so far away as other horizons, is deep blue, and it gives mooring to distant clouds. Sometimes, in the afternoons, the clouds grow so large that pieces break free and sail over the fort in little puffs. They frame soaring Frigatebirds who patrol the walls of Fort Jefferson and whose languid flight sets the pace on the Tortugas. The fastest things that move here are the tides, and the small, silver-sided fish when they are pursued.

The absence of water did not dissuade the U.S. War Department, which began construction of Fort Jefferson in 1846. The islands were strategic, safeguarding America's soft underbelly and protecting her interests in the Gulf of Mexico. Though hardly a shot was ever fired in anger from its walls, Fort Jefferson served as a military prison both during and after the Civil War. Accounted among its prisoners was Dr. Samuel Mudd, the physician who had the ill fortune to set the broken leg of John Wilkes Booth, assassin of President Abraham Lincoln.

Persistent outbreaks of yellow fever (and a persuasively punishing hurricane) convinced the army to abandon the place in 1874. The structure continued to provide incidental service to the country until World War I. In 1935, President Franklin Delano Roosevelt proclaimed the fort a National Monument.

For most of the year the small garrison of Park Service personnel attends visiting yachtsmen or adventuresome tourists who charter aircraft out of Key West to reach this outermost key, take their pictures, and leave. But every spring and fall, Fort Jefferson's visitor roster burgeons. The place draws hundreds of North American birders, who come to garner exotic birds of tropical seas for their North American Life Lists. And, if conditions are right, to reap a harvest of migrating birds sown by the night sky.

None of this, of course, would have interested the Cattle Egret that was dying. Of far greater interest were the several small warblers, waifs like itself, who were foraging in the trees adjacent to the fountain; he eyed them with hungry eyes. It had become a standoff. The birds—a Black-and-white Warbler and two Blackpolls—wanted the water. The heron had strategic possession of the water. What it wanted, *needed*, was the birds if it wanted to live. And, like all living things, the egret wanted to live very badly.

The birders were interested in the warblers, too. Some were bearded and sweat-stained, birders who had been on the island a week or more. Most were not as weathered, members of a birding tour group that had arrived the previous afternoon. It is a tradition to gather at the fountain as the day heats up and bird activity drops off. What birds are about usually find their way to the water. No sense chasing from shadow to shadow when the birds will come to you. Besides, it's a good place to compare notes. To gloat about birds seen and despair about the birds seen by others. Nobody mentioned the dying egret. What could anyone possibly say that would make any difference?

The tour group, one of several that would arrive during April and May, had arrived on a boat chartered out of Key West. After setting up their tents

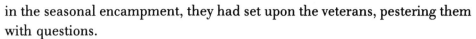

in the seasonal encampment, they had set upon the veterans, pestering them with questions.

Yes, they were told, the Black Noddy was in with the Browns.

Yes, the White-tailed Tropicbirds were still being seen, seen that morning from the walls of the fort.

But no, they were told with undisguised disgust, there hadn't been a fallout worthy of the name in two weeks. The skies had been worthlessly fair, the nights frontless, filled with the call notes of birds that had continued on to the safety of the mainland. Morning searches of the trees within the fort produced only meager handfuls of migrating birds. The spring had been a poor one, they were told.

The great masses of birds that fall from the sky and carpet the Gulf Coast in spring (the fallouts birders pray for) have a tragic side, a dark irony that taints their splendor. The conditions that precipitate birds for birders bring despair for the birds themselves. When the great "blue northers" roll out of the plains, and rain lashes out into the Gulf of Mexico, migrating birds die in uncounted millions. The great coastal fallouts, the toast of birders in spring, are made up of weary survivors.

The absence of rain did not trouble the group of birders who had just arrived and who only had two days to spend, and who were, for the most part, new to the Tortugas. Many still cast excited glances up at scores of magnificent frigatebirds sailing along the ramparts of the fort, and frigatebirds at Fort Jefferson are like pigeons in Central Park.

The news was taken more seriously by the tour leaders, who exchanged solemn and knowing glances. Once the novelty had worn off, once the exotic resident species had been ticked off, the group would be looking for more and looking to the leaders to provide them. Without a good fallout, the Dry Tortugas can be a very hot, dull place.

But not on the first day. Not with one hundred thousand nesting Sooty Terns hardly more than a stone's throw away who day and night fill the air with their excited chatter. Not with the inscrutable Brown Noddys keyed up on pilings and Brown Boobys perched on distant snags. No, Fort Jefferson is too exotic and the birding too exciting to feel disgruntlement on the very first day. It was a tired and happy and hopeful group of birders that retired that evening, beneath a creamy swath of stars portending an uneventful night. Many debated the merits of stretching storm flies over tents or using tents at all. It hadn't rained on the Tortugas in two weeks. By all the signs, it wasn't going to rain for two more.

The first shower at 10:30 precipitated a flurry of hatch battening and impromptu rain fly stretching. The gully washer that raked the island a couple of hours later collapsed one tent, swept another into the night, and found the weak points of many, many more.

But the thunderstorm did more than make a shambles of the Hooverville under the palms. It beat the hosts of migrating birds out of the sky, driving those that could find it to the half-shelter of the island. From midnight on, the air was filled the panicked *squawk* of Green-backed Herons and the sound of large-bodied birds crashing into the palms. Ghost images of Cattle Egrets glowed in the lightning flashes, and tiny warblers sent their searching calls out into a death-filled night that moved unhurriedly toward morning.

A rainy dawn found members of the group already up and about, searching for birds by flashlight. The fort was a treasure trove, and every branch claimed a share. One tree held twelve species at one time: a Yellow-billed Cuckoo, a Gray Catbird, Yellow Warbler, Cape May Warbler, Black-throated Green Warbler, Black-throated Blue Warbler, Blackburnian Warbler, Common Yellowthroat, Black-whiskered Vireo, Indigo Bunting, Bobolink, and a Scarlet Tanager.

Birders moved from tree to tree, shrub to shrub, group to binocular clad group. Some walked, many ran, drawn to close-at-hand views of birds too weary to fly, with no place to fly to. On the parade ground, storm-grounded Cattle Egrets stalked weakened songbirds, and hungry Merlins made off with warblers whose exhaustion had befuddled their wits.

As the morning progressed, as the sun melted the shadows and sent heat waves rippling across the compound, bird and birder activity diminished. Singly or in small groups, the birds took wing, vaulted the fifty-foot walls, and left the island, heading east. There are, you see, no insects worth discussing or pursuing in Fort Jefferson; no food for nutritionally bankrupt birds. So those that are able to, leave. What future they have begins seventy miles to the east, or it will end somewhere short of that. By noon, the only activity in the compound was centered around the water fountain.

The egret, whose strategy was good, was still waging its war of attrition. The warblers, whose strategy was also good, stayed out of reach. With each passing minute, the bird seemed to shrink deeper into itself, becoming less of this world and more of the next. When its legs finally failed it, the bird slumped forward until its bill touched the grass. By the time it finally surrendered to gravity and fell to its side, it had been dead several minutes.

Few among the birders took any notice, and none mentioned it. Later, when the crowd had gone to lunch, a Park Service employee came out of the office, placed the body in a cardboard box, and carried it away.

It was something that happened all the time. Part of life on the Dry Tortugas.

## 8 • POINT PELEE, ONTARIO:

## Impact at the Omega Point

### THE PASSERINE PLAY

*S*PRING MOVES ACROSS NORTH AMERICA IN WAVES THAT crest just a little higher each day. Riding the crest is a family of birds so exquisite that they seem cut from living crystal. These are the wood warblers, the true birds of spring.

Their colors are enough to make an oriole or a tanager pick up and move to another perch, and their voices sing rings around the thrushes. Their frenetic energy could make a hummingbird pant, and with fifty-two species distributed across North America, their variety humbles even North America's diversity of waterfowl.

Every morning finds new treasures deposited by a night sky—flame-throated Blackburnians; jade-colored Tennessees; Yellow-rumpeds of the golden crown; and sapphire-backed Black-throated Blues. Every day brings new songs that fall on winter-numbed ears, begging recognition.

It's a festival, it's a treasure hunt. It's baseball, the Kentucky Derby, a concert in the park, and the Easter Egg Hunt on the White House Lawn all rolled into one. In forests and city parks, suburban backyards and desert oases, North America's birders turn out to witness the *Passerine Play*, birding's great rite of spring. In *no* place do they turn out in greater numbers or with greater enthusiasm than Point Pelee, Ontario—the place where spring and birders meet.

## THE PARK THAT BIRDING BUILT

"I guess the welcome mat is out," Linda observed over the top of her muffin, gesturing toward the banner stretched across the road with a steaming go-cup.

"Downtown Leamington *Welcomes* Birders," it read. And well it should! In Leamington, Ontario, gateway to Point Pelee National Park, birding means business. Big business.

But the Chamber of Commerce was not blowing kisses from the roadside—not at this hour of the morning, anyway. Except for the cadre of sleep-drugged attendants in the doughnut shop, most of the residents of Leamington still slept peacefully in their beds.

"What time is it?" I wanted to know.

"Four forty-five," Linda replied.

I eased my foot off the accelerator, coming to closer accord with the posted speed limit. No sense in drawing the angst of the local constabulary—particularly not in a town so accommodating to birders. We'd easily make the park gate by post time, 5:00. Plenty of time to find a parking spot in the parking lot closest to the action.

But birders would do well *not* to arrive late, *not* on the third weekend in May, not at Point Pelee National Park, just the hottest little birding hot spot this side of High Island, Texas. One thousand cars is capacity, and six square kilometers is not a lot of space for six thousand birders (Pelee's standard peak season crowd) to spread out in—not that they specifically try. In spring, birders go where the warblers go, and come May both head for Pelee; seventy-five thousand of the former; forty-two species of the latter (thirty-five of which are seen annually). Linda and I were going to join them both.

We were third in line at the gate. The uniformed park attendant looked as though he'd been wearing those corporal stripes since World War I—and he looked a little sheepish, too, when he learned that we didn't have a season's pass.

"You'll have to pay your four dollars on the way out," he apologized. Normally, the park opens at 6:00 A.M. But to accommodate birders during May, Pelee opens at 5:00 A.M. The cash box, apparently, hadn't caught up with the change, yet. But since it was birders he was dealing with, there wasn't any harm just letting us in on the honor system. There was no question in his mind (or ours) that we would ante up when departing. That's just the way birders are.

We claimed a good spot in the south lot, grabbed our binoculars, and followed the gear-laden assembly to the tram stop next to the Visitor Center. The park operates a shuttle service, carrying birders (and regular visitors, too) a mile and a half down the peninsula. From there, it's another half-mile or so to the tip—the southernmost point on mainland Canada.

Pelee, a narrow, sandy spit projecting south fifteen miles into Lake Erie, is a migrant trap. For many migrating birds crossing Lake Erie, it is the first dry land they encounter. For forest birds, Pelee may also be the last *appropriate* habitat they will find for many miles. Agricultural land dominates the region. So, from the standpoint of a tired woodland bird seeking sanctuary, the projecting spit of green is an oasis in an aquatic and agricultural desert—the only show in town.

This alone would insure Pelee high favor with spring migrants, but there is another point that wins favor with visiting birders. Pelee's climate is affected by Lake Erie, whose cold temperature retards leaf development in the spring. Over most of North America woodlands are already blanketed by leaves during the third week of May; on Pelee, the oaks are hardly out of tassel yet. Birds can fly, but so long as they stay in bounds, they can't hide.

The first warblers *normally* reach Pelee in mid-April. The last straggling subadults move through in early June. The peak species diversity occurs between May 7 and 22, but weather, more than date, determines whether a day's birding will be average or exceptional.

The conditions that precipitate flights at Pelee are like those that cause the massive fallouts along the Gulf of Mexico. The optimum scenario finds a fast-moving cold front colliding with a warm southerly air flow out over Lake Erie, sometime after midnight and before dawn. Pushing headwinds and a wall of clouds squeeze the birds out of the sky, forcing them to descend—onto the land if they can make it, into the water if they cannot.

There are mornings, a handful every spring, where Pelee is simply festooned with brightly colored warblers, gifts deposited by the wind. These are the good mornings, the red-letter days, the days birders hope for. Then, perhaps a few times a decade, there are the spectacular days, the ones that overreach human comprehension and break human hearts. These are the days when birds stack up on the beaches, too tired to make the trees, too weak to move out from underfoot, too spent, many of them, to do much more than die.

I remember the story told by a friend and Pelee regular, Dr. Harold Axtell, who recalled to me one of these great fallouts. It was raining, he said, raining rain and raining birds. In a puddle, on the tram road, he found a warbler up to its belly in water. The bird was asleep, its head drawn deep into its feathers. Harold reached down, rescuing it from the puddle. As he lifted the bird it jerked its head, but consciousness was beyond its capacity. The bird was asleep again before Harold could place it on a nearby branch.

Today, talk at the tram stop was lively. New arrivals asked for news, and veterans of the week gave it freely.

"You should have been here Wednesday," a Pelee regular advised. "The best wave in recent memory," was the most often expressed phrase. But Linda and I were lucky on one count. Had we come a weekend earlier, we were told, we would have "gotten our butts kicked." The second weekend in May is the weekend of choice among the ranks of questing birders—the ones that are more interested in finding a rare southern overshoot (a Worm-eating Warbler, maybe a Yellow-throated) than in hitting Pelee for the spectacle—for lots and lots of birds but maybe little out of the ordinary.

But that weekend it rained. It rained hard and it rained cold. The tram drivers, loading up for their first run of the morning, were still shaking their heads at the perversity of their birding clients. Despite last week's patently horrible weather, the three trams had each carried over six hundred birders out to the tip, and others had chosen to walk.

"How could you tell they were all birders?" I asked our tram driver, a lively young woman with a name tag that read "Stephanie."

"Oh, God," she replied, rolling her eyes a bit for drama and emphasis.

"You can tell them right away," she insisted. "For one thing, they are always looking up. And they don't want to move for you," she adding, expressing what must be, for tram drivers, a professional pique. "Last weekend," she confided, "I really had to lean on the horn for a few of them."

But it was the birders who were leaning on their horns now. Eager to leave, eager to get out to the tip where the morning action would be.

"How can you tell they were birders?" Stephanie repeated, shaking her head, moving behind the wheel of her vehicle, getting underway. "You can pick out a birder a mile away."

Maybe tram drivers can pick birders out right away—not that there is any great trick to picking out birders in Pelee in May—but most people seem to have a great deal of trouble recognizing birders. If this were not the case, then the cherished image of birders as "Little Old Lady in Tennis Sneakers" would not be as pervasive as it is.

I recall, and maybe you do too, a character on an old television comedy series, *The Beverly Hillbillies*, named Miss Hathaway—a cerebral and patently plain-looking bank secretary slipping inexorably toward spinsterhood. Her role was chasing a not too terribly bright (but otherwise eligible) hillbilly millionaire's son, whose delusion was to grow up and be a brain surgeon. Her hobby was bird-watching. Why bird-watching? I suppose because the not too terribly bright producers of the show figured it went with the cerebral, plain spinster image.

This popular image of bird-watchers seems to have been around since Garfield (the President, not the cat) was shot, and may not have had any more bearing on reality then. One of Garfield's successors to the U.S. presidency, Teddy ("Rough Rider") Roosevelt (1901–1909), was a birder, as was Depression and World War II President FDR (as are, for that matter, former President and First Lady Jimmy and Rosalyn Carter).

Whatever the historic roots, today's typical, active birder bears little resemblance to the myth or to Miss Hathaway. As profiled by surveys conducted by Dr. Paul Kerlinger of the New Jersey Audubon Society, the average birder is not "old" (unless you consider forty-seven "old," because that *is* the average). If it does sound old, then realize that the ranks of birders are pretty evenly distributed between the ages of twenty-five and fifty—with nearly one quarter of all birders falling in the thirty-one-to-forty age group. No, birders are not "old"—but a strong case could be made for "mature."

Nor is the "average" birder a "lady"; 63 percent are male. As for tennis shoes—well, if tennis shoes are synonymous with running shoes, then birders are still wearing "sneakers"—birders, and almost everyone else in society. Linda is a Reebok fan. Me? I like whatever happens to be on sale.

The number of birders who come to Pelee to study birds has made it an attractive place to study birders—to try to establish an accurate profile *and* to estimate the economic and resource impacts of birders on a place like Point Pelee.

Dr. James R. Butler of the University of Alberta and several of his colleagues have done extensive studies on bird-watchers, at Point Pelee. They learned that as a group Pelee birders were highly educated, with over 60 percent having bachelor's degrees, as compared to 10 percent of the Canadian population as a whole. They found that birders also tended to be affluent, with an average annual household income of $57,000, as compared to a Canadian household average of $38,000, and that high income correlated well with vocation. Fifty-seven percent of birders are in "professional occupations."

Dr. Kerlinger's figures, too, support both the high level of education and the higher-than-average income. In Dr. Kerlinger's survey, 75 percent of respondents held bachelor's degrees and 38 percent of respondents held graduate degrees. The average *individual* income was between $25,000 and $35,000. Again, well over the national per capita income average (less than $20,000 in 1989, as established by the U.S. Department of Commerce).

The average Pelee birder had traveled 689 kilometers to reach his destination, spent between three and four days at Pelee, and had made 28.6 trips to Pelee in the course of his birding career. What does all this mean to the people of Leamington? Money. Lots and lots of money—about $3.2 million spent locally by birders in 1987. On food (36.7 percent), on accommodations (38.4 percent), on souvenirs (6.5 percent), and on equipment (6.3 percent).

Of course, if birders were just an eccentric fringe of society, numerically insignificant, merchants and retailers could ignore them with impunity. But this is not the case, and to ignore them courts missing some of the $20 billion birders spend annually in the name of their pursuit.

Estimates of the number of birders in North America differ, and the variation relates to how strictly or loosely one defines the term *bird-watcher*. The figure most commonly bandied about put the number of birders in North America between 20 and 30 million—a figure that should make the manufacturers of "tennis" shoes very, very happy. A Canadian study conducted by A. Jacquemot and F. L. Filion in 1987 supports the higher range of this estimate. The authors believe that in Canada 13 percent of the population undertakes special trips to observe, study, or photograph birds. If this percentage is applied to a combined U.S. and Canadian population of 275 million individuals, it comes to roughly 36 million people for whom birding is a clear act of volition—a figure that would probably even surprise Miss Hathaway.

In 1989, D. A. Hall and J. T. O'Leary analyzed the results of the 1985 National Survey of Fish, Hunting and Wildlife Associated Recreation, published by the U.S. Department of the Interior. They estimated that the number of bird-watchers in the United States was 61 million—making birding the country's most popular wildlife-related activity, more popular than hunting with 16.7 million proponents; even more popular than that most cherished of outdoor pastimes, fishing, whose ranks include 46.6 million Americans. In fact, when all outdoor activities are rated, birding ranks second only to gardening for the title of America's favorite outdoor pastime.

So, very probably, tram drivers at Pelee really *can* pick out birders on sight. If every fourth person you pass on the street is a birder, there is no great trick to it. Actually, at Pelee in May, a tram driver would be harder pressed to pick out a person who was *not* a birder, because 98 percent of Pelee visitors are just that.

The tram pulled up to a pavilion whose principal features were rest rooms and a large, colorful map complete with arrow and perennial legend: "You are here." Everyone on the first tram already knew where they were.

They were half a mile shy of where they wanted to be—the Tip—and those who weren't interested in rest rooms rushed to amend this geographic shortfall.

First tram passengers are *serious* birders. Their field jackets are weathered and stained, their binoculars expensive and new. Most wore Gortex shells or Capeline jackets. Jeans were the rule. Running shoes almost swept the field. Not a field guide was to be seen (although a few may have been hidden). Here and there in the crowd were quiet groups of men incongruously garbed in Barbour jackets and knee-length rubber boots ("wellies"). These were British birders ("Brits!") whose affection for Pelee (and North America's warblers) makes oceans no barrier.

The crowd was much younger than the national average. Males in their twenties and thirties were particularly overrepresented. These are birding's shock troops, men who are single and serious or coupled but committed—husbands who leave birding widows at home with once-a-week regularity and whose every waking hour orbits around some facet of birding.

These are the crazies.

Women made up less than a third of the first tram passengers, and none seemed to bear the loco brand. Unlike their male counterparts, single, unattached women are the exception in birding. Most are, like Linda, partners in a birding dyad or, when they go birding, go with a group of female birding friends (leaving birding widowers at home) or a bird club, or as a member of a professional tour group.

There was something else about the group that was at odds with North America's social profile. The group was ethnically static, Caucasian to a fault. In fact, over most of North America, the ranks of birders are so filled with people of European extraction that they make professional hockey teams look like models of affirmative action.

Linda and I went with the flow, moving down the main path, stepping around figures that stopped suddenly in their tracks, went rigid with attention, and brought binoculars up like a salute. Unlike tram routes, on a birding path standing birders have the right of way. Itinerants yield.

The binocular salutes were crisp, identifications perfunctory and precise. Only when a feathered subject was moving deeply through the latticework of branches was any time or effort involved. Then, the birder on point would fairly writhe in place trying to negotiate a clear view of the feathered gremlin.

But let a reticent warbler whisper a single phrase—in the presence of the audio elite, a single, audible *chip* note—and the binoculars fell back in place. These were Pelee's finest, sharpshooters who could nail 'em at a glance, could lift them out of anonymity by the ears.

It's one of birding's greatest ironies that a well-trained ear doesn't help birders *see* more birds. The truth is that an identification made by audible clues means that the bird doesn't need to be viewed at all—and many that are so identified never rate a raised glass. But as an aid to picking out rare or uncommon species in a myriad of bouncing forms or of pinning a name to a treetop bird showing nothing more distinguishing than white undertail coverts, it is a skill worth cultivating, a skill worth all the warblers in the bush.

It takes time to tune an ear, and effort, too. It means tracking down every unfamiliar song and welding the visual image of the bird to an ephemeral voice. Unless you are among the gifted few, someone with the auditory recall of Igor Stravinsky, the weld usually does not hold the first time, or the second time either. The bird with the short, bright phrases or the raspy vowels must be tracked down over and over and over. Then over and over again, until *those* phrases and the image of *that* bird fuse and become one.

It helps to be at a place where you can track down American Redstart with reinforcing regularity. It helps to be at a place like Pelee on a good day.

It was a good day, too. Not spectacular, not great. Good. Fun and fast-paced. Filled with color and song. We worked our way down toward the Tip, working slowly at first, gaining a sense of the flight.

In the treetops the high sibilants were pushing the limits of human registry. High, thin notes that all but fall on deaf ears. Black-and-white Warblers wheezed their classic *weesee, weesee, weesee, weesee, weesee* song. This is an easy one for beginners—an audio anchor to hitch a growing repertoire of bird songs to. In the trees overhead Cape May Warblers whispered *seet, seet, seet, seet,* all on the same pitch. From those same trees, Bay-breasted said almost the very same thing. *Except!* Except Bay-breasted split the notes—*tee-si, tee-si, tee-si.*

"Blackpoll?" Linda asked.

I listened for the song that had tripped the name in my wife's audio recall . . . and heard it. The song a Cape May might make if it were running out of breath. A series of notes that lose their substance and fade into space.

"Blackpoll," I agreed.

Then there are the ones with the buzzy vowels. Parula, which drags its feet up the stairs and falls down at the end; Cerulean, which takes 'em two at a time and scales the last six in a leap. Blue-winged Warbler of the asthmatic rising and falling breath (*beeee-buzzzz*); and Golden-winged, which inhales the *bee* and chokes on the *buzz, buzz, buzz. Bee-buzz, buzz, buzz.* Black-throated Blue Warblers slurring their phonetic apology—*I am so lay-zee.* Black-throated Green Warblers, who sound just as lazy (but have a better voice and a two-song repertoire).

There are the warblers that *trillllll*: Pine, Palm, Worm-eating, Orange-crowned, Wilson's. Warblers who repeat themselves, like Kentucky Warblers (*Chory, chory, chory, chory, chory*), Yellowthroats (*witchity, witchity, witchity*), and Ovenbirds shouting for the attention of the *TEACHER, TEACHER, TEACHER, TEACHER.*

There are warblers whose songs have two or three parts to them. Nashville and Tennessee; Northern and Louisiana Waterthrush. Warblers whose songs hold you in limbo until the final notes like Canada Warbler, whose song is a jumble, runs up and down the scale, and only gains *"Wit!"* at the end. And Chestnut-sided who (even more than Yellow Warbler, its musical twin) is *Pleased, pleased pleased to MEET you!*

When all the ones who neatly fall into categories have been labeled, then it's time to track down the rogue singers, the ones that throw the change-up pitches or specialize in Teflon-coated songs—the kind that simply refuse to stick to human comprehension. Magnolia who sings 'em short and sweet; Yellow-rumped with the rambling variations; and, of course, American (when-in-doubt-call-it-a) Redstart. Put them all together, add a few tanagers, orioles, vireos, and grosbeaks, and you have the sound of a Dawn Chorus. The true sound of spring.

Three hundred birders crowded the Tip, a coarse, sandy beach sharpened to a point by wind and waves. Barn Swallows were working the crowd, picking off the insects that had gathered on the lee side of the birders, out of the cold lake wind. Spotting scopes and binoculars raked the Tip and the horizon, turning up the usual assortment of Ring-billed and Bonaparte's Gulls.

But the hosts of tired migrants were not so tired this morning that they couldn't make the trees. Singly or in small groups, the birders, like the birds, turned to the woodlands and began working their way back up the peninsula, through the labyrinth of trails and song.

No, it wasn't a killer fallout, but it was the best morning's birding we'd seen all spring. We savored it, marveling at the birds that stood first in line when colors were doled out at the Creation; listening for a Mourning Warbler's chortle and Wilson's chatter. If ever we heard a song we couldn't identify, we just called it a Redstart.

The Tip was getting crowded now, the trails congested. Here and there, tight knots of people blocked passage; one group of birders attracts other birders, eager to share in whatever fortune there is to share. A Mourning Warbler, perhaps? Maybe even a Connecticut!

"A Connecticut? Where?"

"In there, walking left. Just follow my finger."

"HEY, PHIL. THEY GOT A CONNECTICUT OVER HERE."

[Sound of feet] *crunch, crunch, crunch.* "Whe-Where'stheConnecticut?"

"It's preening now, just to the left of . . ."

"Ohhh, I *see* it," [edging forward, two quick steps into the May apples].
*Crunch, crunch.*

"I still don't have it."

"That branch is probably in your way. Here. Move over a little."
*Crunch, crunch.*

"Got it, now?"

"No."

"OK, here, stand right where I'm standing."
*CRUNCH, crunch. Crunch, Crunch, CRUNCH, Cru-Crunch.*

"What do you people have over there?"

"A Connecticut Warbler!"

"Great! OK. Everyone in my group come up quietly and gather around these people."

*CRUNCHCRUNCHCRUNCHCRUNCHCRUNCHCRUNCHCRUNCH-CRUNCHCRUNCH . . .*

Crunch.

It's a typical scene at Pelee, enacted hundreds of times every day, thousands of times a season. A good bird is found, a crowd is drawn, and another bit of Pelee's vegetation falls underfoot, victimized by a crime of passion.

It's not wanton destruction. It's just destruction. One birder walking off the trails, poking through the underbrush hardly leaves a trace. But fifty birders leave a swath. A thousand birders cut a trail. Seventy-five thousand birders cut a labyrinth. Before you know it, more than half the trail system in the heavily birded areas falls on unofficial paths cut by errant birders.

Dr. Butler's studies (1985–1986) of birding's effect on Pelee also focused on the effects that birding has on a fragile environment. He found that most birders leave the designated trails at least once a day. The average was *112 illicit forages per person, per day(!)*, and damage to vegetation during these rogue excursions occurred 95 percent of the time. (Note: Stricter control measures were adopted at Point Pelee in 1990, and damage to vegetation has been sharply reduced.)

Sometimes these excursions took the form of "margin-viewing impacts," birders stepping off the trail to get a better look at, say, a Connecticut Warbler. Some were extended off-trail rambles. Others were over-hill-and-dale pursuits of "good birds"—pursuits that recognize no legislative or vegetative boundaries. Exacerbating the problem, the birders most likely to leave the trails are the more skilled birders—birding's leaders, its role models.

The negative impacts of pursuit are not limited to vegetation. Twenty-five percent of pursued birds flush, leaving the immediate area. For a normal healthy bird, displacement by an overzealous birder is not a major concern. But what about birds stressed to their physical limits by migration?

Heavy birding pressure has forced birds to alter their activity patterns, at Pelee and elsewhere. Birds have been harried to exhaustion by over eager birders. Birds have been lured into harm's way, where they are picked off by predators and tweaked by recorded playback of their calls until their territorial response goes tetanus. There have even been documented instances where secretive species have been trampled to death by birders whose fundamental concern for birds was eclipsed by their craving to see them.

Birders are not stupid people. They are intelligent, environmentally sensitive, cognizant of cause and effect. This is, in fact, part of the problem. Being both intelligent and benign, they can fairly and accurately assess the effects of birding on the environment, and at most times and in most places this is tantamount to zero. Birding is not consumptive. It is not unduly disruptive. It is one on one with nature, a benign activity, less injurious than a flea bite on dog.

This is how birders see it.

This is why seventy-five thousand intelligent, sensitive, and benign people acting in concert can cause so much damage. Seventy-five thousand flea bites draw blood and present people like park administrators and their staffs with a big problem: How to optimize a recreational activity that draws both world acclaim and millions in income and minimize environmental impacts—to insure that the activity *has* a future?

In response to the mounting pressures, and in response to the needs of Pelee's birding clientele, the park instituted new, stricter guidelines during the spring of 1990. Seasonal bird-watching trails were established to help absorb the peak season crunch and allow access to key birding habitat. Unofficial trails would be closed "for revegetation" and marked accordingly. Off-trail wanderings would be, pure and simple, verboten.

The park has also taken the unusual but necessary step of trying to spread Pelee's birder wealth over a wider geographic area. Dubbed: "Operation Spread Out," birders are encouraged to visit other nearby birding locations. The Windsor and Essex County Tourist and Convention Bureau printed a brochure offering descriptions and directions. A sighting board at Pelee includes birds sighted at these satellite locations.

Nobody wants to drive birders away from Point Pelee. Not the park whose reputation is built upon their interest and support. Not the economic infrastructure that thrives on the annual infusion of cash. And certainly not the birders themselves for whom Pelee is one of birding's most cherished hotspots. But nobody wants to reduce Pelee to vegetative fragments or to place unnecessary stress on birds that have reached their physical limits. And how Pelee deals with the problems and how it meets birding's needs will establish guidelines and set precedents that will become standards. Luckily, its administrators have shown themselves equal to the challenge.

Linda and I returned to the tram depot late in the morning. The dawn chorus and bird activity had tapered off. Birder activity continued unabated.

The trams were running full, full of birders whose enthusiasm for birds was more tempered than the level found in the first tram out—tempered by things like the need for sleep and breakfast, age, wisdom, and, for a few, inexperience.

Late-morning tram riders were older. Older than first tram riders, anyway. Old enough to bring the average age up to forty-seven. Identically clad couples, not rogue males, were the rule now; small groups bearing the brands of assorted bird clubs were well represented. The breakdown along sexual lines was a dead heat. Women may even have had the edge. And the techweenie outer-gear had given way to L. L. Bean and Eddie Bauer's finest (along with the odd windbreaker). Tan slacks and comfortable walking shoes had replaced the jeans and runners. There wasn't a Barbour jacket in sight.

We thought we'd stay . . . and then we thought maybe we'd leave . . . and then we went back and forth a few more times. Lunch won out. Time to start pouring our share of birder dollars into the local coffers. (Besides, we'd already gotten our Connecticut Warbler—several, in fact.)

We caught Stephanie's tram back (and discovered that she really is heavy on the horn). Checked out the sighting sheet in the crowded visitor center. Found nothing that would preempt lunch. And left. We were halfway back to town before we remembered that we'd forgotten to pay our entrance fee when we left. We had to go back.

## The World Series of Birding

E WAITED IN SILENCE, BRAINS NUMBED BY EX-haustion, eyes fixed on Linda's pencil as it hopped and skipped (and sometimes jumped) down the tally sheet. Most of the bird species listed on the page were emblazoned with a bold check. The pencil paused at these, sanctifying each with a tap.

But there were other birds scattered in the columned ranks; birds whose names were unchecked and whose empty boxes mocked us. These were the birds whose stealth and cunning had defeated our best efforts to find them. Birds like Pied-billed Grebe . . .

*How?*

American Kestrel . . .

*Come on!*

White-rumped Sandpiper . . .

*When had we ever missed White-rump!*

Winter Wren . . .

*The little snit.*

And Black-throated Blue Warbler . . .

*Fer Chrissakes! Charles Urner must be spinning in his grave.*

Like a nervous Sanderling pecking along the tide line, the pencil moved down the columns, coming at last to the bottom of the page.

"I get the same number," Linda said, raising her head, meeting our eyes. "Does anyone want to count them a third time?"

Nobody did. After 44 sleepless hours and 588 miles in the saddle, there wasn't enough combined energy in the members of the Zeiss Guerrilla Birding Team to strike a match.

Linda's pencil fell upon the page one last time, drawing a number in the box: 210. Two hundred and ten species of birds, all recorded in one calendar day, all in New Jersey.

The beam of the Cape May Point lighthouse arced across the parking lot, bathing the car and its occupants in light, disclosing for a moment the faces of the team.

"Hey now," Pete Bacinski chanted, breaking the silence, breaking into a tired grin.

"That's a kick-ass total," rookie Don Freiday asserted.

"Pretty good," Rick Radis observed philosophically.

Linda said nothing and her silence expressed the unspoken anxiety shared by all. Yes, 210 was good. Almost unbelievable. But scattered around us—caucusing in their cars, staggering toward the finish line, or clustering at the edge of the marsh, still hoping for *one last bird*—were thirty-nine rival teams, combatants in this year's World Series of Birding.

Yes, 210 was an incredible total. No doubt about it. But would it be good enough to win North America's most spirited birding event? The clock on the dashboard read 11:52 P.M. In eight minutes, we'd know.

Four doors opened. Five figures, two soda cans (one empty, one mostly empty), and an avalanche of corn chip remnants spilled into the night. Leaving our spunky but battle-worn Saab 9000 on the curb, we made our way toward the light pouring from the visitor center's door; toward the finish line, and our friends, and our fortune.

The World Series of Birding, sponsored by the New Jersey Audubon Society, is an annual competition, pitting teams of top birders against each other in a twenty-four-hour blitzkrieg. The objective? To record as many species as possible, by sight and sound, between midnight and midnight. The purpose? To raise money, based on pledges, upon the number of species recorded, *and* to focus world attention upon New Jersey's avian wealth.

Ah, but the roots of the annual competition go deeper, much deeper, almost to the origins of birding itself. "The Big Day" tradition reaches back to the early part of this century, to Charles Urner, god to a host of eager young birders growing up in New Jersey during the twenties and thirties.

As early as 1925, Urner was consciously pursuing long lists of birds seen in a single day. On May 15, 1925, he tallied 118 species in and around his hometown of Elizabeth—a total he apparently regarded as some sort of record. A year and a day later, he noted in correspondence that C. H. Pangburn "alone in Westchester County (N.Y.) got 119 species, the record." On May 15, 1927, Allan Cruikshank and R. J. Kuerzi saw 120 species in the Bronx region—"a new record for the Atlantic Coast."

Urner regarded the Bronx record as a thrown glove. Four days later, on May 19, 1927, he teamed up with Ludlow Griscom (whose enthusiasm for Big Days equaled Urner's). Setting off before sunrise, they started their feathered treasure hunt in Troy Meadows, a large freshwater wetlands twenty miles west of Manhattan. From Troy the pair moved on to the woods and farmland surrounding Boonton . . . to the Essex County Reservation, finally anchoring their effort in the tidal marshes of Newark and Elizabeth. Different habitats produce different species, and their total of 130 species eclipsed the short-lived record set the previous Sunday in the Bronx.

One year later, the route was extended south to take in Manasquan and its larder of coastal species. The modification added three hours of driving time (but 15 more species). In 1929, Urner's ambitions drove him all the way to Brigantine, adding even more coastal species.

Several years of tinkering and fine-tuning ensued, and by May 14, 1933, Urner was ready for his Big Day—an all-out assault, man versus bird. Surrounding himself with the talented likes of Ludlow Griscom, J. Lee Edwards, Joe Hicky, Richard Pough, Urner and an *eleven-member hit squad* scoured the state, running up a party total of 173 species, a remarkable total.

Urner's addiction has become birding's tradition. The Big Day has become an annual rite of spring. The American Birding Association, codifiers of birding's rules and regulations, gave it uniform standards so that Big Day totals might be compared. In 1972, the Long Point Bird Observatory of Ontario,

Canada, gave the Big Day higher purpose by turning it into a fund-raising event, a birdathon, where money pledged on the number of species seen goes to benefit conservation. And in 1984, New Jersey Audubon gave it a common arena, the state of New Jersey's 7,800 square miles of forest, fields, swamps, streams, wetlands, estuaries, and tidal flats (give or take a little urban erosion).

It was Roger Tory Peterson, the premier birder of our age, who gave the event its name—"something that will demonstrate its competitive spark." He suggested "The World Series of Birding."

On midnight, May 19, 1984, thirteen teams carrying the banners of assorted conservation organizations fanned out across the Garden State and did battle in the name of fun, glory, and conservation dollars. Twenty-four hours later, it was the Guerrilla Birding team of Pete Bacinski, Bill Boyle, Roger Tory Peterson, David Sibley, and me who carried the day with a total of 201 species—a New Jersey Big Day Record.

But that record, like all records, was not built to last. The field was destined to grow; teams and their fortunes destined to change. Only once again in what remained of the decade would a Guerrilla Birding Team win the prestigious Urner-Stone Cup. The cup and the decade belonged to arch-rival Bausch and Lomb, a ruthlessly efficient band of birding mercenaries (disguised as a newspaper editor, a hospital administrator, an environmental consultant, and a realtor).

This year, the Guerrillas wanted it back.

This year, we vowed, we would come home carrying our tripods or skewered upon them.

*Ave Urner, morituri te salutamus.*

And now . . . this year was almost over.

Gravel crunched underfoot, not the quick, emphatic crunch of steps smartly placed; the long, tortured scrap of gravel stirred by feet that no longer have what it takes to break gravity's bond.

"How are you doin', Mr. Bacinski?" I asked, turning toward my long-time birding companion and only other surviving veteran of the original Guerrilla Birding Team. Pete's a big man, and twenty-four hours of hard birding tears hell out of his ankles.

"Oh, I'm fine. I'm fine," he assured, lying gallantly. "You know . . ." he said, changing the subject.

And I *did* know—guessed what Pete was going to say. But I wanted to hear him say it anyway. Because it was Pete, and I love to hear him talk, and now that the day was over, and we'd done our best, and our best had been pretty damn good, it felt wonderful just to ease back and listen to Pete say . . .

". . . I *knew* 210 was possible. Didn't I say before we started that 208 was guaranteed on this route and that all we needed was . . ."

Yes, Pete had indeed said that, just the evening before, in Rick Radis's kitchen, just after we'd dismantled and rebuilt our new, top secret, Big Day route for the eighth or ninth time that spring. But three months earlier, when the members of the Guerrilla Birding Team had first met to pool their talents and plan their assault, 210 species in twenty-four hours was nothing but a pipe dream, was . . .

"Crazy," said Rick, peering down at the New Jersey road map and a route, freshly marked out in red felt pen. "But doable," he added, with more confidence than the great big red question mark etched over the face of the state inspired.

Charles Urner and his cronies would have thought otherwise. In fact, Charles probably would have taken one look at the prescribed five-hundred-mile Big Day route and stroked out. Ah, but Urner was born in an age before interstate highways, Saab 9000 Turbos, birding hotlines, and optics that bring the horizon within mortal reach.

Urner didn't know about Clinton Road and its pocket of northern breeders, or have a Brigantine National Wildlife Refuge to sop up lingering waterfowl, or command a working knowledge of South Jersey to snag those southern specialties like Yellow-throated Warbler and Summer Tanager.

Urner didn't have the cumulative wisdom imparted by sixty-plus years of Big Day tradition and six straight World Series of Birding Competitions. Most of all, Urner did not have the members of the Zeiss Guerrilla Birding Team at his command:

Pete "Golden Ears" Bacinski, whose repertoire of bird songs is only exceeded by his prize collection of 45 rpms. A man who can identify any bird song or any rock-and-roll tune cut before 1965 in three notes or less.

Rick "Linnaeus" Radis, birder and botanist, heir to New Jersey's naturalist tradition clear back to Charles Urner's living room; a walking index of every fen, field, and bog in the state of New Jersey.

Linda "10x" Dunne, a transplant from those wide open western spaces, who doesn't seem to understand that people aren't supposed to be able to see birds behind trees. So she just does it.

Don "Our Man" Freiday, young, talented, and willing to lose his job and court divorce for the privilege of putting in two weeks of scouting prior to the event.

I was driving.

There was, however, one thing the Charles Urner had that we didn't have—and that was migrating birds. Fifty years ago, a May morning in any New Jersey woodlot would have been met by a flood of songbirds. No more. Songbird populations have fallen to only a vestige of what they were in Urner's time. The flood has become a trickle, and migrant traps, the cornerstone of Urner's strategy, have lost their clutch. If Charles Urner and his cronies were to head for their favorite dawn site today, chances are they would be met with a daunting wall of silence.

Some blame tropical deforestation. Some ascribe the decline of North America's thrushes, vireos, and warblers to development in the Northeast. Both levy a toll, and there may be causal factors that have yet to be identified. For whatever reasons, the sputtering flow that is spring migration today is too unpredictable to anchor a Big Day strategy. The only way to feel confident about finding birds like Hermit Thrush, Solitary Vireo, and Black-throated Blue Warbler is to search out nesting birds prior to a Big Day run and link these feathered points together along a carefully crafted line.

Our line, in the grand tradition of New Jersey Big Days, began at Troy Meadows, at midnight.

Potholes chewed at our wheels and headlights flickered and danced down the dark tunnel of trees. At the far end of a well-puddled parking lot we parked and stepped into the night.

"Damn," Pete Bacinski observed.

"What'sthematter?" Don asked fervently and not without basis. Far too often in the history of Big Days, a sudden expletive at the first stop has been followed by: "I left my binoculars sitting on the kitchen table."

"Oh," Pete intoned, "I put my foot in a puddle."

Treacherous things, puddles.

Like children, like moths, we followed Rick's flashlight across the meadow, striking out toward the finger of trees that reached deep into the marsh. Troy was Rick's home turf, and his hours of scouting had turned up a special prize, a Long-eared Owl.

Big Day totals may be grounded in the common, everyday birds—the "must gets." But Big Day records! Ah, to set a record you have to reach deep into the night and draw from it birds that lie on the rim of possibility.

"Stop," Rick commanded.

"We're still pretty far from the trees, aren't we?" I challenged.

"Yes, but I'm standing in water," Rick said placidly. "The marsh must be flooded."

Treacherous things, marshes.

Moving to higher ground we stood, silent as the shadows cast by stones, seining the universe with night-sharpened senses.

"Five minutes," Pete said, looking at his watch, bringing us back to earth.

The air was heavy with the sound of distant traffic. Ambient light spewing from the urban corridor spread an oily sheen across an overcast sky. More light and more sound than Urner had known in his time. Still, it was a perfect night for listening, still as a bird poised for flight, silent as a held breath—a wonderful night for picking out the cries of distant night birds.

"Three minutes," Pete said.

"*Sora*," four voices responded in chorus, pinning a name to the descending whinny that had ushered from the marsh.

"No good," Pete intoned, calling the first pitch of the World Series a foul. No birds could be counted until midnight. We'd have to wait and hope it vocalized again.

"Two minutes."

Somewhere, in the Hackensack Meadows, in Kearny Marsh, in the Great Swamp, at Turkey Point, at a dozen sites scattered across the state, thirty-nine other teams were also poised and waiting. Teams that had schemed and dreamed a year for the next twenty-four hours. Teams from as far away as California and the United Kingdom.

"One minute."

Somewhere, waiting in the darkness, was a state filled with hidden treasure, every bird a prize. Some would come easy. Some would be hard. And now, with the second hand bearing down on the other two hands of Pete's watch that were already joined at midnight, all we had to do was:

"Count 'em," Pete commanded. But if teams gain points by identifying birds, birds gain points by remaining anonymous. In the first several minutes of our vigil, the birds gained a respectable lead.

Birds must go about the business of being birds. Part of their job is communicating their whereabouts to other members of their species. Gradually, one by precious one, the birds of Troy surrendered their identities.

"Virginia Rail," five voices whispered as one.

"Swamp Sparrow . . . Marsh Wren . . . Sora . . . Killdeer . . ."

"(American) BITTERN! . . ." Don Freiday more or less shouted, pointing off to the left where the sound had emanated, the sound of a bassoon with a limp and . . . "Hey!" Don added, hesitating, committing himself no further.

"That was King Rail," I agreed, putting the name to the grunting sound heard by all.

Cheers, rebel yells, and high fives all around. Bittern and King Rail! Whew! Tough ones. Two birds that could make all the difference. The Guerrillas were rolling.

But in birding, as in life, loss is never far from gain, and of Long-eared Owls there were none to be had. No Long-eared but . . .

"Great Horned," Pete said abruptly, gesturing toward the west.

"I didn't get it," Linda said, speaking for the majority.

This is where things get dicey. According to competition rules 95 percent of all birds tallied *must* be recorded by all team members. For every twenty birds a team is allowed one bird that is not unanimous—a wild card. More than this and the bird must be dropped from the total.

We listened, hands cupped behind ears, senses strained. *Sometimes* I *thought* I could hear the sound that had reached Pete's hypersensitive ears. *Sometimes*. But not enough for certainty.

There is in birding an unspoken code of honor. A birder's word is his bond, and not even something like a World Series of Birding can shake this unshakable ethic. Reporters who cover the event invariably want to know "how everyone can be certain that everyone else is telling the truth."

The answer is very simple. Because they just do.

We would have to get another Great Horned Owl somewhere else. Or else this one would have to claim one of our precious wild cards.

"Time," I said, cracking the temporal whip. Without protest we raced our unseen shadows back to the car. Headlights gleaming, the Saab sped back down the tunnel of trees, sidestepping puddles and branches that reached out to rake her enameled sides. (Many of them, anyway.)

BMW won't put up cars for the event anymore, not after an inexplicable (and very expensive) scratch was discovered running the length of the 735i we used in 1985. Mercedes-Benz has flagged our applications, too (but then, it's likely that nobody else has ever dipped one of the cars from their loaner fleet in a salt marsh, either). The Swedes have a much better attitude about these things—perhaps because birding is a very popular pastime in Sweden.

In the copilot's seat, Pete poured a stream of coffee that fell, for the most part, in the cup. In the back, Linda tallied our earnings.

"Nine up . . ." she announced, giving the total, ". . . one down" (the Long-eared Owl that had eluded us).

*And Great Horned Owl in the hole*, I thought darkly. It was too early to be in foul trouble; too early to have that hanging over us.

Five minutes later, we were speeding west through a dark New Jersey night en route to scheduled rendezvous with Barred Owl, Screech Owl, Least Bittern, and American Woodcock.

"American Bittern and King Rail," Don chanted, digging into our cache of munchies, lifting the wrong end of an opened bag of Dorito chips. "Boy, talk about . . ."

". . . luck," Peter B. concluded, keeping his eyes turned toward the ground, filling the air with the measured sound of footsteps churning on gravel. All anyone needs to reach the stars is luck.

Yes, that's what Pete had said, all right, over twenty-four hours ago. But luck is an elusive commodity. Now you have it, now you don't, and no team rides on its coattails for twenty-four hours. There is a lot of emotional up and down on a Big Day.

"We didn't seem to have much luck after Troy," I pointed out. "We couldn't get a rise out of that Saw-whet Owl."

"That was a bust," Pete admitted.

"And we never did get that snipe or the nighthawk. *And*," I added, to cement my case, "the rain at three A.M. didn't do us any favors."

"That was the pits," Pete agreed, shuddering. "But," he said, brightening, straightening, smiling widely, "we rallied at sunup. At Stokes State Forest, we conquered."

Do you remember how it is when you stand and watch the sun rise after a long night without sleep? They come so rarely, these mornings. They are bound to great events and purpose—the milestones that mark the memories of a human life.

Perhaps you recall a lover who swept you through the Long Night, on a trestle built of talk and touching and possibility so great that hopes danced freely across its span . . . turned left at the Milky Way . . . and went right on 'til morning, 'til sun and the stars and the moon,

> *'til the cat ran away with the spoon,*
> *forever, and ever and ever . . .*

Maybe your life has known the Long Night of birth, the bloody struggle that forged the corporeal union of you and another in living form. Or maybe you have experienced the Long Night of flight, where a life mired in complications set itself free upon a dark highway leading east.

Or west.

Or south.

Leading to a new horizon.

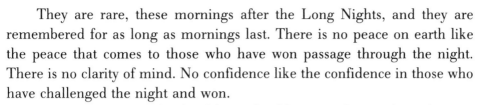

They are rare, these mornings after the Long Nights, and they are remembered for as long as mornings last. There is no peace on earth like the peace that comes to those who have won passage through the night. There is no clarity of mind. No confidence like the confidence in those who have challenged the night and won.

We stood, side by side, shoulder to shoulder, poised—watching the stars above the meadow surrender without terms. And we knew, as thirty-nine other teams knew, *knew* without question or doubt, that this day was ours.

One by one, impatient to be heard, the birds of forest and field announced themselves, begging audience with their songs.

Barn Swallows twittered a greeting from the bridge beneath our feet, and Song Sparrows sang for their pleasure and ours. Least and Willow Flycatchers dueled for our attention; Blue-winged and Chestnut-sided Warblers vied for our countenance.

*One by one* the common birds of New Jersey's fields and woodlands offered themselves to our growing list: Downy Woodpecker . . . Northern Flicker . . . Eastern Wood-Pewee . . . Eastern Phoebe . . . Blue Jay . . . Amerizan Crow . . . Black-capped Chickadee . . . Tufted Titmouse . . . White-breasted Nuthatch . . .

With them came the uncommon birds, the must-gets, the ones that could be missed. Solitary Vireo (seen by less than half the teams on the average), Golden-winged Warbler (ah, saves us the trouble of digging one out on Clinton Road later on), and . . . Alder Flycatcher, tallied by less than ten percent of all teams as a rule.

All the common and all the uncommon birds. All present and accounted for. It was a glorious dawn.

"Time," I called, leading the charge for the car.

"About sixty-five," Linda announced, "with lots of holes to fill."

"No problem," Don assured.

Stokes State Forest had been part of Don's assignment; the location of a half-dozen critical species placed squarely in his hands. But anyone who has ever done a Big Day knows that "no problems" have ways of becoming *big* problems over the course of a day. Even the surest birds can fall through the cracks, making big, unfillable holes in Big Day lists.

So, just to be safe, Stokes State Forest had been double-teamed. Rick "Linnaeus," who probably knows Stokes as well as God does, had worked it over, too.

I glanced in the rearview mirror, catching Rick's eye. But Rick was on Don's side.

"No problem," he assured and . . .

By golly, there was *no problem*. Not with *this* team. Not on this glorious morning. Turkeys gobbled their encouragement from opposing hillsides and Pileated Woodpeckers knocked on wood for our behalf. Wood Ducks flushed with pride to be accounted among the birds on our growing list and a grouse thumped out a measured tattoo synchronized to the beat of our drum.

There were Brown Creepers at every crossroad, Cerulean Warblers at every full stop. Hermit Thrushes sang from roadside perches, and a maddeningly intermittent Acadian Flycatcher belted out a greeting. All were birds that might have been missed—had been missed by our team before. It was a matter of getting them here or possibly go wanting.

No time for backtracking on a Big Day.

"Eighty-five," Linda announced as the car and its occupants hit Route 23, the northernmost point on our route, and turned east.

The clock on the dash read 6:30 A.M.—right on schedule.

The silver Saab leaned into the corners and breezed through the straightaways. Forested ridges receded in the rearview mirror and farmland engulfed the windshield. Dogs on white-washed porches smiled their doggy smiles as we passed. Cows, solemn as judges, flagged us by with wisking tails.

But Sussex County's pastoral charm was undermined by anxiety. This was uncharted ground for the Guerrillas, virgin territory, beyond our collective ken. No World Series Team had ever tried to tie this out-of-the-way corner of the state into a Big Day route.

"Too far," the analysts said. "*Impossible*," the ghost of Charles Urner hissed in our ears.

The man on the spot was Don, the rookie. It was Don who had scouted the area in the week leading up to the event. It was Don who had convinced the team to scrap our plans at the last minute and go with his modified route.

The potentials, as Don described them, were tremendous—but so were the risks.

What if it took longer to dig out Don's special prizes than anticipated?

What if we got lost in the rural maze?

It would cost time.

It would cost birds.

It would mean that we'd get creamed at the finish line. Our man Freiday was on the spot, all right.

Don leaned forward, almost joining Pete and me in the front, eyes fixed on the highway. "Turn here," he commanded, a feat that would have been impossible in a car of lesser engineering. When the world was more or less level again, and it was reestablished that Linda was indeed my wife (and not Rick's), Don directed us to stop in front of what even the most generous eyes would regard as a dispirited clump of bushes.

"I really think this spot is worth a couple of minutes," Don said, addressing four teammates whose expression suggested that we were being asked to buy a certain infamous bridge.

"*I wouldn't even sell this to a developer*," I thought darkly.

Peter B. was a shade more blunt. "What's here?" he wanted to know.

What was *here* was just about the whole world and everything in it—Black-billed Cuckoo, Eastern Kingbird, Swainson's Thrush, Brown Thrasher, Northern Parula, Tennessee, Yellow, Chestnut-sided, Magnolia, Cape May, Bay-breasted, Blackpoll, and Wilson's Warblers. The migratory mother lode.

"How did you find that place?" a newly converted Pete Bacinski asked five minutes later.

"Well," Don explained, "I drove by it several times while scouting, and suddenly it hit me that every time I went by, the place was filled with singing birds. Stop . . . *here!*" he commanded. "Kingfisher and Green-backed Heron should be on that pond."

And they were, too.

Several miles and unsigned roads later, we drew up across from a newly disked field.

"Keep your fingers crossed," Don tutored. "This is our best first shot at Vesper Sparrow *and* where I had American Pipits. It took half an hour for the pipits to show up," he cautioned.

We didn't have half an hour to waste on one bird or two, not even prizes like Vesper Sparrow and pipit. But it didn't take half an hour. It didn't take half a minute and it didn't stop with Vesper Sparrow and American Pipit, either. This comely little corner of the planet produced Savannah Sparrow and Eastern Meadowlark, too. (Grasshopper Sparrows and Bobolinks were technically around the corner.)

"Mister Freiday," Peter B. intoned, "I've got to hand it to you. That was a masterful performance back there."

"One hundred and nine," said Linda.

Seven-thirty, said the bank clock in Vernon, New Jersey.

Roll, team, roll.

Now it was Pete's turn: Peter B. "Lord of the Highlands," batting cleanup on our woodland roster. The Jersey Highlands was our backup site for woodland species, a place that boasts many of the northern breeding birds that Charles Urner used to catch in migration. Peter B., as coordinator of the Highlands Breeding Bird Survey, is on a first-name basis with every nesting bird in the place.

Carefully, Linda read out the names of the birds unaccounted for. Pete listened and nodded.

"Pull up at the first pine grove on 517," he ordered. "There are Red-breasted Nuthatch in the trees on the right, and," he added, savoring the disclosure, "this is where I had a flock of White-winged Crossbills yesterday."

Finding White-winged Crossbill on a New Jersey Big Day is the birding equivalent of going into your attic and finding a Picasso. But Pete, who is almost never mistaken when it comes to avian matters, was wrong on two counts. The Red-breasted Nuthatches were not on the right side of the road. They'd shifted to the left. As for the attic, well, the things had gotten moved around there, too. The flock of crossbills that swept down upon us were not Pete's White-wingeds but a flock of *Red* Crossbills. Somebody had switched the Picasso with a Van Gogh.

"Well, that was pretty amazing," said Rick, after we'd climbed back in the car.

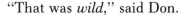

"That was *wild*," said Don.

"Red or white—still counts as one," said Linda.

Peter B., smarting under the double-cross done to his honor, studied the items left on our shopping list and refrained from comment.

"Stop at the next grove," he ordered. "Yellow-rumped Warbler was singing there early in the week. Listen for Red-shouldered Hawk, nesting somewhere on the left."

The beam swept across the parking lot, illuminating our team for a minute, then passing on in search of others. It found some huddled in isolation and others joined in conversation with teams that had already ceased to be rivals.

"Clinton Road sure didn't do us any favors," I said aloud, giving voice to my thoughts.

"Clinton was somewhat underwhelming," Pete agreed.

"Do you suppose anyone got Winter Wren?" I asked.

"That little creep," Pete muttered, falling silent, and I knew he was brooding about our biggest miss of the day. Not the wren but . . .

"Black-throated Blue was the worst," he said, shaking his head at the treachery of birds and the injustice of it all. "B.T. Blue was the *pits*."

Yes, we'd struck out on that one. Big time. If Charles Urner's spirit had been watching our efforts from the celestial stands, he would have climbed onto the field and thrashed us.

"Hell, it wasn't your fault," I soothed. "You had him pegged. We just got there too late and the bird had probably been pished out by a dozen teams already. It wasn't your fault that the little creep wouldn't sing."

"Oh, I know it," Pete admitted unhappily, and I hoped that if someone else won this thing that it would be at least by a two-bird margin.

"Besides," I continued, "Clinton Road wasn't a total loss. It gave us Black-throated Green and the Cooper's Hawk and Broad-winged."

Pete sighed, his self-recriminations assuaged but not purged. The misses are the ones you remember, and B.T. Blue was a miss, pure and simple. When the Guerrillas left the Highlands, there was a cloud hanging over us even a Saab 9000 couldn't outrace.

I have heard it said that history is moved by the hands of great men, that in times of need a hero will rise to rally the oppressed, filling hearts and minds with hope and courage. So it is with Big Day teams.

Clinton Road had shattered our confidence, sabotaged our enthusiasm. The "Big Mo" was gone. Suddenly, all of us realized that we were tired. Suddenly, it was too cramped in the back, and too hot in the front, and there wasn't enough roast beef to go around so someone was going to have to have turkey.

And I had to go to the bathroom real bad.

And Route 517 doesn't have any shoulders that you can pull off on.

Then Don dropped a well-mustarded bun that made a brief stop on Linda's lap on its way to the floor. Then Linda remembered that Don was supposed to be sitting in the middle, anyway.

Yes, if ever a team needed a hero, it was ours.

"If we're going to find a Black Vulture, this is where I've been seeing them," Rick ventured, leaning forward, drawing our attention to the cliffs ahead.

The ruse worked. All eyes focused on the sky, searching the clouds for aberrations or flaws.

"I've got two birds," I announced, pinning the lowest level of identification to two minute specks. "At eleven o'clock, right in the top left corner of that largest cloud."

"Igotem," said Pete.

"Lookin' good," said Don as the distance narrowed and the specks became dots, and the dots grew wings, and the wings turned white at the tips.

"Yeah!" Linda "10x" shouted. "Way to go, Rick!"

Two minutes later, too short a time for excitement levels to have fallen, Peter B. pulled a passing Red-shouldered Hawk out of thin air, pulled it right out of the lost column and into our hands. Congratulations were still being expressed when Linda fairly leaped through the sunroof, screaming, "NIGHTHAWK."

The sudden application of brakes sent Dorito chips flying like shrapnel throughout the car's interior, and our front suspension never did feel the same after that drop off the embankment—not that it was a matter of great concern. We still had lots of Dorito chips.

On the seawall at Liberty State Park two fishermen slouched in their chairs and stared at the lines lying slack in the water. Their friendship probably went halfway back to the dedication of the statue, and their intimacy was so complete that with a raised eyebrow or a measured nod they could communicate more to each other than most people can convey with speech.

As they sat, a car that might have been pale blue beneath its coating of mud wheeled to a halt. Four doors opened, drawing five identically clad figures into the light. In less time than it takes to raise an eyebrow, five telescopes were sweeping New York Harbor, each wielded by a silent observer.

"Caspian Tern," shouted one, giving directions.

"Got a Spotty on the breakwater," shouted another.

"Brant in front of Port Liberty," directed a third.

"Great Corm on the barge—fifth bird from the left," shouted a forth.

"All right? Everybody got 'em?" a voice demanded. "Let's get out of here."

Tripods clanked and car doors thunked and the car and its occupants prepared to disappear.

The two fishermen turned, each studying the face of the other. One raised an eyebrow and after a little more consideration, raised the other, too.

"What kind of shit comin' down here?" his companion was heard to say.

We were close enough to hear the sound of voices coming from the Visitor Center door, close enough to see movement within, almost close enough to recognize faces. I wished Peter B. would say something. Just to keep the conversation going. Just to keep my mind from turning to all the birds we'd missed. That's a funny thing about Big Days: all the birds you find, well, they're just expected. But everything you don't find becomes a "miss." These are the ones that haunt you.

"There's Kevin Karlson," he said, offering a reprieve. I could see them, the members of the Woolrich Team, heading, just as we were, for the Visitor Center.

"He doesn't look very happy," Pete ventured.

"They don't look any worse than we do, I'll bet."

"*T-that's* for sure," Peter B. agreed. "But Mr. Karlson didn't look very happy at Brigantine," he added, recalling a part of our day that I would have been happy to avoid.

"Nobody looked very happy at Brigantine," I said, hoping to close out the subject.

"That is for sure," Pete repeated absently, his voice and his thoughts suddenly somewhere else. If I had to make a guess, I'd wager that his mind had backtracked forty-five miles north and nine hours in time. To a place lying in the gilded shadow of Atlantic City, New Jersey's answer to Reno, Nevada. Officially, it is called Forsythe National Wildlife Refuge. Birders know it as Brigantine.

"Brigantine was a bust," Pete said suddenly.

We had hit Brig with 165 species in the bag, twenty minutes to spare, and visions of 215 species staring us right in the face.

And we were rolling. We were *hot*. Hotter than Atlantic City dice on a Saturday night. Hotter than the casino slots the day after Social Security checks clear the mail.

Hot! And Brig is the place to play some time against some very good odds. No place offers quicker access to more new birds than Brig. No place offers a greater surfeit of herons, egrets, waterfowl, raptors, shorebirds—all for the price of one spin around an eight-mile auto loop.

Ah, but Brigantine can be a risky place. There are *so* many birds in its estuaries and impoundment pools. The chances of finding just one more bird for the list are *so* good. So Big Day teams gamble, betting the time they have (and sometimes the time they don't have), hoping for one more bird. Very risky.

So you've got to have a system, see? You can't just go into Brigantine without a game plan, or the House will kill you. The strategy is to know precisely the birds you want and precisely where to find them. When you get them, get out. Quit winners while you can.

That's the way to play Brigantine.

We didn't. And we got killed.

The dikes were crowded with Big Day teams, slowing traffic. Water levels in the impoundment pools were high and the tide was low, spreading flocks. And, to top things off, the wind was blowing a gale, making spotting scopes useless. All these things worked against us, worsening the odds. There were birds found, but they took too much time. There were birds that couldn't be found. These took more time still.

You know how it is. Once you've invested so much time in finding a bird, you don't want to leave without it because without it, why, you've just thrown all that good time away, haven't you? All that time spent is just a waste.

So you risk a little more time and take your chances.

Then you gamble a little more, figuring you'll make it up later.

Until, suddenly, all the time you'd allocated for Brig is gone. The time allocated for the next stop is gone, too. And if you have any wits about you, you get out while you still have a shirt, get out before Brigantine eats you up. Brigantine . . .

". . . was the *pits*," Pete said, summing it up nicely.

"I can't believe we blew forty-five minutes looking for a White-rumped Sandpiper," I said, shaking my head. I said "we," but that was a dodge. That was a lie. "We" should have read "I" because *I* was driving, I was calling the shots at Brig, and I have done enough Big Days to know better than to get sucked into the time trap of searching for one, stupid, insignificant (dung-colored, mud-sucking) *bird* that we just might have gotten somewhere else. If we'd had the time.

*If I hadn't blown forty-five (God Damn!) extra minutes at Brig.*

Laughter rolled out the Visitor Center's door, spreading into the parking lot. The gravel turned to grass, and in the sudden silence, individual voices could be picked out of the din—cheerful, boisterous voices. The party sounded like it was in full swing.

Pete sighed, one of those long, deep, soulful, purging sighs that's as good as saying: *"Yes, that's how it is all right, and that's how it's going to stay."* Then he brightened, flashing a grin that shed exhaustion and misgivings the way friendship sheds doubt.

"Ah, but Mr. Dunne," he intoned grandly, "when we hit Cape May, we were back in the saddle again. We conquered," he exclaimed, raising his hand for a high-five salute.

Pete was right. There are four quarters in every football game, nine innings in baseball, and twenty-four hours in a Big Day. Fortunes rise and fortunes fall. Sometimes they rise again. When a route is good, it's good— good enough to absorb the little defeats and stay on track. Good enough to produce, whether luck goes along for the ride or not. And our route *was* good. Maybe it was even the best.

We were heading south, into the home stretch, and now it was our turn, Linda's and mine. South Jersey was our assignment, the location of its bounty of southern breeders our special charge—and South Jersey's birds are old confederates. Eleven years spent as director of the Cape May Bird Observatory instilled in me an intimacy with their habits and haunts that few other teams can match.

The Yellow-crowned Night Herons on the back side of the Stone-Harbor Heron Rookery winked at us as the Saab eased by. Why, we didn't even stop. The American Oystercatchers at Nummy Island screamed to be recognized, and a Red Knot stepped away from an amorphous flock of shorebirds as we drew up, raising its wing in a salute.

The last Purple Sandpipers in New Jersey waited patiently on the concrete ship, Lake Lily's perennial coot reclined in his favorite spot, and at Higbee Beach a sympathetic chat chortled a greeting, falling silent as another team approached.

And . . . there was luck, too. A high-balling Merlin picked off by Our Man Freiday as we were gassing up on the Garden State Parkway. A female Bufflehead sitting in a tidal creek along Stone Harbor Boulevard that didn't escape Linda's 10x eyes.

With Cape May Point behind us, Linda did a count. It didn't seem possible, so she did it again.

One hundred and ninety-five species!

Pete did some fast calculations, based on what was missing from our list and what was possible.

"The best we can do is 212," he said. "The worst we can," he continued, trying to keep the satisfaction out of his voice (and failing), "is 206."

"Is the record," I said, trying to keep the satisfaction out of my voice (and failing just as badly).

"Awlll right," Linda chanted, not trying to keep the excitement out of her voice at all. (Linda's pretty competitive.)

"I say we kick the record right in the pants," Pete challenged. "Two-ten or bust."

The sound of our high-five salute reached the Visitor Center, turning heads, conveying a clear message to discerning minds. Zeiss was pretty happy. Zeiss must be up there this year.

But how high? And how high was *up*? What was it going to take, to *take* the Urner-Stone Cup from Bausch and Lomb . . . to ward off a hungry Woolrich squad . . . to foil Canadian dreams of conquest? The answer lay beyond that door.

*Jeezus*, I thought, *if we could get 210 out of a jury-rigged route and after all the mistakes we made, what does that say about the fortunes of other teams?*

Another burst of laughter flowed from the doorway, followed by a wave of exclamations and a rush of congratulations. Somebody must have scored pretty high. How high? What's it going to take? Will 210 be good enough?

Now it was a race to the finish, a race against time. Two hours of daylight left. Thirteen species to claim before darkness pulled them out of reach. Five additional nocturnal species that might be pried from the night.

North on 47, up along the Delaware Bayshore. Out of the Gingerbread Belt and on toward Cumberland County, to swamps and marshes and forests that stand untouched by time. To:

The Blue Grosbeak in a field with no name. The Orchard Oriole on a road that leads to nowhere. To the . . .

Shsssssh. Listen! "Did everybody hear the . . ."

"*Bobwhite . . . Bobwhite . . .*"

"Yeah!"

"AwlllRIGHT!"

"HOT-damn."

"Whew!"

"OK. Let's get out of here."

Over to the bay side. Down roads deep in ruts and lost to memory. Searching for:

A Kentucky Warbler that would not sing.

A Red-breasted Merganser that would not show.

Then . . .

"OK. Let's do it." Back across the peninsula, chasing hope, chasing a gamble that might not pay. Might not be worth the risk. Might cost too much time. Too much time . . . *too much ti-ime* . . . shades of Brigantine . . . folks, we-got-to-get-*Out-of-herrrre* . . .

"*THERE!* RED-HEADED WOODPECKER FLYING TOWARD THAT TREE. LANDED! GOT IT?"

"Gotit."

"GOT IT!"

"Got It."

"GOTIT!"

"LET'S GET *OUT* OF HERE!"

Rounding the Dennisville turn. Into the back stretch. Out of the pack. Goin' for broke; goin' for three, here, folks. Three out of three; win, place, and show. "*Come on Jake's Landing.*"

And it's . . .

Pine Warbler by an ear.

Yellow-throated Warbler right under our noses.

And Northern Harrier . . . "*In front!*"

"OKletsgetouto'here."

Faster than tired minds can think. Faster than reflex. Faster than anything but the night bearing down upon us we fled west, racing to catch the last birds of May from the failing day.

Some, with luck, were found. Some, by fate, were not. By the time the Whip-poor-wills fell silent, by the time the lesser stars blazed, we had run out of options, run out of energy, and run out of time.

The Visitor Center was packed with teams and their sponsors. The excess spilled into the night, overflowing the wooden porch, teams boasting to other teams about their exploits. Teams recounting their defeats for catharsis and the pleasure of all listeners. An hour ago, they had been rivals. Now they were World Series of Birding veterans.

Our feet fell on the wooden ramp, making the platform shake, turning heads and bringing up hands in greeting and an onslaught of questions.

"How'd you do?"

"What'd you get?"

"Did you hear what Bausch and Lomb got?"

"We did good," Peter B. said simply, honestly—reluctant to surrender the number that we had worked so hard to get, not ready, yet, to commit ourselves to our fate.

On hesitant feet, I reached the Visitor Center door and paused, skimming the room with my eyes. But there were too many people, too much animation for tired eyes to cull faces from the pack. I looked for Bruce Cavey, our sponsor from Zeiss Optical, Inc., but couldn't find him. I tried to see the posted totals but there were too many onlookers blocking the view of the board.

The rest of the team closed in from behind, and from several points within the room, greetings were shouted.

"Well, Mr. Dunne," Peter B. encouraged.

I looked for and found the eyes of Rick and Don and Linda. Then, on feet that had suddenly lost all reservation, we stepped through the door, across the finish line, and into a room full of friends.

# 10 • ATTU, ALASKA:

## Birding the Fringe

### EVERYDAY PEOPLE

*H*E WAS TALL, AND ORDINARY, AND ONE AHEAD OF me in the checkout line. In his hands were several packages of golf balls. I was carrying socks. Wool socks.

"We're flying to the islands, tonight," he said, turning, smiling. "St. Croix," he added, assuming that I'd want to know.

"That's terrific," I replied.

"A little R & R," he waxed. "A little golf; a little sun. Just me and the wife. Know what I mean?"

I said yes without remorse, but then, I've lied before.

"Going hiking," he said, studying my purchase. It wasn't a question.

"Yep," I said, deferring to his keen powers of observation.

"Vacation?" he wanted to know.

"Close enough," I replied.

"Maine," he suggested.

"Attu."

"Ahhhhh," he said, nodding.

I waited, wondering how long it would take before curiosity bored a hole through his veneer.

"Where's that?" he asked, breaking down in something under five seconds.

"The Aleutians," I replied, studying his face, seeing the name pass wide. "Islands," I added.

"Oh," he said. "Well, we're going to St. Croix."

"That's terrific," I said.

## "FANTASY ISLAND OF THE NORTH"

"What did he say?" I shouted to David, over the sound of the props and across a distance of about two feet. In real life, David Narins jockeys DC-10s for American Airlines. But on this flight, he was just a passenger like the other birders crammed aboard our twin-engine charter.

"The pilot said, 'It looks grim,' " David relayed.

*No shit*, I thought, peering down at the unbroken blanket of clouds. Somewhere down there was an island and a runway (not to mention an ocean). But chances were, unless we could find a break in the clouds and find it fast, this was as close as we were going to get to our destination. Our fuel was getting low, and Adak, the closest friendly landing strip with radar, was 350 miles back.

"He seems like a pretty competent guy," David continued (but I noticed that his eyes never left the plane's instruments, or the aircraft radar). The green blob, our destination, was plainly visible on the screen. Unfortunately, the plane's radar was not sensitive enough to depict things like mountaintops and five-hundred-foot Loran towers—the kind of obstructions that can do bad things to aircraft operated by careless pilots.

"He's not the sort to take any unnecessary risks," David assured—which was good news, since neither our pilot nor his copilot had ever seen our destination before, much less landed there.

"Remember," David said, turning, offering me the wisdom of his many hours of flight time, "there are old pilots and there are bold pilots, but there are no old, bold pilots." It was at this wonderfully sublime moment that young Captain Brash made his decision and dropped the nose of our plane into the clouds. The world disappeared.

The green smudge on the plane's radar screen, which, incidentally, also appears green on the world atlas—a *very* significant point—is called Attu. It is one of a chain of islands stretching across the North Pacific from the Alaska peninsula clear to Kamchatka—the Aleutian Islands. Attu is about forty miles long, eighteen miles wide, with a lot of up and down in between. For much of the year, it is miserable and cold. In winter, it is miserable and colder. At any time of year, a sunny day is a matter of conversation even a week later, in part because sunny days are rare, in part because there is little else to discuss on Attu except for the weather.

Unlike St. Croix (and many other islands on the planet), Attu has no regular civilian air service. There is good reason for this. There are no motels on Attu. There are no bathing beaches. No tennis courts. No casinos. No heated pools. No bars with drinks that have pineapples and umbrellas sticking out of them. There are, in short, no services.

There is only tundra. In winter, snow and . . . since 1943, there is peace. Over much of the island, there is also a great deal of rusting military hardware—Marston matt, Quonset huts, gutted vehicles, abandoned equipment, unexploded ordnance—mute testimonies to the wastefulness of war. A Japanese monument, paying tribute to the soldiers who died in the only World War II land battle fought on U.S. soil, attests to the tragedy of war.

The island's human population consists of a small group of U.S. Coast Guard personnel who man (literally) a Loran Navigation Station. A sign welcoming those to "Attu International Airport" painfully allows that the garrison consists of 28 men and 0 women. Most conscripts can tell you to the day how long until their tour of duty ends.

Despite the lack of amenities, the island is not without visitors. During the summer, the U.S. Fish and Wildlife Service sends out the occasional biologist to take nature's pulse. Now and again an adventurous yachtsman is driven into one of the island's bays to escape the region's not infrequent storms. At times Japanese visitors come to pay tribute to relatives and ancestors who died on Attu, defending the honor of the emperor.

But the peak of Attu's tourist season occurs in May and June. Every spring since 1977 the hardest of America's hard-core birders travel to Attu for a three-week treasure hunt. Why here? Because Attu enjoys a very singular distinction. Attu is the westernmost island in the Aleutians—only three hundred miles from the Soviet Kormandorskiye Ostrova (Commander Islands), seven hundred miles from the Soviet mainland (less than half the distance to Anchorage, Alaska). It is an island that reaches so far across the Pacific that they had to bend the International Dateline just to keep Sunday from happening on Attu before it could happen in the rest of the United States. Attu, though politically and geologically linked to North America, is so far west that it is really *east*.

For North American birders, the strategic implications of this are enormous. What this means is that any bird that lands on the Island of Attu lands on North American soil—lands "in bounds" in the eyes of the American Birding Association refs. So, any bird found on Attu, no matter how Asian its origin, *counts* on the North American Life List of any birder who can get out there and see it.

The murk outside the plane got murkier; the green smudge on the radar screen larger. After a long, long time, the gray murk beneath the wings turned slimy and green . . . then the green became flecked with whitecaps. A dark mass loomed ahead of the plane, intruding between the ocean below and the overcast above—a dark mass with patches of snow and most of a five-hundred-foot Loran tower poking up into the clouds. Captain Brash circled once and put her down on the first attempt.

It was raining when we arrived. But then, there is nothing unusual about that on Attu.

"*The first thing you need to know,*" the opening line of Attour's promotional information sheet announces, "*is that our accommodations are Ugly with a capital U. You'll think, 'Am I really supposed to live here?' *" And this is true as far as it goes. What the literature fails to disclose is that this is what you'll think providing the shock doesn't kill you.

Our group, burdened by baggage and gear, more or less walked through the opened door of Lower Base and out of the rain. For most of Attour's history, the principal difference between outside and inside is that outside most of the water is in the air; inside, most of the water lies on the floor.

"It stays a lot drier in here since we ripped up the floor tiles," Al Driscoll noted, "and hung the drop cloth from the ceiling." Al, a retired Air Force lieutenant colonel, is charged with the not inconsiderable task of repairing anything that needs repairing on Attu. This makes perfect sense, since Al is also the wizard who designed and built just about every item of comfort at Lower Base (except the building itself). The U.S. Coast Guard gets credit for this.

And they abandoned it.

*"People who birded Attu before we began improving the facilities even call them luxurious."* It would take a generous heart to accuse the Lower Base of luxury, although it doesn't lack for charm. With its concrete walls, latticework of rusting pipes, bare light bulbs, and stalactites hanging from the ceiling, it looks like the stage set for the oldest floating crap game in New York City, like Cannery Row when Mack and the boys held forth at the Palace Flop House.

"*Jeezus*," one of the new arrivals whispered.

"Excuse me," said a young man carrying a mop.

"Must be a leak someplace," one room's occupants observed dryly.

*"We live dormitory style, in 13 rooms quartering 2 to 16 people (most are 4)."*

Our room, shared with a couple from Minnesota, was named The Rat Hole. Why The Rat Hole? According to sources, once, when the drain clogged, a dead rat was found to be the impediment. Next door was The Swamp, an abode notorious for its problems with percolation.

There was one morning during our two-week stay when I failed to test the substrate before setting foot to floor and discovered that during the night the tide had risen. When we complained to the neighbors that their swamp was encroaching on our rat hole, they apologized and explained that during the night their swamp had metamorphosed into a lake.

"The history of Attu," Larry Balch, the director of Attour, once observed, "is the history of moving water."

"Must be a leak someplace," a passerby noted.

"I'll check upstream and see what the problem is," one of The Swamp's occupants promised.

*"Each room has clean and easily controlled gas heat."*

"Pig heaters?"

"Pig heaters," Al confirmed. "I saw them advertised in an agricultural mail order catalog."

*"Every room also has bunk beds, storage shelves, and electric lighting."* All wrapped in bomb-proof, ventilation-free concrete. The single mold- and leachate-encrusted window was fused shut, but its light did supplement the light bulb dangling from the ceiling. The roof, needless to say, leaked.

"If we leave the door open during the day," our roommate encouraged, "it helps evaporation."

"These conditions," observed one of our fleet of birding physicians, "make the spread of infection inevitable."

"It used to be tough in the old days," Jerry Rosenband, one of Attour's leaders, remarked.

*"Three outhouses provide the toilet facilities for the lower building."* Three outhouses, one with a Plexiglas porthole and a lovely view of Casco Cove, are supplied (daily) with (dry) toilet paper stashed in watertight cans. All are braced to withstand natural calamity; this was done after one outhouse was blown one hundred yards from its base by a winter storm.

Not mentioned in the literature is the comfort station "designed and constructed by (Dr.) Gerald Maisel for the comfort of his fellow male Attuvians." As urinals go, it is convenient but . . .

"Jeezus, this place stinks like hell," one patron couldn't help noticing.

"What do you expect from a pissoir built by a doctor instead of a roofer?" Sandy Komito, roofing contractor, asked. "A roofer would have run a drainpipe through the trench."

"The history of Attu," said Larry, "is the history of moving water."

Larry Balch is an energetic birder from Highland Park, Illinois, whose years have failed to suppress a boyish charm. Larry is also a lister. A serious, certified, hard-core, card-carrying lister who collects new birds with the enthusiasm that ten-year-olds lavish on baseball cards. It was this penchant for avian aggrandizement that brought Larry and two companions to Attu in the spring of 1977—this, and certain tantalizing discoveries made by birders who visited Attu the previous year. Discoveries like: Oriental Greenfinch, Rustic Bunting, and Eye-browed Thrush.

"*Good Birds!*" as they are known in the old birding vernacular. *Asian* birds. Birds of such lofty allure that the mere rumor of one anyplace in North America would cause lines to form in front of the nonticketed passenger counters of every major airport.

As Larry tells it, he and his companions stepped off their plane and walked one hundred yards smack into a male Brambling, a Eurasian finch, feeding on the runway. For Larry Balch, it registered number 638 on his North American Life List. In the ensuing two weeks, Larry and company accrued such heart-stopping rarities as Olive Tree-Pipit, Gray-Spotted Flycatchers, and Common Reed-Bunting—birds that might take a lifetime to encounter on the North American mainland. Birds that any dedicated lister would pay any amount and suffer any privation to see.

However, the birds that cemented the bond between Larry and Attu were *not* Asian overshoots but two birds that proved to be resident. One rare, clear day, two large birds of prey appeared overhead. They were eagles, that was apparent enough. But there was something very special about these eagles. They weren't Golden Eagles, that was obvious. Their tails were white, like those of Bald Eagles. But they weren't Bald Eagles either.

The birds proved to be White-tailed Eagles, a mated pair, and as the birders watched, the birds grasped talons and tumbled, end over end, to within fifty feet of their astonished heads. Two years later, twelve birders paid $2,950 each for the privilege of seeing North America's only White-tailed Eagles and the chance to pack their North American lists with Asian booty. Attour was born.

If the history of Attu is the history of moving water, the mission of Attour is that of accommodating people. It is no small feat to transport upward of eighty individuals to a cold, wet, inhospitable, and functionally uninhabited island and offer them a measure of comfort. The Coast Guard maintains the runway, and, to a degree, the roads hurriedly laid down half a century earlier by the Army Corps of Engineers. Otherwise, it has adopted the prudent position of innocent bystander with regard to island visitors.

Early Attour efforts to utilize old military structures to house the group more or less failed. Larry finally secured use of the old, abandoned Loran Station from the U.S. Fish and Wildlife Service, who had assumed jurisdiction once the Coast Guard abandoned it. Attu's climate is tough on things that rust, rot, warp, weather, or wear; so, needless to say, little in the derelict buildings inherited by Attour worked. Electrical wiring, plumbing, and heating fixtures all had to be installed anew. When it was discovered that the building housed pipes covered by asbestos, Larry had to become a licensed asbestos contractor to deal with the problem in a manner that satisfied federal officials.

Year by year, room by room, improvements and comforts came to Attu—washbasins, showers, hot water, three-speed bicycles (to replace the torturous and soundly cursed "red ones"), even a drying room. The toast of Attour is its cuisine. Housed in its own facility, orchestrated by Jennifer Jolis, a professional chef, Attour's meals are not just hot, not merely ample, they are downright epicurean. Attour's dining hall is the only establishment serving veal breast stuffed with hazelnuts this side of Petropavlovsk (and that side of Dutch Harbor). The enchiladas aren't half bad, either.

By the time Linda and I and our group arrived, Attour could offer visiting birders amenities that Attour veterans never even dreamed of, and tales of the "bad old days" are legion, bandied about at dinner and whenever the weather is so bad that even an Attuvian won't venture forth. Accounted among the Attuvian ranks there are birders who have returned to Attu five and six and eight . . . up to eleven times. They aren't conscripts. They aren't penitents. They are physicians, lawyers, businessmen, mail carriers, nurses, college professors—*birders*—all willing and eager to spend $4,200 each to live in a facility that were it a prison would precipitate a riot!

All for the privilege of birding North America's fringe. All for the chance of adding one more precious species to their North American Life Lists. And maybe it all sounds too outlandish to be true. Well, it is true. Not only that, it is wonderful. "The Fantasy Island of the North" is how one Attuvian describes it, "Summer Camp for Adults" in the words of another.

One thing I can tell you. There is no place in the world where birding is so much the focus of lives. There is no group of individuals who work harder and more diligently to find the birds they want. And you would have to go a long way to find a finer group of people. In fact, you would have to go back the way you came (because when you reach Attu, you've reached the end of the earth).

These are North America's most serious birders, driven to the literal and figurative fringe by their passion for birding. They are the creme de la creme. They are the finest. They are the elite.

The Few.

The Proud.

The Attuvians.


## THE DAY ROOM

When breakfast was over, all the "official trips" were under way and the last straggling birders had departed, activity in the day room fell to almost nothing. Those who had elected to stay settled into the familiar pattern of waiting. Waiting for the rain to taper off. Waiting for some reports to trickle in. Waiting for a few birds to be found. Waiting to make up their minds about leaving.

Waiting.

Eli Elder, eleven-time Attu veteran, her North American Life List total poised at 735, was settled into her chair by the fuel-oil stove, reading a mystery.

Sandy Komito, roofing contractor (T = 778), had commandeered part of a couch and was trading insults with a slipper-shod Louis Banker (T = 744), who had taken up position near the radio.

Alone at the card table, Dan Guthrie (T = ???), biology professor, was playing solitaire with the passion of a sphinx, while James (aka: Casper the-friendly-ghost) Huntington, postman (T = 742), stalked the room, trying to decide whether to venture out into Attu's sub-Arctic gruel or hold himself in reserve. Sam Madison, retired attorney (T = 696), was making snoring sounds at the ceiling, and Jack Wright, the CIA psychologist (T = 611), was sitting on the couch, staring at the opposing wall, sometimes the floor, but mostly the wall.

Stan Heath, decked out in his diagnostic red suspenders, was pawing through the reading material—an eclectic assortment that included *Aviation Week & Space Technology, The Atlantic, Natural History, Science, Time, The Living Bird Quarterly*, several dog-eared copies of *Crossword Puzzles Only*, and five copies of *Conan the Barbarian*.

"So what do you think, Sandy," Stan drawled. "What sort of things they gonna find for us out there today?"

Sandy Komito, who can probably boast at least a few bunco artists in his lineage, closed his eyes and assumed the pose of an entranced swami.

"Ahhhh," he intoned, giving expression to his vision. "Yessss," he promised. "I see . . . I see . . . a *bird!*" he exclaimed, his face contorted by chicaned exaltation. "Ex-excuse, please," he said, effusively apologetic, his hands imploring patience. "Your language is strange to me. But do you maybe have bird with name . . . La-Lapland Longspur?"

The effort got the chuckle it deserved. On Attu, Lapland Longspurs are only slightly less regular than tombstones in Arlington. A birder would have to be deaf, blind, drunk, dead, and three days buried to be on Attu and not find a Lapland Longspur in fifteen seconds or less.

"One minute to the check," Louis announced, flip-flopping his way across the room to rinse his Circle K go cup.

"Uhhh, that's ok, Banker," Sandy admonished. "We c'n awl tell tyme heeah," he assured, falling back into his normal speech, a voice that cuts corners on consonants and burns rubber on the vowels, the way people who speak New Jersey do.

Louis turned upon his traditional Day Room adversary with staged dignity. "Well, Sandy," he tutored, "some of us are more attentive to these things than others. And," he added, dredging deeply into the old debate coach's bag of tricks, "anyone who wears pants like that would do well *not* to criticize anyone about *anything*."

"Wh'a, wh'a," Sandy responded with a grin, "wha's wrong with these pants?" he pleaded, spreading his hands, inviting appraisal of a pair of polyester trousers so tasteless that they wouldn't have been allowed on a golf course.

*"Base, this is Jerry,"* the radio suddenly announced.

Heads popped up around the room and filled the open doorways. Books and magazines dropped into assorted laps. The ten of hearts, in Dan's hand, stopped halfway to the table, waiting.

Louis strode across the room, reaching for the mike.

"This is Lower Base. Go ahead, Jerry," he invited.

*"Louis, our group is at Kingfisher Creek. We have nothing to report yet."*

"Roger," Louis sighed, "Jerry at Kingfisher Creek with a negative report."

The ten of hearts went down, with an audible flip. Dan drew another card from the deck. Two of diamonds.

*"Base, this is Terry [Savaloja]."*

"Go ahead, Terry," Louis encouraged.

*"We are at Murder Point. Visibility is good. So far we have seen Black-legged Kittiwake, Short-tailed Shearwater, and distant, repeat distant Laysan Albatross."*

"Roger, Terry. I copy you on Black-legged Kittiwake, Short-tailed Shearwater, and distant Laysan Albatross."

*Flip.* Dan drew again. This time it was the one-eyed jack.

*"Base,"* a nasal New England accent directed, *"this is Nob'l [Proctor] behin' Big Lake. Nothing to rep'rt."*

"Roger, Noble," Louis drawled, his Missouri-softened syllables smoothing the edges on the Down East diction, "you are behind Big Lake and have nothing to report."

*Flip.* Up comes the king of spades.

*"Ahh, BASE, this is PETE [Isleib], at the north end of the runway. NOTHING to report."*

"Roger, Pete," Louis soothed, "you are at the north end of the runway with a negative report."

Louis replaced the speaker and finished his notations in the log. Slowly, the room's occupants returned to whatever it was they'd been doing before the radio turned their heads. To books or cards, to conversation or dreams. But their minds lingered on the ten o'clock report—weighing the implications, holding the portents up to the light of their experience. These are Attu veterans.

"No birds found," they were thinking. Well, it was early, yet. Still early. Too early to tell anything for certain. The trips were just getting under way, just getting into position. All it takes is one bird, after all. One new bird to make the day—make the whole trip! The 10:30 check would be critical. Ten-thirty would be the real test of it. That's what the Attu veterans were thinking.

"Where's Pete headed?" Casper demanded.

"He's on his way to Alexai Point," Dan said, putting the king of spades in his proper place.

"Oh, God," Casper moaned, expressing the near universal sentiment. "Not Alexai!"

Pete Isleib is an Alaskan commercial fisherman who looks like Socrates decked out in Helly Hansen rain gear. Endowed with the endurance of a billy goat, Pete has earned a reputation for finding good birds at distances that orbit the rim of mortal endurance.

"Oh, I wouldn't worry, James," Sandy counseled. "Noble Proctor's the one to watch out for. Noble can *smell* a North American record."

"That's what I *am* afraid of," Casper explained. "Noble will find something good all the way out on Krasni Point and then Pete will turn up something all the way out on the other end of the island. Oh, God," he moaned again, retreating to the safety of his bunk.

"I can't understand an attitude like that," Sandy lied. "Imagine somebody willing to pay all this money to come out here and then not want to die of exhaustion," he said, leaning back, succumbing to exhaustion, or maybe ennui. A short time later, he left, wandering back to the rooms but staying within earshot of the radio.

With all parties accounted for, the room lapsed into silence—silent enough to hear the turning of Dan's cards; quiet enough to hear the hiss of static on the radio and the periodic intrusion of Japanese commercial fishermen.

But it was too early for silence. Conversations sprang up—discussions about this bird or that; conjured accounts of days that began with everything stacked against them and then turned into red-letter entries.

That day in '87 when all hell broke loose . . .

The day Jerry discovered the Red-breasted Flycatcher on Infarction Ridge . . .

The last day in 1985 with the 6:00 P.M. greenfinch . . .

Grim tales of assorted "death marches" out to Alexai Point.

Most of the people in the room could recall these episodes and others. These were veteran Attuvians. People who had traveled everywhere. People who had seen everything—every regularly occurring bird in North America. What people like Sandy and Louis and Eli and the other Attu regulars haven't seen probably hasn't touched down in North America, yet. But might at any second. Might be here *right now*! "The Big One" might come heralding over that radio at any second.

That is why they were here.

The clock on the wall ticked off the minutes. At 10:25, the room began to grow animate. Fingers began to drum. Pocketknives appeared; nails cleaned. Coffee cups that had been empty for half an hour suddenly needed filling. Every crackle of static, every Japanese fishing vessel reporting its catch, brought the room to sudden silence.

And as the minute hand closed in on the half-hour mark people outside the Day Room began to filter in, filling the perimeter. At 10:28 Louis moved closer to the radio and stood there with his eyes out the window and his hand on the mike.

*"Base. This is Nob'l."*

Once again heads snapped erect. Books and magazines dropped into laps. Pocketknives froze midsweep. James, decked out in full field gear, ricocheted off the doorjamb and into the room. Two Attuvians coming in from the drying room side, carrying their conversation with them, were shushed to silence.

"Go ahead, Noble," Louis encouraged.

*"We are at South Beach an' have n'thing to rep'rt."*

"Roger, Noble," Louis said, completing the litany, "you are at South Beach but have nothing to report."

Somewhere in the room a foot is shuffled, a chair creaked, a throat cleared. Dan pulled the six of hearts.

*Flip.*

The two of clubs.

*Flip.*

A string of diamonds.

*Flip . . . flip . . . flip . . .*

*"Hello, base, this is Jerry with a negative report."*

Then Terry followed suit.

Flip, went the four of spades.

Flip went the ten of hearts.

*"BASE. This is PETE. Do you read me?"*

"Go ahead Pete,"

*"Ahh, we have JUST reached the TRIANGLE . . . NOTHING to report. Have the other parties checked in yet?"*

"Roger, Pete. All reports are negative."

*"THANK YOU, base. PETE clear."*

"Base out."

Nothing. A bad sign. If there had been any kind of bird movement overnight, somebody should have run across something by now. Still . . . it only takes one. One bird could break the day wide open. The Big One. The $4,200 bird. The one that pays for the trip. All it takes is one. Maybe the next check . . .

Silence gains an upper hand. Silence is the norm now. Silence and people dozing in chairs. One voice addressing another commands everyone's attention. Dan shuffles his cards and draws a room full of stares—"The Aleutian Stare," a disorder first diagnosed during the army occupation of the Aleutians in 1942.

James renews his final preparation to leave, thinks better of it, heads for the stove and backs up against it, storing up some precious BTUs before venturing into the cold.

Sandy Komito reenters the room, looks out the window, grimaces, stares with hands in his pockets, walks out.

Eli places her book face down on the table, then, finding no greater distraction, picks it up again.

James, overcome by second thoughts, reconnoiters back to his room.

*Silence.* And in the silence, the static on the radio becomes more pronounced. The voices of Japanese commercial fishermen break into the room. Excited chatter. Idle banter. Issues and items beyond the ken. This is the way the time goes.

The Attuvian hopefuls come wandering into the room earlier this time. By 10:50, heads start poking in the doors, checking the wall clock, counting down the minutes. At 10:55 Casper drifts back into the room and wanders over to the window, usurping Sandy Komito's position.

Shuffling his deck with the air of a mystic reader, Dan starts a new game just as the minute hand reaches to claim the hour and the radio crackles to life. James beats everyone to the radio by half a length. But it's:

Terry at Murder Point: "Negative."

*Flip.*

Noble at Krasni: "Negative."

*Flip.*

Jerry at Henderson: Other than "one Wood Sandpiper," the word is "Negative."

*Flip. Flip. Flip.*

Now only Pete is outstanding. Peter the Terrible. Peter who was heading out to Alexai. Peter who could find those good ones like nobody else. He'd make you pay for them. Make you suffer. But boy can he dig out those good ones.

"Come on, Pete," James whispers, staring out the window, across the bay, toward Alexai Point. Come on.

But Pete doesn't come on. Perhaps he's out of range. Maybe he's distracted. Maybe he's got a bird—is busy getting his group onto it. Pinning it down. Making sure the identification is airtight before calling it in. Damn, isn't it just like that Isleib to find something way the hell out and gone on a day like. . . .

"BASE, this is PETE; do you read me?"

"GoaheadPete," Casper pleads.

"We have . . ." but the transmission is broken up, jammed by another voice—speaking Japanese.

"PETE!" Casper shouts into the mike. "Pete! Somebody walked all over your last transmission. We did not read you. Repeat. We did not read you. Over."

But the interference continues. The Japanese fishermen have more powerful units and their transmission washes Pete out of the air.

"Base," a new voice intrudes, an English-speaking voice. "This is David Narins at Lower Henderson."

"Go ahead, Dave," James said.

"James I can relay for Pete. His last transmission was 'negative.' He is approaching Alexai Point. Over."

"Thank you, Dave," James says. "I read you with a negative for Pete. Out."

The voice of the Japanese fisherman continues, but the room remains silent. James replaces the receiver. Makes a half-step toward the door, then changes his mind and leans against the wall, staring out the window.

Dan Guthrie scoops the cards off the table, stacks them without shuffling, and pushes away from the table.

Jack Wright, the CIA psychiatrist, still sitting on the couch, stares at the wall, sometimes the floor, but usually the wall. Not that there is anything unusual about that.

## NOTES ON THE FLY

"Terry's waving his radio," Jerry shouted, stopping my retreat.

Sure enough, down where the road turned west along Gilbert Ridge, about a quarter-mile away, Terry was impersonating a metronome, frantically trying to catch our attention.

Struggling out of his pack, Jerry removed his walkie-talkie and turned it on.

"Go ahead, Terry," he encouraged.

"Go to Channel 17," Terry said, evasively, ending any immediate thoughts I might have had about following Linda, who was already lining out in the direction of the Common Rosefinch. Channel 17 is the "leader's ears only channel." The "I got a good bird but *itsa otna orfa ommonca olodgekna, etya*" channel.

Jerry obliged and listened closely to Terry's relayed account of . . ."a small flycatcher . . . feeding in willows . . . Upper Henderson . . . [someone] still with it. Out." And *gone*. Transmission over, Terry was off like a shot, peddling like hell, racing deep into the valley, the valley he'd just spent an hour slogging out of.

"Why don't you go for the rosefinch?" Jerry suggested. "I'll go investigate this flycatcher. If it turns out to be something really good, we'll call it in on the next half-hour check."

Then Jerry was off, standing on the peddles of his three-speed, making the muck on the roadbed fly, leaving me very much between a puddle and a wet spot. The rosefinch was a sure thing, a Code 5 bird (and they don't get any better than that). But the critter was also four miles away—four miles on Attu roads. If I went for the finch and the flycatcher turned out to be hot, I'd have to turn right around again. Four miles out, four miles back . . . and God only knew how many more miles into Henderson Valley to the mystery flycatcher. Henderson was a long, long valley, and the road, even by Attu standards, was bad, bad, bad.

And I'm not going to lie. I was tired. Leg-twitching tired. Frankly, I wasn't sure I was up for chasing either bird, much less both. The fact is, it had already been one hell of a day. One exhausting, madcap scramble for birds that had popped up all over the island, sending birders racing in all directions then back again. Feast or famine is the standard fare on Attu, and today fortune had rolled out a banquet.

Things had started leisurely enough (but then, on Attu, they usually do). Linda and I were soloing, mopping up some of those first generation "Attu specialties" that had eluded us in three days of birding. There was a Slaty-backed Gull and a Black-backed Wagtail staked out near Navy Town. A Yellow Wagtail was hanging out at the east end of the Coast Guard runway, and somewhere we hoped to run into a Common Sandpiper. All of these were good birds, Codes 3 and 4 on the 1 to 5 rarity scale. Birds that could be missed if you weren't careful.

We found the gull and the wagtails and chased a Common Sandpiper all around Casco Cove until we finally got the kind of look that doesn't make consciences squirm. Then the island began to hop. Things began to catch fire.

First, Bill Mueller found a Bluethroat (Code 4), precipitating a rush that rivaled the opening of the Oklahoma Territory. The campaign to corner the skulkiferous little chat involved forty birders, and its like has probably not been seen on Attu since the Japanese surrender. At the very height of the campaign, just as the troops were closing in on the bird's last-known position, [Gunga] Dan Gibson, Attu's ranger scout, radioed in a little flock of Brambling (Code 4), dividing the loyalty of the troops, sending half those present hotfooting it for the west end of the runway. Those who stayed at their posts (i.e., those who already *had* Brambling on their North American Life Lists) were in much better field position when a short time later an Eyebrowed Thrush (Code 4) was glimpsed out near the Pyramid. By the time the Black-tailed Godwit (Code 4, again) sailed over, heading toward the mouth of the Peaceful River, any pretense of coordination was a shambles. Attu had succumbed to mob rule, overrun by needy listers peddling from one bird to the next and back again.

By the time Gunga Dan unveiled the rosefinch, a top-of-the-line Code 5 species (right back where the Brambling had been, earlier), everyone was far, far away—out at the Pyramid, deep in Henderson Valley, or collapsed in chairs back at Lower Base. There were few on Attu who had not already bicycled twenty miles and more, and fewer still who weren't pretty bushed.

The good news about the rosefinch was that, for most Attuvians, it was, at least, on their way back to base. Oh, it was a grunt of a trip at high speed, all right. And it was a gamble (moving out of position while there were still troops in the field). But *certainly*, at five in the afternoon, nobody was going to have the poor social graces to find *another* good bird.

Or would they?

The rosefinch or the flycatcher? A Code 5 in the hand or the bird behind door number 3?

*I'll bet it's that son-of-a-bitch Mueller who found the bird*, I thought darkly, watching the little blue speck on a red bicycle that was my wife disappear over the hill, out of East Massacre Valley. It was Mueller who had found the Bluethroat and Mueller, I seemed to recall, who had headed up into Henderson. Mueller was hot today! Mueller was on a streak.

If it *was* Bill, why report just "a flycatcher?" Bill was a good birder. An eight-tour Attu veteran. If *he* was reluctant to pin a name on the bird, it could only mean one thing. It had to be something good, *real* good, something he wanted confirmation on before going public.

*Mueller*, I thought wearily, *I'll get you for this. I'll write an article in* Birding *and depict you as a Chickadee maven. I'll start a rumor that the Barnacle Goose on your Life List is a suspected escape.*

There really wasn't any choice in the matter. None at all. What kind of birder would turn his back on a really good bird—even the rumor of one? No birder who ever came to Attu, that I can assure you. (Besides, I could still try for the rosefinch on the way back to base after getting the flycatcher.)

The road into Upper Henderson, such as it was, turned to soup, then into a long, rutted puddle. But this was OK. This was fine. At least puddles have bottom. After a couple of days on Attu you learn to steer into the puddles, not avoid them. Hit them hard and fast and you'll be all right.

But then the road began to climb. The puddles returned to soup and the soup turned to gruel—a thick, viscous, bottomless gruel that sucked on tires, making thighs ache, calves throb, and breath come in gasps.

I tried the other side of the road, forgetting, momentarily, one of Gerry Maisel's Attuvian Axioms, etched on the walls of Lower Base for the edification of junior Attuvians: *The other side of the trail always looks smoother until you switch over.*

*Attu, Alaska*

It did. And it wasn't.

Moments later, I was brought to recall another of Gerry's gems: *If there is a rock in the road and you try to avoid it, you are sure to hit it.*

There was. And I did.

But the most ominous axiom of them all would not be tested until later—not that I doubted its veracity. This one has to do with Attu's wind: *When you go out in the morning,* Attu's sage confides, *the wind is always in your face. But when you return later, the wind will still be in your face.* Thus spake Gerry Maisel, Attuvian, who has been chasing birds into the wind all his birding life.

At the top of a long rise, a mile past the point where I first considered giving up, there was a pile of bicycles, hastily dismounted. A hundred yards farther on was a tight knot of birders studying field guides . . . and a small, gray bird sitting in a knee-high patch of willows. The bird was quite calm. The birders were ecstatic.

The story becomes fragmented here, because the story of a good bird is really many stories, woven together into a single thread, all leading to one place.

Sandy Komito was back at Lower Base when the call came in. He *ran* for his trusty three-speed and was a hundred yards down the road before he realized he'd left his binoculars behind.

Jim Kuethe was heading for home, tired and happy. He'd seen five Life Birds, had an incredible day, and "didn't want to be greedy." Sandy, en route to the bird, passed him the news.

Immunity from greed is one thing. But a Life Bird. Well, a Life Bird is after all, a Life Bird—to a true Attuvian, a life-and-death matter.

*Semper fidelis.*

Kayo Roy was with Pete Isleib, still looking for the Bluethroat, when Terry came on with a couple questions about flycatcher plumages for Pete. As Kayo tells it, Isleib was off like a missile. They reached their bicycles in something approaching a tie but "three minutes later, Pete was a mile ahead and pulling away."

Dan Guthrie was way up on the bluffs east of the west runway. He turned and saw a distant armada of bicycles speeding up the north-south runway. His first thought was of the radio sitting with his pack a mile and a half mile away. His second thought was probably unprintable.

Mike Toochin got to the Bluethroat spot and found it disquietingly empty. He knew something was up, something big. But without a radio, he hadn't a clue as to what or where. Luckily, Eli Elder, coming up from Lower Base, gave him the scoop.

Winnie Conway had it easy. She was with Al Driscoll and had just been chauffeured out to see the rosefinch aboard one of the house Honda three-wheelers. Off-road vehicles make light of distance (though they aren't immune from deep, deep mud).

Sam Madison didn't have it easy at all. In the course of his day he had already peddled from the east runway, where he'd seen the Brambling, to the Pyramid, where he *didn't* see the reported Eye-browed Thrush, then all the way back to the east runway for the rosefinch—a fair workout for a seventy-six-year-old retired attorney. Dan Gibson told him about the flycatcher all the way back at Henderson when he showed up for the rose-finch. Like a trooper, like a true, true Attuvian, Sam turned his bicycle back into the wind, peddling back along the route he'd navigated four times that day. With rosefinch on his list, the Siberian Flycatcher became more than just a Life Bird. It became Number 700—the magic number. Providing, of course, he saw it. Providing, of course, he made it.

Linda got to the rosefinch just about the time everyone else was leaving. There was talk about a mystery flycatcher back at Henderson, but nobody was hurrying—not yet. It wasn't until she caught up with Dan Gibson and the rosefinch that the import of the bird was finally established.

"You better go look at it," Dan urged. "This is only the third North American record for Siberian Flycatcher." Although Dan was crying to chase the bird himself, he was honor-bound to remain on post in case anyone else showed up for the rosefinch. On the other hand, Dan Gibson was about the only person in North America who could afford to be generous about this particular bird—he was the one who had recorded North America's first Siberian Flycatcher.

One by one, and in small groups, all the disparate lives wove a path up Henderson, drawing to a point high up in the valley. From all across the island, from wherever their ambitions had carried them, the tribe was gathering, drawn by a single will, a single bird. Some bulled their way through the muck, fighting the Henderson Highway to a standstill. Others cheated the slime, discarding their bikes along the route and walking the grassy shoulder. Larry Balch and Al Driscoll operating their ORVs shuttled in the most distant members of the tribe.

One by one, the weary Attuvians straggled in, breathless, frightened that the bird would disappear before they could arrive. One by one, as they reached the group, they were ushered to spotting scopes trained on the bird . . . and the breaths that came in tired gasps were drawn through sudden smiles. They had passed across the invisible threshold that separates those who have seen the bird and those who have not.

Initially the flycatcher, taking its notoriety in stride, moved from thicket to thicket, never traveling more than a hundred yards from its point of discovery. But as the crowd and the clamor grew, so did the bird's nervousness. Once it crossed to the far side of the road and disappeared, raising the anxiety levels of late arrivals. It returned but withdrew into a canyon and sulked, making detection difficult. Looks that once were generous became momentary, glimpses at best, not the kind of looks that satisfy. Not the kind of look you want for a Life Bird.

But birders are a tribe bound by common interest and shared need. It was the duty of the tribe to see that everyone got this bird. A dozen scopes following its every evasive move were surrendered to the needy, hoping that their eyes could pick out the small gray form before it flew. First one leader then another tried their hands, directing anxiety-clouded eyes to this patch or that branch. Their instructions were augmented by some, contradicted by others, and by and large muddled past the point of usefulness.

"I have the bird down here," a voice would herald. "Here. In the scope." And the tribe's needy would run down there.

"Wait!" another voice would shout. "I have it here. Perfect view." And the needy would run over there.

One by one, the glimpses were had. One by one, the have-nots joined the haves, crossed over into the arms of the tribe. Only a handful remained. One of them was Sam Madison.

Suddenly a radio crackled. A voice brought ears and heads erect. "There's an Eyebrowed Thrush in a willow thicket about a quarter-mile up the road. I'm on it now."

*God damn that Bill Mueller*, I thought joyfully.

Like some great multilegged beast, a mob of Eyebrowed Thrush aspirants fled up the valley, leaving the flycatcher hopefuls to fend for themselves. Tribal unity is one thing. But a Life Bird, well, a Life Bird is something else again.

EPILOGUE: Dinner was late, hours late (since even chefs get to see third records for North America). People were too tired to talk and too talkative to eat, so in the interest of saving time, everybody was talking and eating at once. There were toasts and there were cheers. There were stories of individual trials and hardships surmounted that had already attained the stature of legend. There was great joy in Mudville.

Later, but not much later, a tired Sam Madison crawled into his bunk and was asleep almost immediately. Though there was no one in the room to see it, if any had chanced to look they would have seen the face of a very tired Attuvian, but one that was creased by a smile.

## THE LONE EAGLE

The bird was perched upon a lichen-stained crag on a mountain that anchored the west side of Temnac Valley. She was a large bird, even by the standards of eagles, but to a human eye the bird would have been invisible, so well did she blend with her surrounding. The head was pale as lichen, the white wedge of a tail indistinguishable from snow. The feathers that encased the great lump of a bird were the cold, brown color of stone—in fact, the bird might easily have passed for stone, so lifeless did she appear —except for her eyes. The eyes were yellow, and deep, and very much alive.

From her vantage she could see the beach and the bay and the group of human intruders still two miles away. Her eyes looked up the valley, along the river, stopping momentarily to rest upon the silver bird, then on to the great wall of rock that supported what remained of the old nest. If she chose, she could have turned her eyes west, up the valley, until the mountains choked it into a gorge. But she rarely looked west anymore.

For a short time, yes. In the spring following the winter that her mate had died, she looked west. But she was old by then, old even by the measure of her kind. It was too late for looking west, now.

Temnac Valley is a beautiful valley, uncomplicated and remote, just the way White-tailed Eagles like their valleys. It had been the anchor of her universe ever since she had arrived, a spirited young adult from a distant coast who had wandered here an eagle's lifetime ago. Here she had met the one who would be her mate and they had played and sparred, binding their talons and spirits in the skies over Attu. Here, they had spent their lives, built their nest, raised their young, surmounting the hardships and reaping the bounty of life. Here they had been young and here they had grown old. And here, five years ago, he had died, the only selfish act committed since the day they had paired, but one that he, like all living creatures, had no control over.

Her eyes swept her valley, sifting the world for signs of change. They settled, again, upon the great, silver bird resting by the river. This time they stayed. More and more, it seemed, she found herself regarding the silver intruder, although it had been part of the valley almost as long as the valley had been part of her life, although it had never stirred since the day it had come screaming out of the fog, skidding to a halt. Seeing it recalled the day, the sound of it, the fright of it—how she and her strong young mate had taken to the air, screaming their anger, united in their defiance against another great bird of prey in their valley.

The whole island had been an eruption of sound and anger that spring, and the silver bird had been a part of that anger, wounded by that anger, felled by it. The eagle did not know, and would not have cared, but the silver bird had a name. It was called a P-38 by the manufacturer, a Lightning by the pilots who flew it. The eagle did not know and would not have cared to know the circumstances that pit two nations against each other on a desolate island that neither particularly wanted but neither wanted the other to have. It is not an eagle's burden to be concerned about these things. All she knew was that one day the silver bird had come to the valley where nothing changed more permanently than the seasons or more quickly than storms. In coming, it had frozen a moment in time.

Years stood between her and that day, now. Years and young, and all that was all of her life (all except the little that remained). Now, her days were long. Long and uneventful. Sometimes she fed. Sometimes, when the skies cleared, she took to the air and soared to other parts of the island to give her eyes something else to gaze upon for a while. But most days were filled with hours of sitting and watching in the valley, where nothing really changed at all.

Sometimes, for no reason she could understand, she would look at the great silver bird, and it would call to mind the day and the noise and how it once had been. Several times she had flown to it, circled it, challenging or maybe encouraging it. But the silver bird remained as rigid as the body of her mate on that morning he did not rise to mount the skies with her.

Now, she merely studied it. The only other bird of prey, now, in a valley that had always known two.

The human intruders were close enough, finally, to nudge her interest. In time she might fly closer to investigate. Then again, she might not. It wasn't an eagle's concern.

# 11 • ARCTIC NATIONAL WILDLIFE REFUGE, ALASKA:

## Birding Beyond the Ken

### LISTENING FOR SILENCE

HE ENGINE OF OUR SINGLE-ENGINE BUSH PLANE revved until the roar turned to a snarl, to a scream. Mew Gulls wheeled in frightened circles over their gravel bar nests, and a pair of Red-breasted Merganser turned the shallows to froth trying to make their escape. With a shudder the plane lurched forward, picking up speed. For one bad moment, it looked as though gravity would not surrender its hold. But then the wheels broke free of the gravel's clutch, turned south over the river, and fled toward the distant peaks. We stood and watched it for a time, then moved to arrange our gear.

The name of the river is the Kongakut, a braided strand of meltwater and gravel bars that winds its way to the Beaufort Sea. The mountains are the British Mountains, part of the Brooks Range, the northernmost major mountains in the world. From our vantage, on the gravel bar, the mountains filled the horizon, cutting deep into the Arctic sky, cutting us off from the world. Just an hour earlier, we had flown through those peaks en route to the Arctic National Wildlife Refuge in northeast Alaska.

Fairbanks was four hundred miles behind. Even the taiga had foundered in its northern advance, broken against that wall of ice and stone, surrendering to tundra. There had been times, as our plane had threaded its way through valleys and passes, that gray talus slopes and rust-colored spires closed in upon us, buffeting us with updrafts, threatening us with a stony end.

But our small, heavily loaded plane was not enough, apparently, to shake the great indifference of mountains—not this time, anyway. And though the gravel bars that serve as wilderness landing strips often shrug off bush planes or throw them on their backs, this one was in an expansive mood. It accepted the plane and its passengers on our fourth pass. Even the Arctic weather let us unload our gear unmolested.

In a short time, the frightened gulls returned to their nests. The mergansers returned to their courtship. And the roar of the plane became a growl, a hum, a peevish, persistent snarl that lingered long after the plane had passed from sight.

You'd think that a wilderness would simply swallow a sound like that, muffle it with grandeur. But the reality is, you only wish it were so.


## OF MUSK OX AND AMERICAN ROBINS

The bird stepped away from behind a boulder, surprising us both. As near as I could tell from the most recently published range maps, the northern limit of the American Robin's breeding range fell short of our present latitude (but then there is no shortage of things whose breeding range falls short of 69 degrees, 30 minutes north latitude). The bird's surprise was also excusable. It had almost certainly never seen a birder in this corner of the Arctic before—a fact that might also account for the discrepancy in the range maps.

"What's that?" Linda said, her binoculars pointed in the direction of the willows on the far side of the river, drawing my attention away from the robin.

"That," said Bob of the dark brown mass half hidden by a latticework of branches, "is a musk ox."

"That's what I thought," Linda confirmed, and settled deeper into the tundra, digging in for a long, savoring appraisal of a Life Mammal. So did Bob and so did I. Musk oxen are not exactly stock items over much of nature's shelf. Even here, in Alaska's Arctic National Wildlife Refuge, they are a treat. The robin could wait.

"Way to go there, *Linda!*" Bob chanted. "I thought we might run into one or two somewhere around here."

That's what I like about "Burly" Bob Dittrick. The man has confidence. But then, when you decide to go birding in the Arctic, this is the kind of quality you like to find in your guide—not that many birders actually do go in for wilderness birding. Not yet. That is something whose time is coming.

In the seventies and eighties, thousands and thousands of people discovered birding and through birding discovered the world. First Jim Lane's guides and later a host of state and local bird-finding guides directed birders to natural areas that travel agents never heard of. Hotlines with their detailed directions offered out-of-town birders an intimacy with forest service roads and box canyons that even local residents envied. Through books, through magazines, through tours, through field trips, through word of mouth and all the intricate tendrils of birding's grapevine, North America's great birding locations fell into the general pool of knowledge.

Everybody went to these places—the *right* places. If you wanted to see Green Jays, you went to Bentsen State Park, Texas. If Snail Kite was your heart's desire, Florida's Tamiami Trail was your destination. Warblers in April? High Island, Texas, of course. Warblers in May? Try Point Pelee, Ontario. In this way everyone saw everything—all the wonderful birds a continent has to offer. In this way the public went birding. Birding the circuit. Birding by the book. Rediscovering all the discoveries, and finding all the birds that had been found before.

But birding by the book has a dark side. It made birds easy to find, but in doing so it made discovery cheap. The circuit led birders to a continent full of birds, but a circuit is, after all, just a circuit, just a wheel, and wheels have a certain monotony about them. Even though the Great Places *are* great, after five trips to Pelee in as many years, birders found themselves wondering whether there might be other places worth birding, too.

Just for a change of pace. Just for a year or two. Someplace a little less crowded. Someplace new. Someplace undiscovered. Someplace off the beaten path that they could have to themselves.

For some, there was another stick stirring disquiet into contented souls. This stick was wielded by time.

You wake up one morning, just before the alarm, and walk to the bathroom, favoring the ache in the knee you screwed up jogging, mincing your steps until the kinks work out of your hips.

"Arthritis," the doctor had affirmed. "Your father's got it and you'll have it, too. Take aspirin."

You step on the scale, grimace, and say, not for the first time, that you're really going to do something about that, and then you step to the mirror. In it is a face. It is yours but not the face you remember; a face that is older than memory and optimism make it.

"It must be the lighting in here," you assure yourself. But it's not the lighting.

"Well then, it's probably the stress at work," or "a poor night's sleep," "or . . ."

"*Allergies!*" That's it. "Allergies." Happens this time every summer. Late summer and early fall. Boy that pollen just raises hell with my sinuses and . . .

But it's none of these things, either. It's Age—the chill wind that shakes the leaves of summer that were once the leaves of spring. It is Time. Where once time ran off that face like vernal rain, now the face is scored with tiny rivulets, channels that cut down the corners of the mouth, deltas that widen from the corners of either eye.

"I'm still young," the heart asserts. But the face says, "No." And this morning the eyes staring out from the mirror side with the face.

"I can still do all the things I used to do; can do anything I want to do," the will shouts at the glass, coming to the rescue of the heart. But the glass refuses to be faced down this time, and then your bum knee jumps into the argument, weakening your stand.

"Just wait one minute, pal," the knee squeaks. "You think you're gonna start jumping out of airplanes or scaling cliffs or somethin' and you got another think coming. And don't blame me. *You* were the one who insisted on running after I *plainly* told you that . . ."

The eyes holding yours weigh the opposing truth. The eyes that speak for the wisdom that you bought with your youth.

"I can do it," you plead. "I can."

This time . . . the eyes side with the heart, surrendering to the force of your will.

"Yes," they say. "You can still do those things," they agree. "*But do them, now,*" the eyes say urgently. "*Do them quickly,*" while there is still time in the world.

Time is slipping away. Time is building a wall between you and possibilities. Time is snaring you in a trap. "DO IT NOW!" the eyes urge.

"*Or you will never do it at all,*" a thin, dark voice whispers from some corner of your soul.

Big as a dumpster, shaggy as a buffalo's mane, deliberate as Eeyore in a thistle patch, the musk ox browsed his way through the willows, nibbling the tips flushed with spring. Musk oxen were extirpated from the North Slope during the 1800s and reintroduced in 1969. Now the population in the refuge is close to five hundred animals.

There was not a great deal to be seen of the beast at this distance, at half a mile. Just a large, front-heavy ungulate moving in and out of view.

Maybe this explains my sudden diffidence.

Or maybe I was just overwhelmed by all the things vying for my attention all at once—caribou on hillsides, courting golden plover behind, tundra flowers beneath, a river below, the mountains beyond. Nineteen million acres of Arctic wilderness, and all that it contained.

Or maybe it was because I was falling under the spell of what Bob calls "Arctic Time"—a peaceful sense of nonchalance that is poisonous to urgency, priority, and demand.

Or maybe it was just something as simple as shaken expectations. A musk ox was something that I was prepared to see in the arctic. But American Robin . . .

Though I have seen tens of thousands of robins in my life, and not a single musk ox, I found myself after a minute or two putting my binoculars back on the bird, watching it walk, as robins all over North America walk, just as the ones that stalked earthworms on my parents' lawn had walked. I watched it walk over a place where I never expected to see one.

In this lifetime.

And you know, I can't recall ever having seen a more handsome robin than the one who lives near Caribou Pass on the slopes above the Kongakut River. I know that I've never appreciated one more.


## PUSHING THE LIMITS OF CONVENTION

"Everybody ready?" Bob inquired.

I nodded, and I guess Linda did too, though her head, and almost every thing else about her, was blocked from view by a pack that would have crippled a camel.

Dittrick and the pack that was Linda took a last look around, casting appraising, professional eyes over what had been our campsite. Both seemed satisfied. When Linda was an instructor at the National Outdoor Leadership School in Lander, Wyoming, she taught the school's ethic of "Minimum Impact Camping." Bob, to state it plainly, lives the ethic. By the time our camp was taken down, the area policed, the rocks that had secured our tent lines returned to their place of origin, there was nothing about it that hinted of human intrusion.

Zero impact in a fragile land. The only ethic that should be tolerated in the Arctic.

"OK, then," Dittrick said, turning a big pearly grin our way. *"Let's get out there!"*

"Out there" led across the gravel bar, up the riverbank, past a pair of Smith's Longspurs that were duking it out over boundary rights and onto open tundra. The direction was up.

Bob set an easy pace, first because there wasn't any hurry, and second because neither Linda or I are as burly as Bob. He's a big man, with a big man's bearing—big enough to shoulder an eighty-pound pack with easy grace, big enough to walk into a bar and be assured that his gracious manner will go unchallenged.

We met, Bob and I, in the autumn of 1976, in Cape May, New Jersey, where both of us had signed on for a season at the newly founded Cape May Bird Observatory. Bob was a hawk bander, I was a hawk counter—common ground enough to forge a friendship that makes light of time and miles. This proved necessary, because in 1978 Bob moved to Alaska, involving himself in things like designing nature centers for the state and surveying nesting raptors along wilderness rivers for the U.S. Fish and Wildlife Service. In 1987, he and his wife, Lisa, a professional anthropologist turned river guide, decided to place their outdoor skills and Alaska's wilderness at the disposal of North American birders. They founded Wilderness Birding Adventures, a company specializing in adventure birding in America's last frontier. Before long, their backpacking, rafting, canoeing, and sea kayaking trips began to attract such regular clients as the Nature Conservancy and the Wilderness Society.

But our trip? Our trip was just for friendship—friendship, adventure, and fun.

"Everybody doin' all right?" Bob shouted back over his shoulder, letting his professionalism show.

"Yep," Linda said briskly.

"Uh . . . huh," I huffed, suddenly very grateful for the two weeks of physical training we'd had on Attu, but guessing it wouldn't be enough.

The footing was soft, but dry. Reindeer lichen cushioned and cradled every footfall, but there was bottom to it—first ice, then, as we got higher, stone. It would have been nice if we had been shod like reindeer. But we weren't. Linda was laced into hiking boots. I was wrapped in knee-high wellies. Dittrick? Dittrick was wearing sandals. Not much ankle support for an eighty-pound pack, but "it makes fording streams easier," he explained. "Keeps your feet drier in the long run, too." This, Linda and I both discovered, was true.

The pack got heavier as we climbed, and breaths came quicker, but I was pleased to note that my legs had remembered the old rhythm of climbing with a pack—a natural, energy-saving plod that makes a body work in harmony, working, without cerebral intrusion, toward one objective: the next step.

It was strange, and it strikes me as curious, still, but the first thing I noticed about the Arctic, the moment we stepped off the plane, in fact, was how wonderfully clean the air was. I am not particularly attuned to air quality. It's not a fetish with me, nothing I give a great deal of thought to, and I'm fortunate in this regard. Linda and I live in a rural part of New Jersey, where the air is clean enough to be the source of envy for urban neighbors. And, of course, we two are no strangers to places where air is so fine that it could be bottled and sold.

In our travels, Linda and I have filtered a lot of North America through our lungs, tasted both the good and bad of it on our tongues. We have known and savored the clean air that smells of pine. The clean air that smells of sage. Clean air that smells of brine. Clean air that carries the hot, flinty, dry, scrubbed smell of desert sand.

But until we reached the Arctic, I had never breathed clean air that smelled like air. Just air. Unless what I was mistaking for the smell of air was actually the cold no-smell of ice. Ice or ice-laden air. I think I understand, now, what people mean when they speak of air so clean that it intoxicates, air so clean it makes you greedy for more, so greedy you think you'll never get enough of it.

This, I will have you believe, is why I was gasping by the time we reached the crest of the ridge.

"How 'bout a rest?" Bob said graciously. "Lot of caribou around," he observed.

A *lot* of caribou. The valley below us was dotted with tawny forms and creased with trails. Not far away, a couple of cows, heavy with unborn young, stared at us with bovine simplicity. In May and early June, the great Porcupine River herd, 180,000 animals strong, moves out of Canadian forests where they spent the Arctic winter, spreading out over the coastal plain. Here is where the calves are born. Here is where they will spend the Arctic summer. Our path to the sea cut right across their path, and caribou would be part of our lives for as long as we remained in the place that is aptly named the Serengeti of the North.

After we had savored enough air, Bob brought us to heel, still climbing, putting caribou to route, flushing American Pipits, Lapland Longspurs, Rock Ptarmigan, Semipalmated Sandpipers, and Semipalmated Plovers at intervals. Below, in a valley large enough to have a name on some map, a Rough-legged Hawk hovered, eyeing the prospects of a lemming-rich patch of tundra. Long-tailed and Parasitic Jaegers vied for supremacy of the air, and their shadows haunted the earth. Baird's Sandpipers flicked white underwings that flashed the message of their presence clear across the tundra. From somewhere high in the cotton-and-cobalt sky, a whistle floated to earth—the ethereal song of Upland Sandpiper.

"Hey, Bob," I shouted, taken by a sudden thought. "According to the range maps, Upland Sandpipers aren't supposed to be around here."

Bob stopped and considered this a moment. "Well," he observed, "there's sure enough of them up here. I'm sure I've seen them every time I've been in the refuge."

There was no question about them being here, in numbers, too. We ran into several Upland Sandpipers that first day, all of them behaving eminently territorial, all of them unconcerned by their renegade status.

We discovered other birds whose breeding ranges seemed to push the bounds of convention. According to the Second Edition of the *National Geographic Field Guide*, printed in 1987, and the Third Edition of *A Field Guide to Western Birds*, published in 1990, the Mew Gulls nesting on the Kongakut also shouldn't have been there. But there they most certainly were.

The very territorial Spotted Sandpipers and Wandering Tattlers that patrolled the gravel bars of the Kongakut shouldn't have been there either; nor should the host of Wilson's Warblers dueling from the willow thickets, or the several Northern Harriers hunting the tundra. According to the most recent range maps, we shouldn't have seen the pair of Sandhill Cranes near Gordon, the American Wigeon beside Demarcation Bay, or the Varied Thrush singing in a willow thicket well out on the coastal plain.

The Tree Swallow hanging around the grounded barge and the female Red-winged Blackbird fifty feet from the Beaufort Sea were probably overshoots.

Over the course of the trip, we were to find fifteen species whose presence, with proper documentation, would nudge the boundaries of their ranges farther north than convention makes them. It's possible that the birds themselves have only recently moved into the region. But the fact is that the northern limits of many North American birds are imperfectly defined. Even now, 165 years after the first explorers of European extraction reached the region, 68 years since Margaret and Olaus Murie turned their inquisitive eyes upon the Brooks Range, anyone with the interest and the ambition can stake an ornithological claim in America's last frontier.

We found other birds, too, "rare" birds (if by rare you mean "not commonly seen outside of the Arctic"). There was a Northern Wheatear of the T-tipped tail flitting from rock to rock. It was a bird Linda and I had seen but half a dozen times between us in North America, so we chased it across a scree-covered playing field, where the bird had all the advantage, hoping for a better look. This proved to be a very good strategy, since it allowed us to pass by the next four wheatears we stumbled upon, thus saving time and energy. It also helped us maintain good relations with the wheatear that was a fixture in our camp that night.

There was the stream with no name that threw shards of sunlight back at the Yellow Wagtails hovering overhead; there were Hoary Redpolls whose electric "zinging" made the willows crackle with energy and the . . .

"BLUHTHOWT," I shouted through the avocado and cheese sandwich that was mostly in my mouth, pinning a name to the small brown-backed bird speeding down the stream bed.

"God *damn*, Mr. Dunne," Dittrick observed with a modest measure of reverence, a stick of reindeer sausage clasped in his hand. "How'd you identify that bird so fast?"

"Caught the rusty patches at the base of the tail," I confirmed honestly, accurately, helping myself to a celebratory handful of Burly's own Triple-A gorp. The fact that I'd seen Bluethroats on three continents (including one on Attu the previous week) didn't seem worth mentioning at the time.

There was a Gyrfalcon whose passage wrapped the living tundra in sudden silence, and a Yellow-billed Loon that circled and called. There were ptarmigan and jaegers and shorebirds of many shapes and hues. There were, during our six days in the Arctic National Wildlife Refuge, all the birds of an Arctic summer, and many of the mammals, too. Caribou and grizzlies; ringed seals and musk oxen.

But the birds that captivated us then, and those whose significance lingers today, were the birds whose presence pushed the limits of convention. The common birds whose encounters bear the luster of discovery. The birds that weren't supposed to be there but were.

We found them.

## TOUCHING THE INFINITE

Dinner was finished, the dishes cleaned, everything was safe and secure in the packs or in the tent. We knew we were letting it hang out a bit, pitching camp in the saddle of the ridge like this. If the weather turned contrary we'd be camping in a wind tunnel, and contrary weather is pretty typical in the foothills of the Brooks.

But the view of the Kongakut, a thousand feet below, was enchanting. The shallow rays of the sun made it shiver with light, setting distant cliffs on fire. Bob had quietly insisted on this place, had plainly gone out of his way to be here. Plotting a course that climbed when it didn't have to; passing up potential campsites that offered greater protection and easier access to water. When he suggested we go up to the rocky outlook to watch the midnight sun, Linda and I weren't surprised.

Clearly the place had special meaning to Bob, and this was a special day! Maybe Dittrick believed that Linda and I had forgotten, but if he had, then he had also misjudged his friends.

Rested now, unfettered by our packs, we fairly bounded up the slope, sprite as caribou calves that buck and frolic across the tundra. A nesting Rough-legged Hawk screamed insults our way and a wheatear fled at our approach, hopping from stone to stone. American Pipits and Horned Larks took to the air around us, singing of their lust and the land they called their own.

Footing was good. Only for a short time did we scramble through scree; the harsh, brittle sound of it filled the air, hurt the ears, made us feel vulnerable and small, prey to a thousand watchful eyes. On top, on the north face of an ancient spire of stone, the caribou lichen lay thick and matted. We collapsed, Linda, Bob, and I, into the cradle of stone and turned our faces upon the universe.

Smiling like the magician who knew where the rabbit was all along, Bob reached into his day pack, drawing forth a plastic water bottle that glowed with an inner amber light. With proper solemnities and a practiced hand, he cracked the lid and raised the bottle like a chalice. "Here's to us being here, guys," he said, taking a long satisfying pull, passing the bottle on with a wide grin.

"Ahhhh," he sighed, putting whatever spirits might be listening on notice that they were dealing with attentive equals here tonight.

Linda and I have both shared a few bottles of Tennessee sour mash with Mr. Dittrick in our time. But neither of us had ever shared one quite so prized. On a trip where even ounces are measured and shaved, Bob had chosen to burden his already overburdened pack with a generous measure of the finest sippin' whiskey on earth—maybe the universe. A thoughtful addition to help us celebrate universal concepts and earthly milestones. I quite forgave him the extra miles we'd hiked to reach this place by the time the bottle came back to me the third time. The fiery liquid had kindled a warm glow in that place where the heart and the soul overlap and the mind is sometimes tangent.

But I would have thanked him anyway. This spot, in the northern foothills of the Brooks, was enchantment itself, and no words will ever do justice to it. Below us was a great valley, flushed with spring, that opened onto the coastal plain. Bisecting it was a spiny ridge the color of old blood; ravaged by winter, broken on the wheel of time. Once, the Inuit hid in the shadows of those rocky weirs, waiting behind stone-tipped lances for caribou. But that was another age, and today, only the shadows fell upon the herds.

Looking northeast ten air miles away was a great icy rectangle, our destination, Demarcation Bay. To the east, no more than eight miles as the jaeger flies, was Canada. To the northwest, gleaming like a tangled web of silver, the mouth of the Kongakut River.

But the direction your eyes wanted most to turn, even though it hurt to look on it, even though the reach of human vision foundered in the cold, white haze, was north. There, beyond a thin lead of dark water, was the frozen Beaufort Sea.

"Whew," Bob pronounced, zipping his pile jacket up to the throat, taking another pull from the bottle. "Must be some ice around here somewhere."

"How long you figure 'til midnight?" Linda asked.

Bob studied the sun, hovering over the icy horizon. "Oh, lots of time," he concluded. "An hour, I'd guess."

Yes, lots of time. All the time in a day that is at once as long and as brief as an Arctic summer. All the time in the world.

When I was young, there was a dream I dreamed. It didn't have a name, this dream. In fact, it wasn't until I learned how little substance is to be found in dreams that I thought to give it one. I called it the Myth of Infinite. It was part of my heritage, part of my birthright, part of a bigger dream, the American Dream. The dream linked a kid growing up in suburbia to the Land of Our Fathers—to purple mountains' majesty and sea to shining sea. It was a dream whose foundation was optimism and hope.

The dream that was a myth said that North America was a great wilderness, a frontier whose limits had been pushed but never reached, never conquered.

Like America itself.

The myth said that in this land of inexhaustible riches, the sky would always be blue, water would always run pure, forests would always be virgin and wildlife abundant. If a body ever needed more elbow room, why, the myth counseled, it was there for the taking, there for anyone with gumption. And I knew, *knew*, that at any time I chose (say, some Sunday evening before a history assignment was due) I could just strap on a pack, pick up a 30/30 rifle, put it in the crook of m'arm, and head for the wilderness. Live off the land.

This was the Myth of Infinite, and it was very important to me. It shaped my outlook. It made me believe that anything is possible so long as you are wise, and free, and live in a land whose borders are only as finite as people's dreams.

Then I got older, maybe wiser. I discovered that the Myth of Infinite has a dark side. For thirty-nine years, I have watched as the dark side of the myth nibbled away at this great continent. The dark side says that if forests are inexhaustible, well then, it's OK to just cut them down and sell the logs to the highest bidder. Hell, plenty of trees where these came from, right?

The dark side says that if there will always be pure water then it's all right to pollute. Not all of it, of course! Just some. Just enough to disguise the real cost of production. Just enough to get rid of a lot of chemical waste cheaply (and make a bigger profit).

The dark side says, "You know, a little bit of infinity goes a long way. What say we just put a fence around this little corner over here and sell drilling rights to all the rest? Can't let something like a few caribou stand in the way of making the world safe for democracy, can we?"

So I came, in time, to disbelieve the Myth of Infinite because I know, now, that the resources of a continent are more finite than human greed. I discovered that freedom can be twisted, can mean that anything a person can grab is his and to hell with everyone else. I learned that the twisted freedom that allows people to destroy a place conflicts with my freedom to appreciate it and the freedom of other living things to survive.

For a time I believed that wisdom would side with me, would speak for all living things that cannot speak for themselves. But I found that wisdom is rarely a match for profit, or crisis, or water rights, or recession, or national security—things whose needs are always pressing, more immediate, and easier to understand. The infinity that was a dream and is a myth was dammed here, fenced there, ditched, drilled, surveyed, excavated, sucked dry, overgrazed, clear cut, polluted, dumped upon, bought, sold, resold, paved, parceled, and turned into an asset owned by a defaulting bank where the lifeless shell of it became part of the taxpayer's burden. There was never any time for wisdom. So, in time, I stopped believing the Myth of Infinite. I never stopped hoping, maybe. But I did stop believing.

Below, a wheatear mounted a scar-colored boulder and started to sing—phrases, snatches of phrases. It was, I suddenly realized, the only living sound in the Arctic. The world had grown so still. And it was singing a song that I had never heard—a wheatear's song, a series of sharp-edged notes well suited to a land shattered by ice and time.

The entire universe cocked its ears and listened, giving grave audience to a creature so bold that it would court the attention of the universe when most creatures crave only anonymity. And I shivered. A deep shiver that had nothing to do with the chill creeping in from the sea.

"Excuse me, Bob, but I think I need a little more of that antifreeze if you don't mind."

"Oh, sorry," he apologized, passing the bottle from his hand to mine, never taking his eyes or his thoughts away from the horizon.

The sun was clearly lower now, a searing white hole burned through the layers of ice and fog that bound the horizon. Below, half a hundred caribou were sprawled upon the tundra, sleeping the watchful sleep of caribou. Even the calves had stopped their frolicking and fallen to the earth.

"I think it's starting to rise," Linda said, speaking of the sun.

"No, not yet," Bob said, after a moment, maybe two—never taking his eyes away from the horizon. "Not yet."

The breeze that had met us on the pinnacle when we arrived had gone elsewhere. Icy fog, hovering offshore, began to creep over the land, slipping over ridges, filling valleys to their stony rim, then spilling over into the next. First the caribou disappeared beneath the icy shroud, then the valleys, then the earth, then, in places, even the sky.

The fog silenced the wheatear, who fled down a shadowed slope. The edge of it brushed our pinnacle with an icy finger but didn't have the power to reach us, or maybe some power greater than fog defeated it. It fell to either side and pursued the wheatear, leaving us, soon, on an island projecting through an ocean of fog.

"Bob?" I asked, shaken by a sudden recollection, a nagging scrap of memory. "Didn't you tell me once that you'd brought your father's ashes up here someplace?"

"Yeah," he breathed, conferring upon us the gift of his confidence. "Just back there," he added, indicating a stony ledge with a nod, taking another sip from the water bottle, passing it on to me.

I took a long swallow, savoring the burning of it in my mouth and the warm glow of it that spread outward, routing the cold that was creeping down my limbs.

"Did he ever see this place when he was alive?" I asked, handing the bottle back to Bob.

"No," he said, touching the bottle to his mouth, maybe taking another drink, maybe not. "He never did."

The smell of ice was heavy in the air and the silence had grown, gathered strength, since the wheatear's song had been cut short. Silence. Not a breath of wind, not a bird's voice, not a felten footfall marred that perfect silence. In most places, silence is just the absence of noise; is just silence. But in this place, on this pinnacle of stone trapped between the ocean and the sky, caught in the eye of an unsetting sun, silence takes on corporeal form, takes your breath away.

It was a silence so profound that it lost all earthly bearing. Silence so silent that the molecules tapping against your ears became a steady hiss; so silent that hearts could reach across the distance that separates one person from another and synchronize their beats. So incredibly silent that if you closed your eyes and listened very, very hard, you could hear, very plainly the fading echoes of the Big Bang reaching out and up and back all the way to the beginning of time, and the end of it, too.

This was the gift that came to me in the thirty-eighth year of my life, and I pass it, now, to you. There is a pinnacle of stone and it stands in the foothills of the Brooks Range. From this place, if you go there with those you love and those you trust, you can reach out a hand and touch the retreating hem of Infinity. And if there is a God and if He is not Indifferent, then I thank him for letting me see It before It retreats beyond this Earth.

"Time," Linda said, with sudden conviction, breaking the silence, reaching into her day pack, the way Bob had reached into his.

"Yeah," Bob sighed, "I think it's on its way around again."

Linda's hand closed on the prize she sought. A small box with a ribbon that she placed in Bob's hand.

"A present from Lisa," she explained. We promised to be the couriers. "Happy birthday, Bob," she said.

"Happy birthday," I added.

"Aw, come on, guys," he scolded, smiling his big burley grin. "You guys are just too much to believe."

The sun started around one more time, and the bottle went around a few more too. Went around, in fact, until it was dry. The next morning we rose late and left later, descending into the valley where the caribou slept, where the wheatear had been. Where Infinity was last seen on this planet.

## 12 • MANITOBA, CANADA:

## Have Bins, Will Travel

HE COFFEE TABLE SUPPORTED A MOUND OF travel catalogues, all bound by a thematic thread. They described organized birding tours to every corner of the globe, to places and birds that were almost (but not quite) beyond the reach of dreams.

"What about Papua New Guinea?" Linda said, looking up from the WINGS Catalog, reaching for the short straw.

"What about the moon?" I offered.

"New Guinea is a lot cheaper than the moon," she argued. "And it has a lot more birds."

"How many?" I inquired.

"Over 750 species," she promised.

"How much?" I demanded.

"Only about $5,300 per person," she declared. (The "not counting airfare" was a mumbled afterthought.)

"The moon," I said again, playing the heavy. Just because a place doesn't lie beyond the reach of dreams doesn't mean that it falls within a mortal budget.

Linda sighed, shrugged, and reached (just a little too quickly, I thought) for another catalog (that just happened to be open and face-down on the table). The FIELD GUIDES catalogue.

"Well, what about Ecuador?" she suggested, in a voice that suggested spontaneity. "It's a lot cheaper than the moon."

"What about Ecuador?" I invited noncommittally.

"August 15 through September 2 . . . going to Quito, La Selva . . . Ooooo, Lyre-tailed Nightjar . . . Golden-headed Quetzal . . . Andean Cock-of-the-Rock . . . Andean Condor . . ."

"Who's leading it?"

"John and Rose Ann Rowlett."

Yes, I had to admit, Ecuador would be a lot of fun. Neither Linda nor I had ever birded the Neotropics. And it would certainly be more affordable than Papua New Guinea. But still not cheap. And, besides . . .

"I thought we wanted to limit the scope of this book to North America," I reminded her.

"But you can drive anywhere in North America!" Linda objected.

"Not quite," I said, playing my trump card.

There was a pause during which Linda analyzed this scant evidence. As I watched, the tinder behind her eyes began to smolder, then glow.

"No," she agreed, "not quite."

"Sabine's Gull, Harris's Sparrow, Great Gray Owl," I pronounced, carefully selecting the birds I knew Linda had never seen. "Jaegers, Arctic Terns, Stilt Sandpipers in breeding plumage," I added. "Tundra, taiga, Beluga whales," I chanted, watching her eyes glow brighter.

"Ross's Gull!" she exclaimed, and the eyes *blazed*, kindled by visions of ice-colored wings. "Ecuador next year?" she negotiated.

"New Guinea if you like. The moon! You want something to drink?" I invited, rising, heading for the kitchen.

"Sure," she replied.

"Club soda?"

"OK."

"Anything in it?"

Linda considered the options, grinned, and said, "No. Just ice."

Lots of ice.

## JUNE 2: SALT LAKE CITY TO WINNIPEG, MANITOBA

*Chilly morning.*

> *Woke at 5:00 A.M. for the trip to the airport. The flight was on time. No problems. Customs in Winnipeg was hassle-free. We caught the limo and were settled in our room at the Best Western by 4:00 P.M.*
>
> *—LD*

Something happened in the 1970s and 1980s that changed the face of birding. Its popularity grew. Grew a lot! The environmental movement, fueled by all that unspent energy left over from the sixties, brought people to an awareness of the natural world, opened eyes to a planet filled with discovery and wonder. In the process, many people discovered birds.

Almost overnight, binocular manufacturers found that their biggest "user group" had become bird-watchers. New magazines like *Birding, Bird Watcher's Digest, Birder's World,* and *Wild Bird* sprang up, filled with the information that new birders clamored for. Field-identification guides proliferated. Bird-finding guides papered a continent. Birding hotlines spread their tendrils in all directions. The American Birding Association, an organization dedicated to sport and pleasure birding, was founded, and it flourished.

*And,* beginning in the sixties and early seventies, an industry bloomed—the bird-tour industry, specializing in bringing people and birds together. Its model was the travel program developed by the Massachusetts Audubon Society. Its pioneers were a few highly skilled, well-traveled individuals who dreamed of making a living from their passionate avocation.

So now, there is a tour industry that serves the birding market and ushers thousands of birders each year to the distant reaches of the planet. At its core are a select cadre of crack field birders, whose skills are legend and whose followers are legion. These are the professional bird-tour leaders.

## JUNE 3: WINNIPEG. FIRST DAY OF THE TOUR

*Sunny, windy.*

> *Had an introductory dinner—the entire group was there, all sixteen. Renee Miller and Otto Ademec from NYC; Barbara Heizman, also from NYC; Mary Ann Kern from Tuckahoe, New York; Ed Amerman of Doylestown, Pennsylvania; Flora Patterson from Ottawa, Ontario; Connie Price from Cleveland, Ohio; David Oliver from Fort Worth, Texas; Bruce and Alice Smith from Stamford, Connecticut; Bob and Maggie Wharton from Green Valley, Arizona; and Ralph and Bobby Lee Davis from Maitland, Florida. Group seems OK. One person's luggage hadn't arrived. Oh, oh! Sat at the end of the table with Ed, David, Otto, Renee, and Dale Delaney, one of the leaders. Otto is a panic. Dale is a real character.*
>
> *—LD*

A *real* character. A company man. Diamond Jim Brady decked out in a T-shirt, a safari jacket, and a white Stetson. Dale Delaney, fortyish, VENT leader since 1985, was an engineer living in California whose life hit a middle-age bump and careered off into the weeds (and the tropical rain forests and the Arctic tundra). His calling cards are a quip and a smile. His concern for the welfare of clients is peerless, and any bird that gets away from his group without looks that offer 100 percent satisfaction is a personal affront.

"Da Mail Man," Otto, a Dale worshiper, lauds. "Da Mail Man da-liVahs," he promises in consummate Brooklynese.

Kim Eckert, our other leader, was Dale's straight man on the tour . . . but only by default and not by very much. Transplanted to Minnesota from his native Illinois, Kim pretty much invented birding around Duluth, where he is revered as something of an ornithological Apollo. He is sly and folksy; Garrison Keillor with a groove from a binocular strap worn in his neck.

Kim and Dale are fairly typical of professional birders. Fit, thirty to fortyish, crippled by a passion for birds that has swept most (if not all) of life's other options aside. Their workaday uniform is a crusty pair of jeans and one of their fleet of T-shirts—shirts emblazoned with names like "Explorer's Inn, Peru," "La Selva, Costa Rica," "Kenya," "Mile-Hi,"—silk-screened campaign badges attesting to their geographic conquests. Around their necks are expensive optics that look like they've been drop-kicked up and down the Baja, then soaked in pickle juice. Their knowledge of North America and its birds is complete.

All bird tour leaders have their idiosyncracies, traits that set them apart from their peers and garner instant recognition from clients. There is Jon Dunn of WINGS, a Cray computer with John Denver's smile, who can take any North American bird down to the feather edges in thirty seconds and then rebuild its image in a client's mind in a fashion that lasts and lasts.

There is Rose Ann Rowlett of FIELD GUIDES, who caps each good bird found with hugs all around, and Kenn Kaufman of VENT, birding's Pun-Gent, whose facile wit has driven many a tired or frustrated group to distraction (and groans and laughter).

Susan Allen, John Coons, Victor Emanuel, Gary Rosenberg, Will Russell, Bret Whitney, David Wolf, Barry and Kevin Zimmer, and others; a select band of birding mercenaries, binoculars for hire. Their skills only begin where those of consummate birders end. Professional bird tour leaders are not just accounted among the finest birders on the planet. They are teachers and counselors, father figures, and the ones whose job it is to make certain that everyone gets a box lunch.

## JUNE 4: WINNIPEG. SECOND DAY

A.M. *sunny but cold;* P.M. *cloudy/windy.*

> *Had an early buffet breakfast and hopped into the vans. Tried to kick up a Gray Partridge right behind the motel—no luck. Found some at the next stop, though! We went to Oak Hammock Marsh—beautiful place. Black Terns, Yellow-headed Blackbird, Virginia Rail, and lots of other birds. Cruised some of the farmlands around Winnipeg looking for Sharp-tailed Grouse, etc.*

*Back to the hotel around 11:30 A.M. to check out and have lunch.*

*Off to Brandon in the vans via Carberry Hills. Beautiful Krider's Red-tailed and Mountain Bluebirds!*

*Checked into the Royal Oak Inn in Brandon. A nice change from Winnipeg.*

*—LD*

A group is a curious thing, an organism of individuals, and although no two are completely alike, in many ways they are similar. Every group has quiet members and ebullient ones; thoughtful members who *never* step in front of someone's spotting scope and not-so-thoughtful ones who pull motel room keys out of their pockets twenty miles out of town.

In every group there is *one* person who is always buying cookies to pass around and another who is perpetually late for meals, field trips, and meetings. And in most groups, there is the odd person out: the *one* person who is just a little too whiny, a little too peevish, too boastful, too noisy, too aggressive, too dissatisfied with the way the tour (and life in general) is going. In brief, the one person nobody can tolerate.

"You hope to have one person like that on your tours," an Australian tour leader once explained with a smile. "They draw everyone's angst and it takes the heat off the leader. But," he added, "you pray you don't have two."

Our Churchill group was not vexed by vexing personalities. It was dominated by tour veterans, as professional in their own right as Dale and Kim in theirs, people who have birded everywhere and seen (or aspire to see) everything! People who have birded with "John" here and "David" there. People who know that the best way to get the most out of a birding tour is to surrender a measure of individuality and keep friction to a minimum.

## JUNE 5: AT BRANDON. DAY 3

*Light rain and cloudy.*

*Had an early buffet breakfast and headed outside of Brandon to look for Sharp-tailed Grouse (primarily). It was like looking for a needle in a haystack, though one van got a rear-end, flying-away view of a bird.*

*"Not a typical VENT view," Dale said. [Sic.]*

*We went to another road and saw Sprague's Pipit and Baird's Sparrow. Fantastic!!! Went to a few other spots and saw Orange-crowned Warbler and Alder Flycatcher.*

*Back to the motel (late) for a buffet lunch. We had the afternoon off and took a nap. There was an early dinner and then it was off to see the Yellow Rail. A Life Bird! Got to bed around 12:30 P.M. Whew! What a long day!*

*—LD*

Birders sign on to tours for many reasons—for convenience, for companionship, for the freedom that comes of letting somebody else make some of life's decisions for a little while. But most do so for the harvest of good birds reaped through the skills of their leaders. Yellow Rail is a case in point.

The bird is a *mouse*. A frustrating, feathered mouse, no more inclined to be seen by mortal eyes than your average leprechaun. Smaller than a boccie ball, nocturnal to a fault, the reticent wraith breeds in the grassy expanses of the north. In winter, the entire blessed population disappears into the trackless estuaries of the Gulf Coast. *Rarely* is it heard from, and almost never is it seen in between. Almost always, the finding of a Yellow Rail is a major, major effort.

Captain Dale and Captain Kim kept us awake 'til dark by recounting an endless series of anecdotes. But their jocular mood belied an underlying anxiety. Douglas Marsh—the "World Famous" Douglas Marsh, Dale insisted on calling it—was a good deal less aquatic than the name implies. As a matter of fact, it was dry. Neither Dale nor Kim had ever seen the place so parched. Neither knew whether Yellow Rail would cotton to this kind of tinder-crisp condition.

But if the group sensed any of the leader's anxiety, they didn't share it. The day had been a good one. Life Birds plentiful. The evening was warm and still and filled with the sound of Red-winged Blackbirds and LeConte's Sparrows. Besides, why worry? That's what leaders are for.

"Hold it!" Da Mail Man demanded. "Kim. Did you play the rail tape?"

"Nope," the straight man said with laconic accuracy.

"I hear a Yellow Rail," he announced, turning, cupping his hands behind his ear, straining to hear the distant sound—a sound not unlike the one that haunted Captain Hook of Peter Pan fame. Yellow Rails sound like the tap of two small stones being struck together (or the *tick, tick, tick* of a crocodile that has swallowed a clock).

Yes, there could be no doubt about it. Somewhere out on the grassy expanse, beneath a starved sickle of a moon, a Yellow Rail was calling. Quickly, Kim and Dale laid out their battle plans, putting order into our ranks. It was their professional opinion that our best option lay in moving out across the marsh in an interception line, executing a pincer movement as our host drew near, trapping the bird in a ring of birders. When the bird was surrounded, we'd close in, tighten the noose, hoping to catch the creature in the beam of Kim's portable light. It was a masterful strategy, one any field commander might have been proud of (and certainly none the worse for having been used here before).

The marsh was dry but treacherous. First one member of our troop then another went down, felled by hostile hummocks.

"OK," Dale whispered. "Let's close it up."

Slowly, one careful step at a time, the line curled at the edges, flanking the ticking bird, meeting as a circle. In its center, hidden beneath the dark mat of grass was a singing Yellow Rail.

What does a Yellow Rail think at moments like this? Is it the shaky fear of the hare or the coy glee of the fox when the clamor of distant hounds rises to a chorus? Does it say: "Oh, poop! Another pack of birders," or "Bless my soul, not Eckert and Delaney again! I guess that *must* have been FIELD

GUIDES out here last night. Huh, could have sworn the tactics stunk of VENT."

More likely they don't give it the benefit of thought. They just react by instinct the way skilled fighter pilots react in combat. For each and every military action, there is a defensive reaction. And our bird's reaction when confronted by our plainly superior force was textbook Jomani (with just a touch of Chairman Mao). In the grand spirit of self-preservation, as the troops moved in, the bird moved out.

"I guess we got a Flyer," Captain Eckert said to the cluster of disappointed faces that met, railless, in the center of the circle. The bird, now calling a hundred yards way, confirmed this supposition. Clearly, we had engaged a rail that had seen a few campaigns before.

A little more slowly, and a little more respectfully this time, we closed in on the bird again. But the last rail in Douglas Marsh had another trick up its sleeve. It made a preemptive flight before we could close ranks! Kim caught a piece of the bird in the light as it escaped through a gap in our line.

Twice more we tried containing the bird. Twice more it eluded us. We stood, catching our breaths, listening to the siren song—ticking coming from the spot we'd just left—wondering whether one quick glimpse of a bird caught in the Q-beam was all our effort would buy us.

"Hey, Dale," Captain Kim hailed, "why not try hitting the tape?"

As ideas go, it wasn't a bad one (and it sure beat thrashing around in the marsh). Dale hit the play button on the cassette, cranked the volume, challenging the heir to Douglas Marsh with an ersatz rival.

And the Yellow Rail who would not stand his ground picked up the audio gauntlet and *charged!* A vengeful, yellow missile clearly intent on taking our leader out. Dale ducked (that is, feinted to the right). Kim found the bird in his light and marked where it landed. Running, stumbling, we closed on the site—looking for a patch of color, looking for any movement in the grass.

And, very suddenly, we were looking at a Yellow Rail.

"What other tour company could bring you to a drought-stricken marsh and find this bird?" Da Mail Man demanded of his circle of happy clients.

Whatever thoughts the rail might have had it kept to itself. But before our retreat had covered half the distance to the vans, the heir to Douglas Marsh was *ticking* away, again. Inviting company, taking on all challengers.

## *JUNE 6: BRANDON, MANITOBA. DAY 4*

*Cloudy and windy.*

> *We got to sleep in this morning with an eight o'clock breakfast. Got a late start to Riding Mountain, a heavily forested area, and made it by mid-afternoon. We stopped into the visitor center for checklists and by the time we checked into our Mooswa Bungalows we only had forty-five minutes before dinner.*
>
> *—LD*

Days three and four are a critical time in the gelling of groups. It's at this point that friendships firm up, that rituals and roles become locked in habit. Before day four, there is a group filled with people whose names are an effort to recall. After day four, the same people maneuver to sit in the same van together, or prefer one leader over another.

You ever want to start a mutiny? Try initiating a rotation system in the vans four days into a birding tour.

## *JUNE 7: RIDING MOUNTAIN. DAY 5*

*Some sun; some clouds.*

> *It was cloudy and cold this morning. We left early, right after coffee, and before breakfast saw a bunch of Canadian Zone warblers—Nashville, Yellow-rumped, Black-throated Green, Blackburnian, Connecticut, Canada, and a spectacular view of a Mourning Warbler! It is so incredible*

*seeing them on territory, again. It is like a spring morning that just goes on all day!*

*Had breakfast by Whirlpool Lake in a picnic shelter. Thureya Weedon, a local guide, made a splendid breakfast for us—fruit, homemade jam, muffins, oatmeal, sausage, and coffee. It helped to cut the cold. After breakfast we birded the lake and had an excellent view of an Olive-sided Flycatcher. The white flank patches just billowed!*

*At lunch, a flock of White Pelicans flew over and a Downy Woodpecker was excavating a cavity. The big hit of the day was the Ruffed Grouse. It was so* tame!

*After dinner, Dan Weedon (Thureya's husband) met us. We saw Spruce Grouse, Black-backed Woodpecker, and A GREAT GREY OWL ON ITS NEST!!! Spectacular evening—*nice sunset.

*—LD*

The life of a professional bird-tour leader is not an easy one. Exciting, yes. Challenging, yes. Satisfying, yes . . . and no. There are tasks that bracket their days that sleeping clients never hear of: flight schedules that must be checked, arrangements with local guides that must be made, contingency plans formulated, vans cleaned, and always, always, problems that must be dealt with.

There is nothing lucrative about their business; nobody gets rich as a bird-tour leader. There is also a piper to be paid for living the vagabond life. Life on the road puts a strain on families. Many, perhaps most, leaders are single or divorced.

Leaders have apartments somewhere that they sometimes return to, if their schedules allow. There they will find bills to pay, correspondence to answer, and a packet containing airline tickets and a list of participants on their next tour—to Peru . . . Costa Rica . . . Kenya . . . or the Texas coast.

Some burn out, succumb to leader fatigue. Most stay with it, pioneers in a young industry. They stay for the excitement, the challenge, the satisfaction that comes of making people happy . . . and for the birds of Peru, Costa Rica, Kenya, and places they have never been. Yet.

## JUNE 8: RIDING MOUNTAIN TO THOMPSON. DAY 6

*Sunny but chilly* A.M.; *warm* P.M.

> *A 6:00* A.M. *start to a long, long day that included a flight to Thompson and a dinner at the Burntwood Motor Hotel at 9:30.*
> *We had coffee and muffins in the van en route to a place that Three-toed Woodpecker was supposed to be "guaranteed." Nope. Ed lost his ring and we had to search. Went to several different places but no woodpecker or Yellow-bellied Flycatcher. Bummer.*
>
> —LD

A group before it has inhaled its coffee is a fearsome thing. Leaders, maneuvering coolers and equipment into the vans, move like an unhappy couple who seek release in separate tasks. "Good mornings" are reflexive; responses automatic and unheeded. Conversation that is unavoidable is drawn right out of the minimalist coffers.

"Otto?"

"Yes, Renee?"

"Otto. Coming?"

"Yes, Renee."

It is on mornings when bodies are herded aboard van before the harshness of life has been softened by coffee that van windows fall off their tracks and are swallowed by doors. Binoculars are left back at the lodge on such mornings, rings are lost, and those special staked-out birds cannot be found.

"Guaranteed," Dale muttered to Kim at the first stop. And Kim muttered to Dale at the second stop. And both muttered to each other at the third.

"Guaranteed."

But nothing is guaranteed. Just as no morning when coffee comes late lasts forever. Soon, the aroma rising from thermoses cleanses the air and the sharp bite of brewed coffee loosens tongues that cleave to the roofs of mouths. Soon, the sun tops the spruces, disclosing warblers at the height of plumage, and lust, who fill the forests with song.

"Connecticut Warbler!" Kim chants, starting off into the trees, and the group files behind. "There," he directs. "Teed up. Thirty feet up in the large spruce in front of us. Everybody got it?"

Shouts of "Yes!" (And "No".) Much jockeying for position as a pair of Kowa scopes are brought to bear. Eager eyes fuse to the eyepieces, and faces that until this moment have been masks of displeasure crack with smiles.

"Bee-utiful."

"Wow!"

"First Life Bird today!"

"Who else but VENT could have gotten a Connecticut Warbler to sit out this way?" Da Mail Man demands.

A group in the wake of a good bird is a wonderful thing. Leaders beam and exchange happy, pregnant glances. People say "good morning" all over again (and this time they mean it). Rings that were lost become found. Windows that are broken fix themselves, and if they don't, well, what difference does it really make? It's not a long drive and . . . hey, it's only a rental.

"Otto?"

"Yes, Renee?"

"Otto? Did you get a good look at the Connecticut Warbler?"

"Did I get a good look? Renee, I had it in *Vent-o-vision!* Hey! Good work, Kim. What's next?"

Thureya's muffins, lined up and waiting beneath the cook shelter, are sweet and warm—the best you've ever tasted. The coffeepot has no bottom. And sometimes on mornings this good, even birds that are "guaranteed" may be found.

## JUNE 9: THOMPSON AND THE TRAIN. DAY 7

*Sunny, warm* A.M.*; cloudy, windy, and rainy* P.M.

> *Had a 7:00* A.M. *breakfast that was preordered in the interest of saving time. Went first to several stops along the road for Tennessee and Magnolia warblers.*
>
> *Walked a trail where a Winter Wren was doing some wonderful singing. Dale called in a pair of sapsuckers. Went to Paint Lake for Common Terns and Sandhill Cranes.*
>
> *Had lunch near Grass River. Beautiful Common Mergansers.*
>
> *The train to Churchill was an hour late getting into the station. Pete and I each had a roomette across from each other. It was a marvelous experience. We had a glass of sherry together and then I read and watched the world go by until it was dark (around 11:15). Tomorrow: Churchill!*
>
> *—LD*

There is something wonderfully seductive about sleeping berths on a train. These utilitarian chambers recall an age when leisure was taken seriously. Time wasn't something to outwit, but something to make the most of. Conversation wasn't a means to an end. It was an end in itself (or maybe just the beginning of an end).

So, from the comfortable confines of our sleepers, we savored the world, watching spring and the forest fall farther and farther behind. At first the tundra appeared as pockets that intruded into forest. But the miles whittled the taiga away and soon it was the forest that was the intruder—cold-stunted spruce brought to bay by crouching willows and withered moss that reached clear to the horizon.

By the time we got to Churchill, it was midmorning and winter, again.

## JUNE 10: CHURCHILL!!! DAY 8

*Cold A.M.; P.M. pleasant.*

>Breakfast in the dining car at 6:30. Then our group moved to the bar car and watched for birds—ptarmigan, Short-eared Owl, and caribou. In some places the water was still frozen and there were great snowbanks left.
>
>The train backed into Churchill. It was blue sky and brisk at the station. The temperature 32 degrees. Dale got our green schoolbus and we loaded all our luggage and drove to the hotel, checked in, and went birding immediately!
>
>Just past the grain elevator, Dale picked out a Sabine's Gull. Had great looks at two others sitting on the water right near shore. Such neat stuff! Eiders, Red-throated Loons, Pacific Loons, Arctic Terns. The ducks and shorebirds are all so handsome in their Arctic finery.
>
>After lunch we had an extended break, then went out with the group at 4:00 searching for the Ross's Gull. Pete finally found a bird way out there. Dale drove the bus around so that everyone got an excellent fly-by view.
>
>Headed to Cape Merry—neat place. The group seemed more enthusiastic today. Or was it just me projecting? I had a great day.
>
>—LD

There are, on all tours, those make or break birds—the ones, and sometimes just *the* one, that everyone wants to see and the success or failure of a tour hinges upon it. Ross's Gull is such a bird.

Dale and Kim wasted no time in getting us settled and getting us out. Though our tour called for five days in Churchill, Arctic weather can eat up ambitions in week-long chunks. Since it wasn't snowing, raining, or blowing a gale, they wisely elected to go for the gold immediately. They decided to head for Akudlik, home of the Ross's Gull.

The birds were in—but where? They had just recently arrived, so territories were not yet established. All we could do was stop at all the traditional locations, scan, and sift the horizon to the limits of our capacity and maybe even beyond. You couldn't go to Churchill and not see Ross's Gull.

And we didn't. We found one. *Waaaaay* out there. A pale, flickering dot so far away that when Dale peered through the scope trying to calculate the bird's whereabouts he had to allow for the curvature of the earth.

"What do you have over there?" someone wanted to know.

"Oh," Dale said, smiling, sidestepping (like a true professional), waving his arm in a gesture of dismissal. "Probably nothing. Pete had an interesting possibility *way over* on the other side of the marsh that's probably worth driving over and checking out."

A true professional. As any leader can tell you, a less than universal sighting of a key bird is far worse than no sighting at all. Not only was Dale's soft sell saving the group from disappointment, he was saving Linda and me from ostracism and maybe worse *just in case* the bird could not be found again.

We clambered aboard the bus at Kim's and Dale's urging and took our seats. If the members of the group were attentive, and maybe they were, they might have noted a certain heightened anxiety in our leaders—noticed that Dale banged a few gears during our retreat, noticed that when he and Kim conferred, their speech walked carefully around the use of any bird names (and they conferred often).

The bus careened onto the RX Road marking the western border of Akudlik, then turned again, navigating a careful path between flanking frozen lakes.

"Stop," Kim suggested.

It's not a very long word, *stop*, four letters, one syllable, but I think Dale managed to effect Kim's suggestion even before he finished speaking.

"There's a Ross's Gull out over that lake," Kim said after a moment's study.

"OK, everybodyoutofthebus," Dale instructed, "we'll set up a couple . . ." But he might just as well have been trying to put order into a bread riot at the warehouse door. There is nothing quite so uncontrollable as a bird-tour group on the verge of the bird of the trip. And in recounting their stories later, at least one of the members of the group mentioned three doors. But the truth was that our bus only came equipped with two.

## JUNE 11: CHURCHILL. DAY 9

*Fog to light overcast to sunny to cloudy; freezing to pleasant.*

> *Got up at 5:00 A.M. to shower. Breakfast at 6:45. By the time Pete climbed into the shower, the hot water was gone! FIELD GUIDES has a group here, too, so there're lots of people showering at the same time.*
>
> *On the road at 7:30. We went out to Goose Creek. Crossbills, grosbeaks, redpolls—neat spot! Went further and saw Little Gull, Tundra Swans. Lunch at 1:00.*
>
> *FIELD GUIDES found a hawk-owl in the Twin Lakes area so we went right out there after lunch. Didn't find the hawk-owl but we did find a white phase Gyrfalcon!!! What a handsome bird!*
>
> *Checklist in Otto and Renee's room.*
>
> *—LD*

We are social creatures, we birders, and our interactive lives are bound in ritual. One of them is "the checklist" ritual. Every evening of the tour, just after tummies are tight and just before eyelids droop, the troop gathers to recount the birds encountered during the day. It's a breaking of bread that lets a group savor the bounty of the day.

By couple, by clique, by individual, the members of the tour gather "in the lobby" or "in Room 101" or "on the patio." Each carries a carefully columned sheet, inscribed with a trip-tailored list of bird names. Following a period during which chairs are moved, pens and pencils borrowed, and tour participant X, the one who is always late, finally arrives, the leader calls the troop to attention. And the evening ritual begins.

"Red-throated Loon?" the leader chants. "Did anyone see or hear Red-throated today?"

Yes (or no) the assembled host responds.

"Pacific Loon?"

"Yes," the respondents affirm with a word and a nod and a notation on columned pad.

A remarkable thing happens as the names are called, as the heads bob in unison and voices meld in chorus. All the little frictions and barriers that distance one individual from another disappear—vaulted by common purpose. Everyone is a player in the checklist ritual, and everyone plays a part, and all are a part of the whole.

When the last bird is accounted for, the pencils stop flicking and faces are raised. The day has become encapsuled with consensus. A memory to savor and hold.

"Now *tomorrow* . . ." the leader explains.


## JUNE 12: CHURCHILL. DAY 10

*A.M. cool and foggy; P.M. cold, sunny to quiet and pleasant!*

> *What a day! Churchill is a great place!! Breakfast at 6:45 A.M. That was early enough for me. From there we went toward the airport to look for longspurs and Hoary Redpolls. We did see a grand Harris's Sparrow. What a handsome bird. That's it for Life Birds for me this trip. We had a wonderful view of Parasitic Jaeger and a fly-over Ross' Gull as well. Very pink underparts. Great look!!! We also went to Cape Merry again—highlight was a White-winged Scoter. The loading docks brought a close-up of a Red-throated Loon.*
>
> *Lunch at 12:30—spaghetti. Went out at 3:00 for Hoary Redpolls and Smith's Longspur. Had the most amazing look at one—a male at eight feet. Incredible! It made me weak in the knees. Had a nice char dinner. Went out to photograph afterward. I blew through seven rolls of film! Phalaropes so close I couldn't focus. Baird's Sandpipers running toward me. Least Sandpiper at six feet. Incredible. I have my fingers crossed!*
>
> *—LD*

Churchill, latitude 58 degrees, 44 minutes north, is a frontier town transported into the twentieth century. The main street is wide and unpaved. Pedestrians are few, vehicles scarce. Buildings keep a low profile. Dust is everywhere.

Bound to Canada by a single set of tracks and to the world by three months of open water, the port of Churchill served the needs of Canadian grain growers until 1988. Then the shipments stopped and the mighty grain elevators that dominate the skyline west of town ceased to dominate its economy.

More and more, tourism has come to play a key role in Churchill's commerce. In the spring, there are birding groups, and for a time the motels run full. In the fall, tourists with cameras come to the "Polar Bear Capital of the World." The motels run full, again, and whenever one of the great white bears blunders into the town, both residents and tourists run for safety.

But even without stray bears, the streets of Churchill are seldom troubled by traffic. Only eight hundred people are accounted permanent residents these days. "The lowest yet," a motel owner confided, as he stared out the window of his lodge, toward the abandoned grain elevator. Eight hundred residents with their backs to Hudson Bay and an uncertain future before them.

## JUNE 13: CHURCHILL. DAY 11

A.M.—*sunny, warm to cloudy and warm; evening sprinkles.*

> *Breakfast at 6:30. Oatmeal again. Yum. On the bus at 7:15. We headed out to the Twin Lakes area to look for hawk-owl (nope), Northern Shrike (saw two, one with something in its mouth); saw nine Pomarine Jaegers together, Bohemian Waxwings, and a Spruce Grouse displaying!!!!*
>
> *Had lunch at the Northern Studies Center, then headed back into town. Went to the end of the road to look for beluga whales but it was cloudy and choppy so hard to see. Went for an ice cream cone. Yum.*
>
> *Kim spotted a female Harlequin Duck—Ed's 499th Life Bird!! Everyone's trying to help him see 500 birds. No belugas or other new trip birds.*
>
> *Dinner at 6:30—chicken and free wine.*
>
> *—LD*

If you are on a tour and someone misplaces a lens cap, well, it's everyone's lens cap, and everyone must search for it. If a couple that is part of your tour comes locked in a bitter marriage, then a measure of that bitterness spills over into the group and their unhappiness becomes your unhappiness. If someone arrives on tour with a stinking head cold, be assured that by the time the trip is over, it's everybody's head cold.

But there is another side to the coin. Just as a group shares its burdens, it shares its joys. When someone sees their Life Willow Ptarmigan, their excitement washes over you, no matter how many Willow Ptarmigan have crossed the path of your life. And if one gracious eighty-five-year-old man has his heart set on seeing five hundred Life Birds while he and life ride in the same cart, then his quest becomes your quest, becomes everybody's quest—even to the point where it moves personal ambitions aside.

## JUNE 14: CHURCHILL. DAY 12

*Scattered clouds to sun, warm, beautiful; our last day (sad).*

> *We went out in the morning specifically for Hoary Redpoll and Gray-cheeked Thrush. Either would be a Life Bird for Ed. Dale tried to take the pressure off by insisting that we were just going birding, but we all knew better. It was a success, too! Several thrushes cooperated (more or less), so Ed got his 500th bird! He was so proud; and everyone congratulated him. Bruce saw it for a Life Bird as well.*
>
> *After lunch we went back to the docks for one last look and everyone saw beluga whales. Neat. That makes the trip complete.*
>
> *We were all reluctant to say good-bye to Churchill, although it was fun watching the plane land on the gravel runway. We were back at the Best Western in Winnipeg by 5:00.*
>
> *After dinner we adjourned to a conference room to do the checklist and say good-bye. To bed near 11:00 and a 4:00 A.M. wake-up call. Yuk.*
> —LD

All tours come to an end. Good-byes are said. Promises to keep in touch are made. Airline reservations are checked in the privacy of rooms. Lives that have been wedded to others go their separate ways—to jobs, families, and coffee tables supporting a mound of travel catalogs.

As for Dale and Kim, they might go home, too. If another tour isn't imminent; if they aren't staying on for a few days to go birding. Ultimately they will return to rarely seen apartments. To pay their bills, draft a tour summary, answer correspondence, and pick up the manila envelope containing a new list of names—and airline tickets to Peru, Costa Rica, Kenya, or maybe some exotic place that they have never been before.

## 13 • THE PAWNEE GRASSLANDS, COLORADO:

## Prairie Summer

### SONG OF THE SHORTGRASS

JUST BEYOND OGALLALA, NEBRASKA, TANGENT TO THE Colorado line, I-76 breaks away from I-80, the great east-west highway that binds New York City and San Francisco by a tarmac strand. The truckers mostly stay on 80. The vacationers mostly tack south. Some, in their overloaded minivans, may be heading for Denver, even Los Angeles. It's a free country. But in June, many, probably most, are heading for Rocky Mountain National Park and the tourist trap that is Estes Park.

For a time excitement replaces boredom in the vehicles of vacationers. Nebraska is a long state, and crossing a state line means progress, means that you are one state closer to your destination. But not much distinguishes southwestern Nebraska from northeastern Colorado. The hills are the same rolling hills, green where they are irrigated, dead and brown where they are not. The highway is the same monotonous river of asphalt. The guy towing the trailer is the same jerk who has been alternately crowding you from behind or blocking your lane since North Platte. And in the back seat, the kids are restless.

"How much farther, Daddy?"

"Not far, honey, not far."

"Daddy, that's what you said a whole hour ago!"

"I know, honey, just be patient. It's a big country."

A big country. Empty, too. By the time vacationers reach the town of Sterling, boredom and edginess can reach life-threatening proportions, and some, in desperation, reach for a map. "Anything," they conclude, "would be better than two more hours of *this*."

"How about *this* road, hon?"

"What road?"

"This one—Colorado 14. It goes west. It even looks quicker than staying on the highway. What do you think?"

"I don't know. Is it paved?"

"It's red . . . no, pink. I guess that means it's paved."

"Well, if you want to take it we can."

"I didn't say I wanted to take it! I asked *you* what *you* thought."

But there's nothing to think about, is there? The decision has already been made. *"Anything would be better than . . ."* They get off at Sterling (Elevation 3939), find C-14 in the center of town, and head west, across the high prairies, eager for the first glimpse of snow-covered peaks.

The land rolls out from either side, cut by fences, dotted at intervals by windmills that dance in the rippling heat of midafternoon. Afternoon sun has leached all the color out of the land, coating everything with a hot, silvery sheen. On the fence wires, small black-and-white birds crowd the posts for shade, and they pant.

"Daddy, is this a desert?"

"No, sweetie, it's just dry, that's all."

"But aren't deserts dry?"

"Deserts are drier, honey. We'll see real deserts when we visit Uncle Frank in Los Angeles. There are some *real* deserts. Out there."

But it *looks* like a desert. It's hot. It's dry. And it's lifeless in the afternoon sun. The wind, unopposed by anything more obstinate than a cottonwood, sends desiccating blasts of air through car windows and ushers legions of dust devils across the countryside.

Yes, the wind is a force to be reckoned with on the prairies—one of the dominant forces, right up there with heat and cold and space and sun and rain that comes too rarely. The wind whittles hills to a jagged edge, draws the Swainson's Hawk's wings down to points, and strops the thorns on plants that would rather have peace.

Wind. It frays nerves and creeps into minds, making living things edgy and nervous. Once, before television, before neighbors, when pioneers first challenged this land, the wind set upon them, hounded them day and night, eroding the support struts of their minds. Finding no release in the great sameness of the landscape, weaker minds turned in upon themselves, surrendering to madness.

"Can you imagine living out here?"

"Not me."

"It must be lonely. It's so . . . so . . . *empty*. How's our gas?"

"It's OK. We'll get some in . . . what's the name of that next town?"

"Briggsdale."

Sometimes, in the evening, after the sun has gone from white to yellow and some of the heat has left the land, the day wind may slacken for a time. That is when the curlews and plovers that have hidden in the lee and coyotes that have lain in the cool come out. That is when the sickle-winged falcons call a truce and prairie dogs sit bolt upright in their towns, watching the lines of cattle who come down to drink.

At these moments, the grasslands look gentle and rolling and stretch like some great tawny cat all the way to the far horizon. In the light breeze of evening, the prairie grass rises and falls so that the land fairly breathes, and later, when the shadows fill the low places, the nighthawks take to the sky and pipe the stars out of hiding with their reedy calls.

"Dad, does anything live out here?"

"Sure, son, lots of things."

"What kinds of things?"

"Oh, rabbits and coyotes and probably a few birds. Lots of cattle."

*The Pawnee Grasslands, Colorado*

"How about owls?"

"Owls? Probably no owls. Not enough trees. Why?"

" 'Cause I thought I saw one sitting on a fence post back there."

"Probably not an owl. Lots of cattle, though."

When the cattlemen came in 1874 and fenced the land, they had to invent a wire that cut just to keep up with the harsh tradition of the high prairie. They crowded the land with cattle brought up from Texas, and the animals ate the grass that held the land in place just as the buffalo had before—with one important difference. When the grass played out buffalo moved on to more grass. Cattle, trapped behind fences, could not. All cattle could do was stay and chew what grass there was to chew, chew it down to the nub.

By the mid-1890s, settlers, homesteaders, arrived, and they brought with them a plow with a sharp steel edge, one that could cut through prairie sod as neatly as wind through grass, laying the soil naked to the sky. In the wet years, there was water enough to support the farmers and the towns that sprang up to serve them. But then the dry years came—in 1889–1890 and again in 1893–1894. The dry years were a horror, and a warning, and many heeded the warnings and fled.

But then the rains came again, and new settlers arrived to replace those who had left. By 1930, according to those who have researched and written about the Pawnee National Grasslands, several hundred families lived in the vicinity of the grasslands, and more than half of the high plains was under cultivation.

Then, in the 1930s, drought came in earnest and the wind sought retribution. Stripped of its protecting mat of grass, the land lay at the mercy of the wind. Hot, dry gusts in excess of fifty miles per hour sucked the moisture out of the ground and chiseled the flesh off the face of the earth, leaving stony fragments and shattered dwellings behind. The wind carried the topsoil aloft, sweeping it across the country, blotting out the sun in cities on the eastern seaboard.

When the winds finally abated, the families and the land were gone.

All that was left was a shattered ecology, shattered towns, and a catchy name for newspapers to bandy about. The name was the Dust Bowl.

"The sign in the window says 'Closed for the Holiday Weekend.' "
"You're kidding!"
"That's what it says. Maybe there's another gas station in town."
"I doubt it. This place looks half blown away. We're just going to have to gamble; hope for the best."

Beginning in 1934, federal relief efforts were initiated. "Damaged" and "submarginal" farm land was purchased or traded for better land. In 1960, the purchased parcels were given an overlord—the U.S. Forest Service— and a new name. They became the Pawnee National Grasslands. Slowly, with patience and careful management, the land is healing. The policy under which they are administrated is called Multiple Use.

"Hey, kids, do you see what I see?"
"What?"
"What?"
"Up ahead. Look."
"Oh WOW! The . . ."
"Mountains, mountains. Me said it first. Me said it first."

Today, in the land around the Colorado communities of Briggsdale and Grover, much of the grass has returned, and much of the wildlife, too. Birds flourish in the grasslands. Sparrows and buntings and longspurs and meadowlarks; waterfowl and raptors and shorebirds and kingbirds. In May and June, the Pawnee Grasslands teem with birds, birds whose lives are held in the balance, caught between the wind and the grass, just as they were before the coming of fences and the plow. Their nests and their lives are allied with the earth. But their voices! The voices pay homage to the wind, take the reedy sound of it and weave it into their song.

In the evening, when the wind drops off and some of the softness creeps back into the land, the ranchers and the farmers who live in the grasslands come out to enjoy the peace of it, recalling why their parents came to this place and why it is they stay. They sit on their porches, or pause in their chores, listening to the songs of meadowlarks, the Horned Larks, and the prairie longspurs singing of the world as they know it.

A hundred miles away, in the tourist town of Estes Park, a family of four, sitting in their rented efficiency, is preparing to watch a movie on Home Box Office.

One is thinking about how close they came to getting stuck out in the middle of nowhere.

One is thinking how barren and lifeless the land looks without trees.

One is thinking that her father isn't getting the movie on fast enough, not fast enough at all!

One is thinking about a bird that was sitting on a fence post and how it really did look like an owl. If there are any owls that can live in a desert.


## *TAKING THE BIRDING ROUTE*

We turned left, out of Crow Valley Park Campground, past the Loggerhead Shrike that always seems to be there, past the trees where the Great Horned Owls had called off and on during the night, heading north on Road 77. Across from a large white gate, we turned left on dirt Road 96, rumbled across the cattle guard, and stopped. This is Murphy's Pasture, the traditional first stop when taking the Birding Tour Route through the Pawnee Grasslands.

"This road may be impassable during or after a hard rain or heavy snow," the guidebook warns. But even at its sterling finest, few would not hesitate to take their own vehicle down Road 96 (and most people would be hard-pressed to understand why anyone would bother). The road is spartan and the landscape looks as if it's been sacked, burned, and sown with salt. A shadow would starve on what Murphy's Pasture could offer it by way of sustenance.

"Looks like great habitat for plovers," Linda observed.

"It *is* great habitat for plovers," I agreed. "Plovers and Long-billed Curlew. The last time I was here, both of them were nesting here."

But that was five years ago, and then the pasture had been lush and green, primped to a verdant luster by spring rain. But this spring had been a dry one, one of a string. Life comes in cycles in the grasslands, and water turns the wheel. The rains had gone elsewhere, and seemingly so had the Mountain Plover.

We continued up the Forest Service road, two ruts studded with quartz and broken sandstone. If you've spent your life supported by blacktop, you'd probably think long and hard before attempting it. But the road is serviceable and practical; people have forged bypasses around the worst spots. Many of them are landowners, cattlemen and farmers. Though the Pawnee Grasslands encompass 775,000 acres, only 193,000 are administered by the U.S. Forest Service.

The road climbed up a long, sloping grade, past a hunting Swainson's Hawk and a pair of Western Kingbirds who had pushed their territories past the practical limit. Kingbirds are comfortable with open spaces, but they don't nest on the ground. For as far as any practical eye could see, this was the only option open to them. In fact, so poor in elevated perches was the kingbird's pasture that they were standing on cow pies—the only elevated points around.

The lack of perches might daunt Western Kingbirds, but it suits other birds just fine—prairie birds, birds whose lives are so closely bound to the earth that they seem to forget that they have wings. On this morning in late spring, the prairie was a riot of birds and song.

Meadowlarks sang verbal duels from opposite sides of the road; two portly, chevron-bibbed birds engaged in a gentlemanly game of "can you top this." It's a funny song, comical, almost careless, as if a preoccupied Pan were blowing notes down the scale—too lost in thought to realize that someone had switched the order of the pipes around.

"I love Western Meadowlarks," my western wife asserted flatly, giving voice to her regional pride.

"Me, too," I agreed, just as happy to root for the home team.

Horned Larks, furtive as field mice, skulked and bobbed through the short buffalo grass, filling the air with their thin, screechy voices. A Vesper Sparrow added its plaintive notes to the prairie medley.

The road crested the top of a long, sloping hill yielding a view that stretched for miles. To the east the prairie ran all the way to a tall escarpment whose height was reduced to insignificance by distance. To the west, nearly a hundred miles away, the snow-capped Rockies peaked above the horizon. Looking north, along the flank of the Rockies, the prairie extends up through Wyoming and Montana and into Alberta. But today, dark clouds and gray bands of rain blocked the view, cutting off things at, oh, Wyoming. Turning south, on a day like this, you can see all the way to an unbroken forever.

The shortgrass prairie is an arid grassland. The plants that make up the prairie community are low in height and welded to the earth with tough, matted roots. This is no amber-waves-of-grain landscape; no place for plants that lack fiber. Rainfall may not equal ten inches a year on the average, and in drought years less. The dominant grasses, blue gama and buffalo grass, are measured in inches. Flowers such as blazing star, locoweed, and evening primrose bring the colors of an impressionist's palette to the gray-green backdrop of the prairie canvas.

Here and there, taller midgrasses intrude and saltbush flourishes. At intervals, in the creek beds or along the crumbled foundation of a pioneer home, there is a tree. If it is over ten feet tall, it will almost certainly host a nesting raptor—probably a Swainson's Hawk. Like perches, nest trees are a valuable commodity in the tree-poor prairie, and there are not enough to go around. But grassland birds have compensated for this, too.

"Hold it," Linda cautioned. "Is that a longspur singing?"

I listened, caught the silver notes but couldn't find the bird. "Yeah, McCown's. Do you see it?"

"No, it's towering I thi . . . hold it! There it is coming down."

The plump little prairie specialty fluttered to earth; it landed a stone's throw from the van and started to strut his stuff for the female that was certainly nearby. The bird was marked like a Pawnee warrior on the warpath, a ghost-white face, with bold black slashes arcing down either side.

As we watched, the bird began another aerial display, went up like a

NASA rocket, flared its tail, set its wings, then settled to earth like a crippled kite. The bold, diagnostic black inverted T pattern on the tail put the final stamp of identity on it.

"That's wild!" Linda applauded, completely captivated by the bird's aerial acrobatics. "That is *so* great!"

"I'll bet even the Soviet judge would have given him a 9.5 on that one. I just hope he scored high with his intended."

But McCown's is the "easy" longspur. The less common longspur of the Colorado prairie is the Chestnut-collared Longspur—a real beauty, a prairie flame of smoke, ash, and fire. The face of the breeding plumage male is ocher. The collar, the field mark that gives the bird its name, blazes like a sandstone butte at sundown. But the most striking thing about the bird is its breast, black as onyx. Set against the pale prairie backdrop, a keyed-up longspur stands out like an ink spot on a wedding gown. This is how we found them.

Like other members of the longspur tribe, Chestnut-collareds are inclined to plumpness. She waddled more than walked and he waddled right beside her. But in contrast to the theatrical cut of the male longspur's jib, the female's nuptial garb leans toward the plain and practical—basic buff-gray attire embellished with patently nondescript streaks. When she paused, she became part of the prairie itself, a wallflower in grass clothing.

Clearly their relation had passed the preliminary stages. As we watched, she fluttered a short distance and he followed. Copulation might have taken all of two seconds.

"What do you think the Soviet judge would have made of that effort?" I asked.

"He would have been a lot more generous than the French judge," Linda assessed.

"Boy, that's for sure. Small wonder they're so uncommon out here."

Hormones were clearly at high peak on the prairies this morning. Bands of Lark Buntings dove into sight, nomadic birds that once followed the roving herds of bison—a habit that garnered the birds their colloquial name: Buffalo Birds. Wherever you looked, male buntings were throwing themselves aloft on rowing wings—showing off for the ladies. Their silver-dollar-sized wing patches flashed in the spring sunlight. One bird aloft would provoke a half-dozen rival males to sally forth. Each of these, in turn, seemed to incite a half-dozen more. For all anyone knew, these love chain reactions might sweep the prairies clear to Alberta. And just *one* Lark Bunting sounds like a pet shop in full chorus. Imagine what a prairie full of them sounds like.

In a land almost devoid of trees, aerial display, not perch singing, is the rule. In the race to pass your heritage on to the next generation, caution takes a back seat. What fails to gather attention fails. So, in spring, even the stealthy, ground-nesting birds of the prairie throw caution to the wind. This morning, wherever we turned, wherever our eyes fell, the prairie was in motion—a flurry of aerial courtship, dogfights between rival males, and tail chases between almost consenting adults. This is rash behavior in a corner of the world where anything that rises above the level of grass falls prey to a thousand eyes. And where there is risk, real danger is not far away.

The sand-colored falcon crested a rise, shutting down the prairies with the flip of a wing tip. One minute, the sky was filled with birds, the next, it was a vacuum. But the falcon was out for more than mere respect or homage this fine morning. It was out for breakfast. Somewhere, not far away, there were hungry young on a ledge. The falcon was playing for keeps.

From whatever perch or patch of sky the bird had come, it had marked the location of the Killdeer well. As the prairie wraith bore down on a low, wet area near a holding tank, the panicked plover lifted off, executed one futile evasive turn, and then the falcon and plover became one.

"Tough neighborhood," I observed coolly.

Linda merely nodded.

At our first major intersection we stopped to check activity around one of the windmill holding tanks, but we were distracted by something—maybe just the suggestion of something—in the pasture to the right. With its back to you, a Mountain Plover is nearly invisible on the face of the prairies. The tawny back could have been lifted from the earth itself, so well does the bird blend with the grassy backdrop. But facing you, a white-breasted bird draws all eyes. More eye-catching still on a windless morning is motion. The adult plover knew this. But her two chicks did not. This was what had caught our attention.

The adult was agitated—but not too agitated. There was half a pasture and a fence between us and her young. In the careful, stop-and-go fashion of plovers, the adult eased her brood out of harm's way. Not, of course, that we meant any harm. All we wanted to do was appreciate—maybe marvel at—creatures so wonderfully attuned to their environment.

Although classed as shorebirds, Mountain Plovers are the landlubbers of the tribe, fully at home on the dry shortgrass prairie. Lithe and long-legged, preferring to run instead of fly, they move with the grace of antelope. When they pause, pure, frozen alertness cast in feathers, the stance is regal, almost haughty.

Farther along the road, we happened upon another adult plover and her three chicks, right beside the road. Too young or too startled to run, the chicks sought protection beneath the huddled adult. But it was a male on the opposing hillside that drew our attention as we drew to a stop. Croaking loudly, white underwings flashing, the bird carried on as if he'd never even heard of Prairie Falcons. Carried on as I've never seen the reticent likes of a Mountain Plover carry on before. Was it courtship display, or diversion?

If courtship, it was spectacular. An easy 9.9 from the judges. If diversion, it rated a perfect pragmatic 10. By the time we returned our attention to the roadside adult and young, they were gone.

We were heading north now, following the route prescribed on the map, stopping at whim, stopping whenever a particularly obliging Horned Lark, meadowlark, longspur, Lark Bunting, Brewer's Sparrow, snake, skunk, butterfly, or ground squirrel posed along the road.

And we stopped often.

Cattle were being moved out on the range today, to take advantage of whatever grass there was. The nucleus of the herd was the water trough and the windmill. The mills spin in the wind, drawing water up from the earth, and life orbits around the trough. Not just the lives of cattle, either. Birds, and mammals, too, orbit around the large raised water tanks.

Every trough boasts its family of Killdeer, a plover, like the Mountain Plover, but one that has never quite been purged of its penchant for moist habitat. We even encountered waterfowl around the tanks—Mallards and pintails, nesting, improbably, amid the grass and prickly pear. But ducks will be ducks. If you want waterfowl, just add water.

One of the better ways to see birds in the grasslands is to stake out one of the water tanks in the late afternoon, after the sun has crested and started to wane but before the heat has left the earth. Birds that huddled in the shadows all day converge on the tanks to drink and bathe in the late afternoon. They line up along the rim of the tanks and crowd the runoff puddles: longspurs, Horned Larks, and Lark Buntings, shoulder to shoulder. And later, in the evening, when the long shadows cast by windmills lose themselves in the growing darkness, shy animals come down to the troughs to drink—mule deer, coyote, antelope—leaving nothing but tracks to mark their passage.

At a designated turnoff, a faint dirt track edged in prickly pear, we navigated a careful detour. In years past there had been a thriving prairie dog town here. But now the burrows were unkempt and cobweb covered. Clearly the dogs were gone—shot out or, more likely, poisoned. Prairie dogs are not popular with ranchers. They eat the same grass that cattle eat and their towns attract rattlesnakes and badgers whose excavations have pitched more than one rider from his saddle.

But prairie dogs are an important component of the prairie community. Their towns attract and sustain other animals, the most famous of which is the black-footed ferret, North America's most endangered mammal. Here, too, in the grass-clipped dog towns, is where the Burrowing Owl finds a niche. The diminutive, long-legged owls (the only North American owls that don't nest in trees) appropriate prairie dog dens and hunt from their elevated mounds.

But the dogs were gone, the burrows abandoned. So, seemingly, were the owls.

"Hold it," Linda of the western eyes announced. "I've got one."

"Where?" I demanded.

"There," she explained, pointing, trying to direct me from this patch of flowers . . . to that hillside . . . to the end of that long shadow . . . and then over to that green swath opposite the reddish patch of dirt.

"You've got to be kidding me," I said, after finally picking out the diminutive form a quarter-mile away. "Can't you find any close birds?"

Linda shrugged, a shrug that was to criticism what western eyes are to distance.

We returned to what is generously called a road and turned west again, onto what might generously be called baked mud ruts. Others who had navigated this particularly bad stretch before us had cut a fresh track, by-passing the worst spots. We followed their lead, driving past Lark Buntings.

"They remind me of fat little bats in white-tie attire," Linda mused.

. . . and a few pronghorn antelope who watched our van with quiet interest.

"Goats," Linda corrected, using the irreverent western synonym. "They've got a statue of a pronghorn in Lander," she added. "Lord only knows why."

The plains got higher, the grass got shorter, and the McCown's Long-spurs got thicker and thicker, outnumbering, finally, even the ubiquitous Horned Larks. High atop a plateau covered by wiry grass and dotted with flowers, a tiny plover suddenly leaped into the wheel track and crouched.

I guess we stopped in time. At least, after a period that could have been measured in heartbeats (had ours not stopped beating), the wheat-colored puffball treaded to the side of the road, apparently none the worse. The chick's near-apoplectic mother moved to the defense, placing herself between the van and the youngster—a distance of perhaps four feet.

The temptation was great to linger, to use the mother's concern for her young to our best photographic advantage. But the morning had long since stopped being cool. Heat was beginning to make the world shimmer and the horizon go all runny through binoculars. We took several quick shots and left.

En route to the main connecting road, we saw a subadult Golden Eagle mounting its column of air and a Ferruginous Hawk turning lazy circles in the heat-warped sky. On a hillside dusted with flowers, a lone coyote at-tending to business of its own loped a circumspect path just below the crest of the ridge, while over its head a Common Nighthawk went through courtship gyrations, trying to purge itself, one way or another, of the hormones poisoning its brain.

The wind siphoned off energy from the sun, growing hotter and stronger by the minute. It grew so hot that proud flowers forgot their prairie fiber and cowered; so hot that it stole the song right out of the panting mouths of prairie birds. It would be a good afternoon for writing in the shade, and then perhaps this evening there would be time for photography, or exploring, or a trip to Pawnee Buttes. The only thing that there was clearly not enough time for was getting your fill of the Pawnee Grasslands. There could never be enough time for that.

When Linda and I had planned our travels, we had allocated ten days for Colorado—five to be spent in the grasslands and five in the Rocky Mountains. The fact of it was that we spent nine days in the grasslands and one day in the Rocky Mountains. If this does not attest to the magic of the high prairies, I can't imagine what does.

# 14 • SOUTHEAST ARIZONA:

## Eden's Desert

*O*I DON'T KNOW WHAT MOST PEOPLE CALL TO MIND when they think of Arizona. The Grand Canyon, I guess. Sunny skies, allergy-free air, maybe a place to retire. If asked to describe the state, some might dwell on cactus, a coyote's howl, and Yippie-i-o-ky-aye; others might just see miles of flag-pocked fairways. Places to visit? "Well, Tucson and Old Tucson (the movie set), and Tombstone and . . . is it fair to say Grand Canyon, twice?"

But as I said, I don't know what most people think. I only know what birders think, and when birders recall Arizona they think of places like Sycamore Canyon ("Birding's Bataan"), Florida Wash ("Home of *the* Nightjar"), and California Gulch—a place that has chewed more oil pans off more airport rentals than any other spot in North America.

They think of the climb to Scheelite Canyon beneath the gaze of Spotted Owls. They will tell you about Cave Creek Canyon (Valley of the Trogons), and Mile-Hi, where jewels have wings. Unless you stop them (and unless you are really interested you might consider it), they will burble on and gush about the considerable charms of Guadalupe and Miller and Carr Canyons and the "Mighty" Chiricahua Mountains—an island of stone that rises out of the Sonoran desert and reaches clear to the Canadian forest! And, of course, no birder could speak of Arizona and fail to mention the "Famous

Patagonia Rest Stop"—home of the Rose-throated Becard, the Thick-billed Kingbird, and the Violet-crowned Hummingbird, birthplace of the "Patagonia Picnic Table Effect":

"If a spot holds a good bird, it will attract good birders who in turn will find other good birds, which will in turn attract other good birders, who will in turn find . . . ."

*These* are the things that birders recall about Arizona, all the stellar points on the Arizona birding circuit. It's a harsh and beautiful land filled with exotic birds, and plants, and animals, many not found anywhere else north of Mexico. It is not uncommon for birders to discover thirty and forty and fifty Life Birds on their first trip to Arizona. It is a rare birder who comes just once.

My trips to Arizona number six. Who knows? I may get up to see the Grand Canyon yet.

## THE HUMMINGBIRD BELT—SANTA RITA LODGE

The Santa Rita Lodge, forty-five minutes south of Tucson, consists of a series of kitchenettes, a gift shop, and an office—all wrapped in a mountain canyon. The establishment's epicenter was once a restaurant, and its patrons were residents of nearby Green Valley who came up to savor the cuisine. But when the restaurant burned to embers in 1983, owners Dave and Lyle Collister never bothered to rebuild it. By that time, the magic of Madera Canyon had worked its spell upon these California transplants. Nature, not epicurean ambition, had become the focus of their lives, and life at Santa Rita Lodge began orbiting around a new sun—birds.

"In the long run," Dave assesses, "it was the best thing for the canyon."

Dave Collister is solidly forty, thinning symmetrically on top and graying nicely along the flanks of a short-trimmed beard. Santa Rita Lodge is a business, a profit-making enterprise, and no bones are made about it. The land is leased from the U.S. Forest Service; the buildings belong to Dave and Lyle. The interests of both parties are in accord.

"The Forest Service's interest is protecting the habitat," Dave asserts, "and so is ours."

Santa Rita Lodge's clients—individuals and tour groups—feel the same way, and their countenance is expressed in a very tangible way. They rent rooms from the Collisters for a day or a week. Peak season at the lodge runs from March through August, which is strictly off-season in a state where summer temperatures habitually crack 110 degrees Fahrenheit. But during that period when Sunbelt motels are "crying for business," as Dave puts it, Santa Rita Lodge runs at capacity. Reservations, that other test of an establishment's popular mettle, must be made two years in advance.

What's the draw? Hummingbirds! Gems in feathers that sneer at gravity, laugh at physics, and humble the colors of the rainbow. Birds so exquisite that even people who profess to be nonbirders will stop, watch, and wonder.

Why this human fascination with hummingbirds? What is it about them that makes commercial hummingbird feeders almost as indispensable as charcoal grills to suburban living? The short answer is probably also the most accurate. *Everything!* Everything about these improbable creatures fascinates us.

Hummingbirds are tiny—diminutive unto disbelief. At four grams apiece, seven Ruby-throated Hummingbirds could be mailed anyplace in North America for the price of a single first-class postage stamp—not that hummingbirds often resort to postal transport. Fact is, hummingbirds can fly rings around the postal service's emblematic eagle, can fly forward, backward, upside down, and even hover in place. With wings that move fast enough to blur the air, the birds almost, but not quite, move too fast for human eyes to follow (and despite their size, the lilliputian light sabers can put even the blackest-hearted cat to rout).

But the hummingbird trait that draws us most to them is that when approached, the birds do not withdraw from us. Other birds fear humans—walk, run, swim, but mostly fly from us. But hummingbirds are different. Hummingbirds (we like to think) accept us for the good-natured creatures we are. Fearless or friendly, the birds will zoom in to check out the nectar potential of hair clips or power-red ties. Easily attracted to commercial feeders filled with sugar water, they take advantage of our kindness and repay us with hours of enchantment. Secretly and not so secretly, we love hummingbirds. Why, we even exploit them.

Beneath the trees, clustered in front of Santa Rita's string of kitchenettes, are a half-dozen commercial hummingbird feeders filled with clear, sweet liquid—five parts water, one part sugar. These are for public viewing, for birders who may not be staying at Santa Rita Lodge (this time) but who are birding the Arizona circuit and have come to catch the show. Motel units have private feeders. During the long Arizona summer, the feeders at Santa Rita Lodge are besieged by a thirsty squadron of Broad-billed Hummingbirds—dark green beauties of wooded canyons, specialties of the house. Other species occur in numbers that vary with the season and the rainfall—residents, like Blue-throated; migrants, like Rufous and Allen's (the Selasphorus twins), in the spring and the fall—fifteen species in all, although only five to ten species may be present at any one time.

It is a rare occasion when some itinerant birder is not perched within easy eyeshot of Santa Rita's feeders, and usually there is a crowd. The appearance of a particularly uncommon species, a (gasp) Berylline or a (sigh) Plain-capped Starthroat, may send scores of needy birders hotfooting it to Santa Rita in hopes of closing a gap in their Life List. During our visit, the feeders were being staked out by a man from Michigan searching for a reported Lucifer Hummingbird. He had been there an hour, but the bird had not.

The gentleman lingered anyway, even though his schedule was tight and he was hoping to be in Patagonia by midafternoon to catch a Violet-crowned Hummingbird coming to a private feeder there. *Even though he'd already seen everything that might be expected to be seen at Santa Rita's feeders,* he lingered.

It's possible he was still hoping for the lost Lucifer. But if I had to guess, I would say that he was merely watching the show, seduced by the mosaic of birds whose warp and woof are color and motion.

It might be argued, and some have, that Santa Rita's interest in hummingbirds is more economic than enlightened. The lodge is, after all, a business, and hummingbirds are the draw. But the cynics would be hard-pressed to explain why Santa Rita's proprietors supported a two-year hummingbird-banding project on the premises to gather information about hummingbird use in Madera Canyon—information that may affect future land-use decisions by Forest Service overlords. Many patrons complained about the banding, some because the nets discouraged hummingbirds from coming to the feeders. Others were simply intolerant of any activity that interfered with their viewing pleasure. But Dave and Lyle sided with the project and the future, accepting a measure of disgruntlement, even short-term economic loss, in the name of safeguarding the canyon.

Such is the magic of hummingbirds. They can make birders out of nonbirders. They can turn entrepreneurs into environmentalists. They can even force needy listers to give up their chase, for a time, and simply watch birds coming to the feeders (even though they may already have seen them before).

## MILE HI

Some forty air miles east-southeast of Madera Canyon and just below the town of Sierra Vista is Mile Hi preserve—midpoint on Arizona's humming-bird belt. Like Santa Rita, the place offers lodging. Like Santa Rita Lodge, the principal inducement is hummingbirds. Unlike Santa Rita Lodge, the rental proceeds and those from bookstore sales flow not into the private pockets but into the coffers of the Nature Conservancy—a singularly efficient conservation organization whose approach to land preservation is a simple one. They buy it. Mile Hi/Ramsey Canyon is one of the Conservancy's show-piece preserves: some thirty thousand people come to the viewing every year, many going away with books, T-shirts, or a Conservancy membership to accompany their memory of the myriads of hummingbirds that buzz Mile Hi's feeders.

Thirty thousand people a year is a lot of visitors in a place that can accommodate fourteen cars at a time *max*. It often happens that people who travel long distances and who come to the preserve without reservations go away disappointed. In March and April, when the winter tourist season and summer birder season overlap, the crunch at Mile Hi is on. "There are mornings when the parking lot is filled before we can brush our teeth," observes Sheri Williamson, one of the preserve's managers. "And cars are lined up down the hill waiting for space."

Parking wasn't always a problem, of course. Times were, in fact, when a fourteen-car lot was adequate to the task, back when Mile Hi was just one of the esoteric points on the Arizona birding circuit. The problems began in the mid-eighties when Mile Hi was "discovered" by some of the travel magazines and the ensuing popularity threatened to compromise the environmental ethic of the three-hundred-acre preserve.

Mile Hi, you see, is not a zoo. It's not a park. It's not a nature center. Mile Hi is a *preserve*, and the Nature Conservancy has long held to the commitment that their principal clients are the plants and animals who reside on their properties. Accommodating people comes second—and where this conflicts with the prime objective, not at all. People who write articles in travel magazines, and people who read them, sometimes fail to appreciate this.

Couldn't the Nature Conservancy simply add parking space to accommodate the crowds—to increase exposure and profits? Of course! But that would conflict with the Conservancy's prime directive. One of the best ways to protect habitat is to limit access. One of the best ways to limit access is to limit parking space. The best advice to people hoping to see hummingbirds at Mile Hi is to come early, come off- (tourist) season (June–October), or come prepared to wait. Reservations, on the weekends and holidays, are a must.

Although competition for space in the parking lot is fierce, it is *nothing* compared to the scene at Mile Hi's feeders. The scene is a melee, a free-for-all. Hummingbirds are territorial creatures whose sense of eminent domain in the flower patch carries over into feeder defense. Even when there is sugar water enough for all, feeders are defended ferociously and defenders are challenged as if life and death hung in the balance.

Black-chinned and Anna's Hummingbirds had the numerical edge when Linda and I visited in late July. But hot-tempered *Selasphorus* hummingbirds, itinerant Rufous or Allen's (the judges are still out where separation in the field is concerned), challenged their numerical superiority and usually won. The action around the feeders was fast-paced, the air filled with the hyperpitched *snitting* and *snarls* that are hummingbird war cries. One-on-one aerial duels escalated to the level of squadron combat around particularly prized feeders. For a period that in hummingbird terms measured close to a dynasty, one particularly pugnacious adult male *Selasphorus* commanded the strategic right-most feeder. Time after time, tail flared, green and red iridescence blazing, the saucy *Selasphorus* faced down challengers.

But the *Selasphorus* hasn't been born that can stay in the ring when a Blue-throated, a hummingbird that would rather fight than feed, steps in. Two sharp *seep, seep* notes heralded the arrival of the tyrant hummer. The burly Blue-throated routed the *Selasphorus* without a fight, faced back challenges from another Selasphorus, then an Anna's . . . and then calmly drank his fill.

There are lulls in the action, too, peaceful times that permit quiet contemplation and study. Binoculars trained, you can savor the trim, clean-cut lines of perching male Black-chinneds—conservative dressers in purple-trimmed blazers. Anna's are adorned with rose-colored hoods that bloom in sunlight. Male *Selasphorus* are garbed demonically—the devil in red feathers. Aptly named and outshining them all is the male Magnificent—black as onyx in moonlight, adorned with an amethyst cap and a turquoise throat. When a Magnificent arrives on the scene, it draws all eyes and lesser hummingbirds give ground.

There were no shortage of eyes in the Mile Hi gallery. The benches before the string of feeders ran full. Among the observers was a family of five from the Midwest armed with a single pair of binoculars and battered bird book. There were two retired couples from nearby Sierra Vista who seemed to know each other. Several more serious, questing birder types were parked in the Mile Hi lot but were spending their time staking out the feeders at the bed and breakfast just down the street. A family of White-eared Hummingbirds was hitting the B and B feeders—pearls of great price.

Some members of the gallery tried to identify the several species, linking the adult male birds at the feeders to their pictorial likenesses displayed on the panel before them. Female and immature hummingbirds are a whole 'nuther story—they're a shoulder-shrug exercise to most and an identification challenge to the best. But most of those enjoying the show at Mile Hi seemed content just to watch, to let the birds simply weave a web of fascination around them . . . before schedules, or hunger, or antsy children broke the spell.

All, when they left, made the obligatory stop at the gift shop. Some to buy post cards. Some to purchase T-shirts. Some to take out a Conservancy membership. Chances were, none would be going on to Walter and Sally's, last stop on the Hummingbird Belt.

## WALTER AND SALLY'S

Just outside of town, the road bends toward the peaks. But the peaks and their birds are for another day. The drive you want is circumspect, just a rutted break in the mesquite. It's not far and not particularly well marked, and you'll be lucky to recognize it on your first pass. Even if you do nose your car down the dusty incline you'll lack certainty.

The drive bears right, but the house you want is on the left, a ranch house framed by a wooden gate with a placard swinging from the crossbar. Aguila-Rancho, it reads. Another sign, stapled to the left-most gatepost, offers additional assurance. "Birders Welcome," it says. Just park in front of the sign. Walk around back. Take any unoccupied chair. Feel free to move it to a spot that offers more shade or a better view of the feeders. Everyone does.

Don't knock; don't announce yourself! There is no need to ask anyone's leave. Walter and Sally are busy people and over three thousand birders a year take advantage of their hospitality. Even a well-meaning interruption is still an interruption—something that shatters a train of thought or stalls a task that needs doing. If you have a mind to, you can pen your gratitude in the guest book out back. Most folks do, and Walter and Sally appreciate it.

Don't look to *this* book for more directions to Walter and Sally's than erudition has offered. If you are a birder, directions to Walter and Sally's place are easy enough to come by. If you are not a birder, you have no reason to go there. I am not about to compromise their courtesy (or my welcome) by extending their invitation to people I cannot vouch for—nonbirders. But if you *are* a birder, and if you arrive between eight and five, you are welcome to take a chair, sign the guest register, and enjoy the show. Hummingbirds abound at Walter and Sally's too, the last and maybe the brightest point on Arizona's Hummingbird Belt.

We navigated the short walk, past the masonry jars filled with sugar water favored by Scott's and Hooded Orioles; past the house harpy, a semi-domestic roadrunner whose diet reputedly includes hummingbirds. We took our seats among the gathering: a middle-aged woman with close-cut hair; a young couple from California; a neighbor armed with a pair of vintage Bausch and Lombs showing lots of metal; a young, intense man of college age, and, not surprisingly, the gentleman at Santa Rita Lodge who was still on the hunt for Lucifer Hummingbird. What goes around on the circuit comes around. There were nods of greeting and no need for words. To be here is to be welcome here.

There are several things that distinguish Walter and Sally's place from Mile Hi and Santa Rita Lodge. For one, their ranch lies at the mouth of a mountain canyon, closer to the open desert than the wooded peaks. The species of hummingbirds that frequent the respective feeders differ some-what. Broad-billed Hummingbirds are rare, usually absent here; but Costa's, a petite prince with a mutton-chop gorget, is regular. Lucifer Hummingbird, a rare, sickle-billed beauty, is annual—a specialty of the house.

The lighting is different, too. At Mile Hi and at Santa Rita, canyon trees cast the feeders in shadows and the iridescent raiment of the hummingbirds is muted. But at Walter and Sally's, sunlight reigns much of the day and the hummingbirds glitter like broken glass in sunlight.

The key distinction between Walter and Sally's and the other two points does not relate to place, but to people and to motives. Hummingbirds are found at Santa Rita Lodge, at Mile Hi, and here. Visitors are welcome at all three. At one, the motive is profit (and there is nothing wrong with this). At another the motive is revenue. There is nothing wrong with this, either. But at one, and only one, the motive is friendship and shared interest, the coins of tribute in birding's realm. They buy you passage into the ranks of birders. They buy your entry into Walter and Sally's backyard, sight unseen; no reservations necessary. *That*, to my way of thinking, is very special.

Walter and Sally's open-door policy is a holdover from their New York State days, when their yard was the birding retreat for a host of friends. When they moved to Arizona in 1972, the policy came with them. They hoped that some of their old acquaintances might take advantage of their Arizona sanctuary—not that it seemed very likely. New York, after all, was a long way away. As it turned out, they needn't have worried. Their old friends did come, and a host of new ones, too—from all across the country and around the world. Seven days a week (for as long as the hummingbirds last).

"Are birders ever a bother?" I once asked.

Walter didn't respond and Sally's answer wasn't immediate. Maybe she was torn between a gracious denial and an honest affirmation. Honesty won out.

"Oh, sometimes," she admitted. "We finally had to post hours."

"Why do you go to so much trouble?" I asked. "It takes a lot of time and energy to keep feeders filled, doesn't it?"

This time the answer came right away. "Because we love feeding birds ourselves and we'd just be doing it anyway. Why not let others enjoy the birds, too?"

Yes, why not? And we did enjoy them, Linda and I, just two more grateful birders among many. The feeders were crowded and the action frenzied. Black-chinneds dominated, but *Selasphorus* were numerous, and, of course, wherever these hot-tempered tyrants are found, peace seeks shelter. Rounding out the ranks were a few Broad-taileds, several Blue-throateds, one or two Magnificents and . . .

"Lucifer, LuciLUCIFER, LUCIFERSifer!" the entire assembly chanted in something under half a second. Maybe at Mile Hi the gallery is content to merely watch and wonder. But little that flies fails to find a name in the crowd at Walter and Sally's. As if it were aware of its esteemed singularity, the Lucifer Hummingbird fed leisurely, then took a perch, turning its head from side to side, letting sunlight explode upon its rakish, handlebar gorget. It was a beautiful look at a priceless gem of a bird, all bought and paid for at a rate well within the reach of even the most frugal budget. Friendship and shared interest. The coins of tribute in birding's realm.


## SYCAMORE

"Let's hold up for a bit," Linda suggested, sliding out of her pack, finding and opening a water bottle. Her T-shirt, where the pack had covered it, was plastered to her back, wet with sweat. Mine, too. We drank lots of water, because we had plenty and because the best place to store water is inside you.

Linda taught me that. When she was a National Outdoor Leadership School instructor, she taught courses in desert hiking; her intimacy with the desert is complete. She understands, well, the stresses that heat and dehydration place upon living things, and she knows what precautions must be taken to wed deserts and people together. When you are lucky enough to have such a person in your company, you are best advised to listen.

We were better than halfway down the canyon, not far from where we might start running into Five-striped Sparrow, so we decided to celebrate with a couple of PBJ sandwiches. Enjoy the cool beneath the trees, while it lasted. Enjoy the canyon that has come to be one of our favorite places.

Sycamore Canyon is a narrow gorge, 9.4 miles beyond Pena Blanca Lake, maybe 15 miles from the border town of Nogales. Part of the canyon falls in the United States, part lies in Mexico. The vegetation clustered along its rocky corridor is a natural gateway for southern species with northern ambitions. From Hank and Yank Spring, homestead of two army mule skinners who tried to make a go of it hereabouts a century ago (but came up short), it is six miles to the border. A wire fence marks the spot.

Few ever hike as far as the fence. For all of its avian wealth, for all its dark fame, Sycamore Canyon is not heavily trafficked. Chances were we'd walk the canyon and back and never see another soul. Casual birders avoid the place. Needy listers fear it, and many recall their infrequent venture(s) as nothing short of a descent into hell—not, I might add, without basis.

Fact is, there is no trail down Sycamore. There are subtle tracks that shy desert creatures lay down in the night, and this is as good as saying no trail at all. There are times when progress is measured in handholds, where forward means up and over and down—through tangled thickets studded with Spanish bayonet; over rocks with the physical properties of ball bearings and hearts of stone. But the thing that Sycamore veterans recall most is the heat—the incredible, unspeakable heat of an Arizona summer that drains canteens by midmorning and makes canyon walls dance by noon.

No, Sycamore Canyon is not a place to be casual or careless, and penance is paid in broken limbs, dislocated joints, and heat stroke. But if a "good" bird, a Life Bird, is standing on the gates of hell itself, then that's where birders must go to claim it. That was the pole that turned birding's compass during the last half of this century. Birding as chase. Birding as sport. Birding with no holds barred. It was a wonderful time, this episode in birding's history. A glorious time. A time of questing and testing and pushing the limits of the world filled with undiscovered wealth. It was birding's golden age.

Once, birders had been like children, waving empty hands at brightly colored forms, smiling at a world full of sound. Then we grew up. Grew skilled. Grew impatient for more—more skill, more places, more birds, more information, and more and more. We birded right through the sixties, the decade the ABA was born, the decade we shed the old label "bird-watcher." We chased clear through the seventies and reached for the world's horizons all through the eighties.

No island was too far for us, not even Attu. No river was too wide (well, except maybe the Rio Grande). No seawall was too cold and no canyon was too hot and no airport rental line too long to stop a real birder. Not a *real* birder. Sycamore Canyon was one of those places that held out its special prizes, and North America's questing birders reached to claim them—emerging later with tales of conquest, tales of loss, and tales of the beastly horror of Sycamore Canyon—the place they nicknamed "Birding's Bataan."

Few, if any, ever mentioned the canyon's beauty, which is considerable.

A trogon began to croak nearby, and another picked up the chant and carried it up the canyon. Somewhere on the hillside above, a Varied Bunting was singing in the face of a sun that was already heating the west wall of the canyon. But here, on the sycamore shrouded bottom, it was cool.

"Isn't this the spot where the Fan-tailed Warbler was seen?" Linda asked, breaking the quiet, studying the streambed and surrounding trees.

"Somewhere around here," I agreed, looking around, chewing thoughtfully, trying to juxtapose the memory and this place. "Yeah, I think it is."

The year was 1987, the year Linda and I were married, and the year a Fan-tailed Warbler was discovered in Sycamore Canyon—found by two young birders, Troy Corman and Dave Kreuper. The Mexican prize triggered a crusade among those errant knights who needed the bird on their North American lists—a not inconsequential number. Of the first three Fan-tailed records (all of them in Arizona), one was collected and the other two could never be relocated. The Sycamore Canyon bird stuck.

Between June 7 and July 4, scores of needy listers made the trek down Sycamore. Some found the bird, some did not. But here is where the story gets strange. Bidden by some strange compulsion, the birders chronicled their success, and failure, on a stick planted in the streambed to mark the bird's location. It became customary among those who found the bird to decorate the totem with a personal item. Some left hats, others bandannas. By the time Linda and I arrived, the totem looked like a mannequin in a haberdashery.

Also attached to the totem was an oaktag specimen label offering instructions and advice relating to the bird. The last entry on the card, scribed two weeks before Linda and I arrived, read: "What Fan-tailed Warbler?"

I have had several years to ponder that curious totem stuck in the middle of a desert canyon, far from the eyes of any that might not care and many who would. For reasons I do not clearly understand myself, it has come to symbolize, for me, all that was of birding's golden age—all of its fun, all of its challenge, and all of its incredible innocence.

Maybe it is because the thought of grim, set-jawed birders marching down some hellish desert canyon in search of one proffered prize is so classic.

Maybe it was the totem that piqued my fancy, a banner planted at birding's high-water mark, a cross between "I claim this bird in the name of North American birding" and "Kilroy was here."

But I think that the bird and its totem hold such poignancy because they are linked in my mind with another event—one that occurred a few short weeks before the warbler was found. On April 19, 1987, the last free-flying California Condor on earth was pulled from the sky, part of a desperate effort to save the species from extinction. The news was like a razor cut, the kind that is deep and almost painless. You stare at it at first and wonder how a wound like that can be so blood-free. So you go back about your business as if nothing had happened. The next time you look, you wonder how so much blood could ever flow from one small cut.

"I guess the flag washed away," I said, for no reason except to state the obvious.

A White-winged Dove crooned a lament. A trogon croaked a warning. Moments later, sunlight swept the canyon floor, and even the canyon walls seemed to recoil from its touch.

"We better get going if we want to get down near the border while things are still singing," Linda said.

We hoisted packs and continued down the canyon, keeping to the shadows whenever we could. We didn't rush. It's not a smart thing to do in the desert. We didn't miss the sparrow, either. There were several, and well worth the hike.

One thing we didn't find was the totem, and I looked for it too, hoping to spot it along the bank or caught in the cradle of some sycamore. But it was gone. Like the bird. Like the errant birders. Like the last free-flying condors.

It would have made a terrific souvenir—a token of birding's golden age. Who knows. Maybe someday they'll organize a crusade and birders with pure hearts can search for it—if any need an excuse to return once more to Sycamore Canyon. The place they call "Birding's Bataan," home of the Five-striped Sparrow. Where a flag was once planted in the sand.

# 15 • MONTEREY, CALIFORNIA:

## Shearwater Journeys

"OK," A VOICE COMMANDED, "IF EVERYONE WILL GATHER around we can get started." It was a voice that was accustomed to giving orders, one that could belt out arias and shout down a diesel engine running full throttle. In a rustle of Gortex, the crowd assembled around the tall, Teutonic figure standing in the boat's stern, waiting further instructions.

During the interval, birding's Brunnhilde took the measure of her group, smiling at some, trading greetings with others. We, for our part, took hers —blonde, big-boned, smiling widely; hair lashed into utilitarian braids; eyes set wide against an attractive face that blended the greens, golds, and browns of the California coast. In her hand she carried a clipboard. Emblazoned in three-inch Orlon letters across her chest was the legend: SHEARWATER.

"I'm Debi Shearwater," she announced, for the benefit of those who could not read and the fewer who did not know. "This is what you can expect and this is what I expect from you."

With this promise, Debra Love Shearwater launched into her patented spiel—a dockside discourse that covered everything from putting on a life vest to the perils of plastic to puking with aplomb (but more on this subject, later). Many on board listened out of politeness, and a dozen could have recited Debi's lines for her. Pelagic birding has a cult quality, and Debi's litany on the bow, spoken forty-five times a year, goes off with the seductive sameness of *Rocky Horror*.

But there were many among the fifty-member assembly who listened *very* attentively. Standing on the deck of the *Star of Monterey* were birders who had never, ever, ventured offshore in search of birds before. If any of their landlocked misconceptions had survived all the way to the dock, what Debi was telling them now offered assurance that landlocked birding and pelagic birding are two very different kinds of birding.

There are, for example, no trees offshore. No bushes. No thickets. No vegetation for birds to disappear into. Yet pelagic birds—shearwaters, petrels, jaegers, albatross, and assorted alcids—are real professionals at disappearing into troughs, quartering into the sun, and placing the superstructure of boats between themselves and the eyes of hopeful admirers.

No vegetation also means, to a greater or lesser degree, no reference points. No pelagic birder has ever been directed to the whereabouts of a Sooty Shearwater with the words: "It's in the black oak." Why? Because over three-fifths of the earth's surface, there are no black oaks (or hemlocks or elms or baobabs), just water and horizon.

"Use the hour-hand-on-the-clock method to point out birds," Debi tutored. The bow (pointy end of most boats) is twelve o'clock; the stern (the other end) is six o'clock. All the other numbers fall (regular as clockwork) in between. So . . . a bird at one o'clock is slightly right of center. A bird at nine o'clock is 270 degrees from the bow. Simple, no? But for the digitally minded, Debi also offered a fallback procedure.

"Just point and shout," she suggests.

Steep-water birding has another problem not commonly encountered on land. Where land offers a more or less stable platform from which to watch birds, oceans do not. In fact, oceans are most unstable. Sometimes this instability comes in the form of waves, sometimes swells, sometimes tides and currents and commonly, all at once. Ships, which are only imperfectly bonded to their aquatic substrate anyway, absorb a measure of the ocean's energy, and this does two things. One, it makes standing up (never mind finding birds) very challenging. Two, it makes people so sick that they think they must surely die.

But as I said, this is a subject that will be taken up in greater detail later.

Her litany completed, Debi headed for the cockpit to confer with the skipper and lay down a game plan. Whether it was because of something she picked up from the captain or because of some sixth sense, Debi was in high spirits when she joined Linda and me on the bow.

"I feel good karma about today," she confided. "Real good."

But if karma is the source of her demeanor, then Debi Shearwater taps the mother lode. Few can match even her standard geniality, and I don't recall ever having seen her when her karma wasn't in top form.

A Pennsylvanian by birth, dental hygienist by trade, Debi started birding in Texas under the tutelage of "guru" Ed Kutac before moving to California with her army husband. When he left, she stayed. Debi had discovered something very special—something wonderful in fact.

The sea waters around Monterey are a cosmos of marine life. Some accident of underwater geography and tides placed one of the earth's richest seabeds right at the doorstep of one of California's most charming harbors. It was this undersea cornucopia that supported the canneries immortalized by a local Nobel Prize-winning writer named John Steinbeck. It was the scientific delight of Steinbeck's character Doc, the genially parasitized owner of Western Biological Laboratories, who figured prominently in *Cannery Row* and *Sweet Thursday*; he was, in real life, Ed Ricketts, Steinbeck's biologist friend.

Monterey's near-shore waters also support a year-round host of birds and mammals—gulls, pelicans, cormorants, auklets, sea otters, sea lions. But between August and December, the number of resident birds and mammals are augmented by creatures that use Monterey as a stopover point during their nomadic lives. Creatures like the blue whales, whose Pacific population is estimated at 1,500. Creatures like Sooty Shearwater, whose Pacific population exceeds 3,000,000.

In 1976, Debi started organizing offshore birding trips for her local Audubon chapter. By 1978, she was offering the wonders of California sea birding to the world.

"Ever organize anything before?" I inquired, playing a hunch.

"You name it," Debi said, offering us a wedge of pastry from her private stock.

Yes, this too is apparent about Debi—she is a born organizer. One of those accursed, gifted people who can walk into any manifestation of chaos, see an immediate solution, and plot a course through obstacles with the ease most people only discover in afterthoughts.

"She's a marvel," one of her many admirers summarized.

The *Star of Monterey*, a fifty-six-foot head boat, nosed out of the harbor past the old cannery and anchored pleasure yachts; past hillsides crowded with houses and docks burdened by chic—more houses and chic than Steinbeck and Ricketts ever knew. Pelagic birders jockeyed for position at the rail.

Some points at the rail are not as strategic as others, and rival factions argue tirelessly about their merits. Many veterans swear by the bow, where birds kicked up from the surface are most likely to be seen first and well. Others swear *at* the bow because birds are not the only thing kicked aloft. In even moderately rough seas, the bow is also the wettest place on a head boat—undermining both comfort and optical performance.

A rival school lauds the merits of the stern, where the "chum" is ladled out. Stern-firsters argue that you can get more birds with chum than by blundering luck—and there is truth to this. The problem with the stern is that it places birders right in the backwash of the boat's diesel exhaust. It also places pelagic birders in close proximity to "chum," which might generously be described as cold, smelly fish, but more accurately as a gastronomic nightmare held in oily suspension. Sterns (and bows) are also the most unstable points on a boat, and if a birder is feeling even a wee bit queasy, the shortest distance to a séance at the rail is usually by way of the stern. One good whiff of diesel fumes and a glance at the chum bucket is generally all it takes to . . .

But later. OK?

Many pelagic birders finally settle on spots along the port and starboard side rails—for the stability, and for the absence of diesel fumes and (depending upon the wind) spray. Debi never has fewer than two or three coleaders on board, so no matter where preference or fortune find you, birders unfamiliar with pelagic species are rarely far from expert assistance.

Many on board were tapping the experts for help even before the boat cleared the breakwater. For first-time pelagic birders in Monterey, strange new birds were a 360-degree matter of fact. Colorful Heermann's and dark-backed Western Gulls followed in the wake, eyeing the vast amounts of food being crammed into birders' mouths—doughnuts, granola bars, oranges, crackers, cookies, cupcakes, pretzels . . . all the standard antimotion additives. One of the fundamental tenets of pelagic birding is *eat*. A full stomach keeps a gut in place. An empty gut is a loose gut and a loose gut picks up the motion of the sea. For most people, staying comfortable is usually just a matter of staying full. And, if worse comes to worst, a belly full of ballast sure beats a bout of dry heaves.

Black Turnstones and blue-eyed Brand's Cormorant stood at attention as our boat passed a breakwater that looked to be about 60 percent sea lions. Pigeon Guillemot, Common Murres, and "Rino" (Rhinoceros) Auklets swam or dove to safety. A sea otter, in dorsal recline, dined leisurely upon the claw of a fresh-caught crab. The former owner of the claw faced the otter across a furry belly, menacing the usurper with its one remaining claw.

Outside the harbor, half of our feathered entourage fell behind. With few exceptions, gulls are not true sea birds; the term "sea gull" is a misnomer. Gulls cannot process seawater, so the orbit of their lives cannot swing far from the coast. But many other species of birds, *pelagic* species, do have this marvelous adaptation, permitting them an unencumbered life at sea. The seawater they ingest is filtered by special glands, and excess salt is excreted through tubes seated atop their bills. These are the "tubenoses." These were our special quarry.

The sea was slick and glassy, gray and opaque. A low cloud cover nudged the tops of the hills receding in our wake. Perfect conditions for pelagic birding. Debi dropped into the cockpit and returned girded for battle. Around her neck, a salt-scarred pair of 10x40 Zeiss; shading her eyes, a *Bird Watcher's Digest* baseball cap.

"We're heading for a feeding flock," she confided. "The captain has them on radar." There are close to *one million* Sooty Shearwaters operating in Greater Monterey waters every August. Our basic battle plan was to head offshore and scour the south rim of the canyon, then return via the north canyon. But we'd hardly left the canyon before our plan was bushwhacked by fortune, and Debi's voice brought the *Star of Monterey* to a screeching halt.

"mmmMIN-KEEE WHALE!!!" she screamed and if volume were speed Debi's cry would have registered Mach 5. Debi *loves* whales, and this one must have been an old confederate. The little leviathan let us pass so close you could hear the blow.

Soon, small, dark shearwaters began to appear, spawned by shadowy troughs and the mystic horizon. Ones and twos . . . then small pods, then scores, closing on the boat in a gentle frenzy. But these were mere vassals, outlying scouts.

"Look out there," Debi directed with a sweep of an arm that covered most of the horizon. We brought our binoculars up, and if my collarbone hadn't gotten in the way, there is no telling where my jaw might have stopped. "Out there" was awash with a swirling dark mass of birds as far as eyes could see and much farther than human minds could contemplate. Many were in the air, most were sitting on the water—dark mats of birds waiting for a wind to stir them to motion.

Our boat nudged a path through the seabound flocks, putting those in harm's way to indignant flight. Legs flailing, wings laboring, the birds scrambled for safety, but once aloft they were creatures transformed— from buffoons to ballerinas. Silent as a deaf man's dreams, effortless as smoke on a still, cool morning, the dark birds with the silver wing linings swept across the water in shadowy sheets, cutting gossamer-fine lines with their wing tips whenever they banked or turned—*shearing the water!*

Shearwaters and many other true seabirds are masters of what is called "dynamic flight." Some birds, like songbirds, muscle their way through the air on rowing wings. Others, like birds of prey, tap the energy of the sun and ride thermals aloft. But the long wings of seabirds are able to tease lift out of the wind itself, climbing the gradient between air slowed by friction near the ocean surface and faster-moving air above. Wind holds them aloft; gravity pulls them down, and, by cleverly playing one natural force against the other, seabirds can maintain an effortless glide for hours on end. But

even if you fail to grasp the principle of it, few fail to appreciate the wonder of it.

Our boat began to collect a host of feathered satellites, drawn to the Judas gulls in our wake and anchovies tossed over the side by a generous hand. Fifty pairs of binoculars picked through the mocha-colored mass, searching for anything different (while at the same time dipping more or less constantly into their food stocks for morsel support).

"Pink-footed!" "Pink-footed!" several near-simultaneous voices chanted. Debi's shriekers were hot today. Half-eaten sandwiches flew. Crackers were stuffed hastily into mouths as those individuals on the wrong side of the boat hurried to make amends. The boat listed precariously, but stabilized just above the gunnels.

Some caught a glimpse of the pale, gangly shearwater with the loose, floppy flight. Others did not. There would be more, and there wasn't time to dwell on past misfortune, because Debi's basic tenor burst clear through the soprano scale as she screamed: "SABINE'S GULL! thREeEeEe O'CLOCK!

Then 2:00 . . . then 1:00.

Sabine's Gull is a good bird off Monterey, and its fall migration passes through a narrow window of opportunity—now! Sabine's Gulls are also not particularly responsive to chum. Odds were that this bird would be the trip's one and only Sabine's, and this faced many with a moral dilemma. Did they see the bird well enough to *really* say they saw it?

"I saw a piece of it," one patron, seeking assurance from another, noted.

"Well, I saw it pretty good. Good enough to count."

"Well, I only saw a piece of it. I hope we get another."

But there wasn't time to engage in lengthy soul-searching. Not in a place with so many birds. Not when the karma is running at flood tide. Because where there are great concentrations of birds, there are almost certainly great concentrations of food. And where there is a surfeit of food in these waters, there is also very likely to be . . .

"BLUUUUE WHALE," Debi wailed with enough volume to wrap the name around the deck with stereophonic force. "BLUE WHALE . . . BLUE WHALE . . . BLUE WHALE."

---

The steel-colored body seemed to take an eternity to move its seventy-foot length beneath the surface. There proved to be not one but *five* whales feeding in association with Dall's porpoise. Motioning us into the cabin, the captain pointed to the printed readout sheet of his depth finder. The sounding line, which had been etching along on a more or less even keel at about three hundred feet below the surface, had suddenly plunged for the floor. This was the rim of the canyon. This was where the whales were feeding.

In 1987, Debi kept track of the blue whales she found in Monterey. There were 303 sightings of what were believed to be about one hundred animals. An impressive number of sightings.

When the last leviathan sounded, when the tiny dorsal fin slipped beneath the surface, the animal lifted its tail, "showing flukes," to the accompaniment of squeals, gasps, and assorted exclamations. Only the roiling, round "footprint" showed where the great creature had been, and, when the boat passed over the spot, the great exhaled breath of creation's greatest life form washed over us. What does a whale's breath smell like? It is warm and wet and briny, and not far from wholesome.

You can't make a mistake hanging around with whales. Hell, even East Coast pelagic birders know that whales are good karma. And when things are going right, there's no stopping them. This pelagic trip was shaping up to be a tom-wallager (as Steinbeck might have phrased it), and nobody was particularly surprised when Debi yodeled "SABeeeeens GULLS." Not one but three immature birds showed up to ease the consciences of those birders who had consciences.

Everyone celebrated by breaking into the specialty items that they packed. A tour group on board even raided their cache of dessert, and it was only 9:00 A.M.! In fact, out of the entire assemblage, there was only one person on board who wasn't pleased and that was Debi, who appeared back on deck clutching a muffin appropriated from the tour's stock (leader's prerogative). "What are we going to do for the rest of the day?" she muttered. The excursion wasn't even close to midpoint, and we'd already seen most of our target species.

Our boat had overshot the hosts of shearwaters and was entering the "DZ"—the "Dead Zone"—a stretch of ocean lying between the north and

south rim of the Monterey submarine canyon that is almost devoid of bird life. Just as on land bird numbers know shortage and plenty, and just as on land distribution is governed according to principles bound by cause and effect.

From above, oceans appear trackless, but when you peer beneath the surface this impression changes. The ocean floor off Monterey is lined with canyons that form a sort of subsurface highway system. The canyons are the key. They are the source of the great upwellings of life, the phytoplankton that form the base of the ocean food chain. Upon these canyons the great pyramids of life form. The birds are just the visible tip, reaching above the surface.

The locations of the canyons are locked into the guidance system of the ship's Loran (not to mention the experienced eyes of Debi and the captain). Sonar tells the captain exactly when the ship passes over the lip of a canyon. But if things are right, the sonar shouldn't be necessary. The concentrations of birds should pinpoint the location without resort to electronic wizardry.

But between the canyons lie the DZs—those unproductive stretches of ocean where sea life all but disappears. It's a place to catch up on your munching or your sleep. As often as not, the DZ is the place where brilliantly waged campaigns against the forces of *mal de mer* are lost. Because without the distraction of birds, many birders suddenly discover that their tummies are feeling a little uneasy. And uneasy becomes queasy. Queasy becomes ill. Ill becomes sick. And then it is time to bolt and boot.

"In the back of the boat," Debi urges. "Not in the toilet. Not in the waste basket. Head for the rail in the back of the boat. It makes good chum and that's where it will do the most good," she offers as an explanatory afterthought.

Seasickness all comes down to a complicated and not terribly well thought-out balancing mechanism called the inner ear. Without a shred of supporting evidence, I believe that inner ears were eleventh-hour modifications installed in the human unit just before the model was released. It was faulty and we're still waiting for the recall. (Knees fall into this category, too.) It seems that when the circuitry connecting the inner ear to the brain was laid down, they ran the line down right alongside another wire that connects the brain to the stomach. When the inner ear is forced to work overtime, as it does when a ship is rocking back and forth, the volume of impulses running to the brain are so great that they jump the insulation and spark the line running to the stomach too.

Then you throw up.

I love pelagic birding and Linda is cool to it. One of us gets seasick; one of us does not. Can you guess who is who? Bet you can.

Yes, there are remedies. Yes, there are over-the-counter and prescription drugs: Marazine and Dramamine and, recently, Scopolamine patches to slap strategically behind offending ears. Yes, there are all kinds of precautions to take. Get enough sleep the night before a trip. Don't drink alcohol. Don't weigh your gut down with a big greasy breakfast before boarding. Eat lots of bland food during the day.

When you begin to feel queasy, there are emergency stopgap measures. Stuff your face. Get up on deck. Fix your eyes on the horizon. And don't, under any circumstances, look at anyone who is spooning pickled herring into their mouths, or eating cold pepperoni pizza, or engaging in a Technicolor yawn at the stern.

The long and short of it is, there are lots of things that can done in defense against *mal de mer*. All of these remedies and precautions work— up to a point; better for some than others; better at times than other times —and *this* is a slimy bit of treachery. Because *after* you think that you've got the seasickness problem licked, *after* you've been lulled into a false sense of security by a solution that "works" for you, *after* (God help you) you've signed onto a two-day winter pelagic trip heading one hundred miles offshore, *that* is precisely when your "solution" is shown to be a sham.

There are three stages of seasickness, and I quote them from scripture. First, you are afraid that you are going to be sick. Then, you are afraid that you are going to die. Then, you are afraid that you are going to live. And if you are sick, in rough seas, one hundred miles from land, that is a long, long time to live.

No . . . no. I will not indulge myself and tell war stories about some of the more horrible pelagic trips I've been on. Winter trips in wind-whipped seas where birders were so sick that they rolled around in their own gastric

juices until the movement of the ship eclipsed all notions of proprietary boundaries. Trips where dear, close friends pleaded with me to end their lives.

No, when I think of seasickness, I prefer to recall the fortitude and defiance shown by such brave pelagic birders as Brian Moscatello, who cannot draw a glass of water from the tap without getting queasy, yet continues to pay his forty dollars for a spot at the stern. I think of the brave young lad (whose name I never learned and whose pallor was about the color of a scotch pine) who managed, somehow, to muster enough strength to crawl to the rail each and every time a Life Bird hit the chum slick.

I think of Joe Burgiel, who has conditioned himself so completely to feeling wretched aboard ship that he can carry on a perfectly lucid conversation, excuse himself, turn to the rail, barf, wipe his mouth, and pick up his sentence where he left off.

"I think I'm going to go stand near the stern," Linda said, standing.

"LOOOONG-TAILED JAAAAEGER," Debi (saved by the bell) Shearwater shouted to the assembly. "LONG-TAILED JAEGER." So much for the Dead Zone.

The bird crossed the stern, moving fast, never slowing. Taken by surprise, some on the boat got good looks; many did not. But the next bird coming in on the same flight path encountered a fully alerted vessel and a near lethal cannonade of chum. The bird circled . . . went wide . . . returned . . . fell away again, then came in once more, passing right overhead—long tail fluttering, yellow cheek glowing, cold black eye gleaming. There is no seasick remedy quite so effective as the appearance of a good bird.

Debi Shearwater worked her way up from the stern with a face flushed with victory and hands gory with chum.

"Want a sandwich?" she asked. "I made extras."

We hit a patch of drift kelp piled up where two currents collided. A tidy swarm of Arctic Terns and *more* Sabine's Gulls rested atop the floating bed of salad. Karma. A bull-bitch tom-wallager cut of karma, and that's just the plain truth of it. There wasn't even time for a letdown, wasn't even time for a cookie or a muffin, before three Red Phalaropes brought excitement levels back up to high peak. They bobbed around like Ping-Pong balls in party masks, totally nonplussed by the fifty-six-foot boat that had suddenly crashed the party.

Debi pointed off the stern, nodding toward the dark smudge on the horizon. The smudge, at 7x power, proved to be a black cloud of birds. Tens upon tens of thousands of Sooty Shearwaters moving in all directions at once. "The north rim has been the real hot spot this year," she confided.

So everything up to this point had just been warming up?

We entered the feathered cloud, mesmerized by the effortless swirl that enveloped us. The day had been a complete success, target species all present and accounted for. The anxiety that birders carry with them when a boat leaves the dock had been supplanted by great looks at good birds. Then the sun came out. A little wind came up. Second lunches appeared. Slowly, through the combined effects of antimotion drugs, lack of sleep, tight bellies, and lots and lots of success, the boat began to relax. In fact, it lapsed into a coma. After all, there wasn't much more that anyone could reasonably expect. So, of course, what turns up is the unexpected.

There is an electricity about a good bird that actually precedes it.

All right—a karma.

Suddenly, very keen birders raise their heads, look around, lock eyes, exchange glances that say: "You too?"

"You too?"

Motion begets motion, and motion is followed by sound. The sound of someone standing. The sudden bump of something hard and optical hitting the deck. Quick footsteps and whispers that becomes a buzz that coalesce into words . . . directions . . . directed questions . . . a *shout!*

"LAYSAN ALBATROSS!"

The bird spawned by the horizon circled the boat and fifty people followed on an inside track chasing the great black-and-white dream of a bird set upon impossibly long wings. With easy grace it settled in among the gulls floating in the stern—a battleship among light cruisers. As befitting its size and rank, it hogged all the anchovies, of which there was no shortage. Nothing is too good for the first August record of Laysan Albatross in Monterey. The bird sat there until interest and film expired—and that was a long, long time.

We started back in, too exuberant to be tired, too tired to do much more than acknowledge the several clouds of birds—shearwaters, Sabine's gulls, and Arctic Terns—that enveloped us en route.

Well, the squadron of Pomarine Jaegers *did* get everyone on their feet.

The hills, hallowed in sunshine, now drew closer. The yachts had slipped their mooring and sped, like pale imitations of seabirds, to greet us. The sea lions on the breakwaters waved a greeting and cormorant sentries stood at attention.

At the dock, a host of tourists were waiting. They had already eaten lunch. It was too early for dinner. So they were killing time by watching the party boats come in. And they were plainly perplexed to find so many exuberant yet fishless people climbing off the *Star of Monterey*.

Last to leave was a tall young woman with her hair bound in braids and eyes whose color was as changeable as the sea—the other star of Monterey. Across her sweater was a word, or maybe it was a name. The word was "Shearwater."

# 16 • CAPE MAY, NEW JERSEY:
## Birding's Migration
## Main Line

### AT THE BUNKER: FINDING COURAGE

*I*T WAS LATE, DUSK. THE WIND HAD FALLEN, THE SUN had settled, and the hawk flight had ended for the day. We were standing on the old World War II bunker, David Sibley and I, maybe picking out the odd, high-flying harrier, maybe bringing our glasses up to inspect distant flocks of waterfowl, mostly savoring the evening and separate thoughts. David is an artist, and more than this, David is a friend. Others more qualified than I have said that he is the finest field birder in North America. This is something I have believed without qualification for many years.

As the colors began to bleed from the sky and shadows to cement the trees, each of us grew conscious of the host of birds rising over Cape May Point and, at about the same time, realized that the other was aware of it, too. Robins and bluebirds and waxwings and many other late-season migrants, climbing for the stars, circling to find their place in the universe, then setting out over Delaware Bay. First there were hundreds ushering from the fields and woodlots, then thousands. They filled the air with the calls that birds use to encourage each other during the long hours and the long, dark miles. Neither of us had spoken. The spectacle was great, beyond expression or words.

It was my privilege to spend eleven years at Cape May, one of the world's great migratory junctions, and the harvest of my memories are worth anyone's envy. I have seen songbird fallouts so massive that treetop warblers went wanting for perches and Blackburnian and Cerulean Warblers fed shoulder to shoulder with Bobolinks and Indigo Buntings. I have witnessed a sky so black with migrating hawks that it humbled all mortal efforts to pin a number to them.

There was an October night when I woke just before midnight to the clamor of migrating geese that did not diminish or abate until noon the next day, and I recall a silver night in November where frost and moonlight conspired to beat back the stars and a host of migrating owls shed shadows upon the earth. I have seen shorebirds so numerous along the beaches of Delaware Bay that, when they flew, they wove a ribbon whose opposing ends bound the horizons. I have seen swallows over Cape May Point so tightly packed that their wing tips brushed people's faces and their numbers reduced the amount of sunlight reaching the earth.

But I have never seen anything quite so humbling and quite so moving as that great host of birds, rising from the woods and fields that had sheltered them all day, disappearing into a blue-black sky. It must take a lot of courage to be a bird. Courage or faith.

When it was almost too dark to see, I turned to David and asked whether he had ever witnessed anything like this anyplace but Cape May.

He didn't say anything for a time. David is a careful thinker, spare with words, and the places he has traveled in search of birds take a measure of accounting.

"No," he said finally, shaking his head. "There is no place like Cape May."

This, too, is something I have believed for many years.


## COUNTING WAVES FROM THE DIKE

"There's a bunch, high," a distinctly British voice announced.

The knot of observers brought their binoculars up, arching their necks . . . then their backs, to keep the birds in sight.

"Baypolls," a softer, American voice, pronounced—the voice of David Sibley.

"Right," a second Brit, named Paul, affirmed. "And two redstarts," he added, glancing at yet another member of the group, the one making notations on the clipboard who nodded as he wrote.

"And two more," the first Brit, whose name was Julian, instructed, "and . . . ahhhh," he groaned, leaning back, fighting to keep his balance and the high-flying group of birds in view, "a whole boat load of palms."

"Is that an American boatload or an Imperial boatload?" Dave Wiedner, scribe and troop muse, deadpanned.

Luckily, there was a lull in the action so that Dave's mildly sarcastic query could gather the chuckle it deserved. But there was little time for appreciation and none for clever retorts. Another wave of warblers materialized over the trees, enveloping the group, and it was all the counters could do to keep up with the onslaught.

The counters—David Sibley, Julian Hough, Paul Holt, and Dave Wiedner—were poised on an earthen dike set on the northern edge of Higbee Beach, 230 acres of fields and tangled coastal forest owned and managed by the New Jersey Division of Fish, Game and Wildlife. The tract was purchased to serve the needs of migrating Peregrine Falcons and Bald Eagles. (The fact that Higbee Beach also offers the finest woodcock hunting in North America is just a coincidence.) But the *real* significance of Higbee Beach lies in its value to migrating passerines. For a flight-tired warbler or an energy-starved vireo, the woods of Higbee Beach and adjacent Hidden Valley Ranch constitute the only sizable haven left in an otherwise wet (and rapidly developing) stretch of this planet.

David, Dave, Julian, and Paul were part of a project organized by the New Jersey Audubon's Cape May Bird Observatory. Its purpose: to document the scope and magnitude of the fall warbler migration through Cape May both as a scientific endeavor and as a conservation tool; to demonstrate the importance of habitat protection at one of the world's greatest migratory junctions—Cape May.

This morning, there were *many* warblers—waves of them rising from the trees, frenetic groups foraging in the tangled woodlands. It was October

3, and a weekday, but the twenty-car lot was filled to capacity and the excess spilled down New England Road. Cape May's fame is widespread, and today, at least, the fame was wholly justified.

Down woodland trails and along the sunny edges of fields, birders were reaping an autumn harvest. Nearly a hundred people crowded "the corner," a hot spot, playing ocular tag with birds who insisted that the game was hide-and-seek. Rose-breasted Grosbeaks and Northern Orioles crashed about in the trees. Red-eyed and Philadelphia Vireos moved from shadow to shadow, slow as you go. And small, cryptic, hyperthalamic warblers raced from leaf to branch, shadow to vine as quick as two-year-olds in a toy store. Overhead, a stream of Sharp-shinned Hawks were flowing. Sometimes one of the feisty raptors would stoop on a snag full of flickers, filling the air with yellow flashes and angry screams of protest. Sometimes one would go under cover, weaving a course through the trees, searching leaves and limbs for anything that might catch and hold a raptor's eye.

It was late in the season for migrating warblers. Their great journey to the tropics had begun during the last week in July when the first Hooded Warbler and Louisiana Waterthrush had beat a surreptitious retreat through Cape May's understory. The peak of the warbler migration occurs around September 1. Attesting to the late-season quality of the flight were the number of Blackpoll Warblers represented in the fallout. If the Blackpolls were in, could the waves of Yellow-rumped Warblers be far behind?

But the species being studied in the "the corner" might have been deposited by a mid-September sky, so rich was the diversity. There were Northern Parulas, Black-and-whites, Black-throated Blues, a Magnolia, a Chestnut-sided, several Black-throated Greens, many Redstarts, *many* Blackpolls, a Bay-breasted, a Canada, even a Blue-winged Warbler—an August migrant. Altogether they were driving many in the assemblage crazy. Because these aren't the warblers of spring, done up in their Day-Glo finery and belting out their names in song. Uh-uh. These were fall warblers—the "Confusing Fall Warblers"; "LGBs" (Little Green Birds) as they are known in birding vernacular. Identifying fall warblers is a challenge to the best (and a shoulder-shrug endeavor to many).

Some species play fair. Adult or hatching-year bird—winter, summer,

spring, or fall—a Black-throated Blue Warbler always looks like a good old Black-throated Blue. But then, there is the Chestnut-sided Warbler, who treacherously sheds his chestnut side by September, and the unmistakable Yellow-rumped Warbler of spring, *Dendroica coronata*, who abdicates his crown and shows up in October disguised as some mud-colored commoner.

Young birds are even worse than adults; cryptic to a fault! Give or take a couple of wing bars and tail spots, the whole lot of them are hardly more than interchangeable little green parts in a bland mosaic. And in the fall, in Cape May, young birds outnumber migrating adults almost ten to one.

But fall warblers are merely confusing, not impossible. The rules of identification remain unchanged, and for the most part the plumages of spring have just been muted by autumn, not eclipsed. Spring warblers shout their colors, winning popularity and praise. Fall warblers whisper them. Surrounding "the corner" subtle minds and seasonally calibrated eyes were sifting through the flock, gathering whispers with their skill.

Back on the dike, they were shouting.

"Parula (pair-yu-la)!" Julian pronounced, pivoting right, pinning a name on the diminutive form sneaking wide.

"That's Pa-roo-la," the "Weed Man" corrected more for argument's than accuracy's sake.

"A whole bunch of birds going out high," David Sibley counsels. Glasses are brought to bear on the flock, lit by a sun that was just cresting the treetops—ten birds . . . fifteen. At the same time another wave rushed from the trees, a bouncing cascade of forms. Some went right, some left, some cut right up the middle making binoculars useless.

"Blimey!" Paul said, smiling, shaking his head at the hit-and-run tactics of the birds.

"Wow," David Sibley said (which is "blimey" translated into American English).

"What'd you get?" the Weed Man demanded.

"Mostly Baypolls again," David pronounced, identifying the birds and fitting the flight into a conceptual framework. Probability plays a large part in this kind of field identification. What David had just confirmed was that there was a run on Baypolls—either Bay-breasted or Blackpoll Warblers.

The species are difficult to separate in the fall and almost impossible given the limitations of flight ID. Checking a high-flying bird to see whether its field marks are or are not consistent with an expected quantity is *much* easier than sifting through a thirty-five species repertoire searching for a match. Quicker, too. When identifications must be made in split-second glimpses, quick is key.

"Four Parula down here," Paul added. "Two redstarts. I didn't get the ones going right."

"One was Black-throated Green. The other two looked like Red-eyes" [Red-eyed Vireos]," Julian advised.

There were other people lined up along the impoundment dike just north of Higbee Beach—perhaps fifty in all. Some tried their hand at identifying the fast-flying forms. Most were unabashedly "cheating," concentrating on the birds that perched momentarily at the woodland's edge before setting off once more. All gathered on the dike were humbled by the identification skills demonstrated by the cadre of counters, and there was no shame in this.

The acumen of British birders in general is acute, and those who come to Cape May are a select and serious culling. But Julian and Paul are not only accomplished British birders, they are accomplished *Cape May birders* whose skills have been refined by days and weeks of polish. They'd been on hand when the first warblers had started south. They would stay until the last passed through in October.

As for David Sibley, well, David is one of a kind. Son of retired Yale ornithologist Fred Sibley, David began studying birds when he was five, painting them when he was nine. In birds, he found colors to gratify his artist's eye, identification challenges to strop a cutting edge to his uncommon intelligence, and a host of friends who shared his focus and who admired his skills. In short, he discovered a portal to the world.

David Wiedner? Dave is a Princeton graduate with the heart of Don Quixote and the mind of Puck. More researcher than birder, his primary focus, as research assistant with the Cape May Bird Observatory, was collecting data for the project. As for the avian missiles projecting past his head,

"I get them on call," he allows. "Whatever David Sibley calls them, that's what they are."

"Bald Eagle," David called, drawing all eyes skyward. Sure enough, off to the west, just a black dot in a pale sky, an immature Bald Eagle was pumping his way toward Delaware—fifteen miles across Delaware Bay. Through binoculars, the bird's projecting head, relatively short tail, and pale wing linings set against a dark colored bird were diagnostic. But David had probably identified the bird on the basis of wing beat. Nothing is quite so evident at a distance as the cadence of a bird's flight. It is a message flashed to discerning eyes that reaches across miles. The wing beat of an eagle is heavy and measured. Nothing else even comes close.

I'm too skilled a birder to claim that I don't know how David and Julian and Paul and a handful of other birders do what they do—put names at a glance to cryptically colored birds that are never seen long, and rarely seen well. I'm also too honest to claim that my skills are equal to theirs. They are not; they fall short of David's talents by miles (and Paul's and Julian's by several kilometers). The technique they use is the same technique applied to hawk-watching. Identifications based upon hints and clues that are drawn together by quick, sure minds to form a composite whole. And pin a name on a distant, high-flying bird.

*Some* fall warblers, even in flight, are easily mastered. The bold, striped pattern of Black-and-white Warblers holds up at a distance. Worm-eating Warbler has a color all its own. American Redstarts flash tell-tale windows in their tails—and they are slim, and their tails are long . . . flared at the end . . . sort of spatula-shaped (like many Cooper's Hawks).

*You mean that warblers have different shapes!?*

Absolutely. Parulas are tiny, stubby little things. Connecticut Warblers are big, chunky, and have a short-tailed appearance. Baypolls have long, broad wings and . . .

"Nashville. Straight up," David called his binoculars in line with a tiny silhouette at the limit of conjecture.

"How'd you know that was Nashville?" someone in the gallery asked.

"Small. Short-tailed. Round wings. Yellow underparts," David explained. "And it gives a rising flight call," he added, smiling. "I heard the call, and then searched for the bird."

It looks like magic, but it's really not that much different from what birders have been doing all along—observing field marks and putting them together to make an identification. The difference is degree. The things that distinguish fall warblers in flight *are* field marks in every sense of the word. They are merely subtle, undocumented, and often enough very different from the marks that distinguish the same birds at rest.

They are also damnably difficult to see. Shooting from the hip to ID fall warblers in flight is not a leisure pursuit, not a game for eyes that need time to focus, necks that don't like to bend, reflexes that are not *quite* as fast as a mirror can mimic. It is a game that demands precision optics that focus fast, focus close, and filter a great, big, depthful chunk of the world down their prismed tubes. Expensive binoculars. Everyone on the crew was armed with Zeiss 7x42s.

It's not a game for everyone. It's there for those who toe the line that defines the limit of birding skill today—a line that straddles the identification of immature jaegers, and falls short of the narrow gap that separates Rufous and Allen's Hummingbirds.

There is a story, and like the story of Ludlow Griscom and the day he pushed the limits of bird identification beyond the range of a shotgun, it is destined to become a classic. I did not witness the event. I have only heard of it from others, so you may regard it as apocryphal.

One day in September, September 21 in fact, on the dike north of Higbee Beach, David Sibley picked out a warbler, flying wide of the group.

"Golden-winged Warbler!" he exclaimed, knowing well that the bird was uncommon in Cape May and that September 21 (1989) was a late date for the species. But threading a course that navigated the limit of birding's skill, as it did, this is what the bird appeared to be, and this is the name that David assigned it.

The angle was poor, the distance unsatisfactory. Only a few of those present were able to get their binoculars on it before it disappeared.

After a time, it became apparent that David had grown pensively quiet. But there is nothing particularly unusual about this. David is a thoughtful

person. There was something troubling about the bird flying wide, discordant points that did not harmonize with the identification he had made. So he took the bird down in his mind, point by point, and rebuilt it from scratch, mating it, finally, to a name that fit like a six-gun in a use-slickened holster.

"Did anyone get on the bird I called a Golden-winged Warbler?" he asked, turning toward the others.

"Yes," Paul Holt admitted. "I did."

"What did you think?" David asked, inviting his opinion.

"Well, I thought it was Black-throated Gray," Paul admitted. "But I know how rare they are here, so I didn't want to say anything."

"Yes," David said, smiling. "That's what it was."

I think that Ludlow Griscom would have liked David Sibley. Paul Holt, too.


## THE DAY THE PEREGRINES FLEW

Listen.

You are about to hear the story of the Peregrine flight of '89. The place was Cape May. The time was October. And the events of that day have already passed into legend.

It's a *wonderful* story, a great silver lining of a story, spawned by a cold dark cloud. If the tale is marred by just the teeniest bit by despair, well, that just gives it ballast, my friend, keeps poignancy on an even keel.

You know about the Peregrine Falcon, of course, the dark-eyed prince of wind? How the bird once fell like judgment from a thousand eastern aeries, taunted the wind across western skies, and flew in a way that makes *mastery* a shallow description.

You know this bird.

How in the fifties, and sixties, and seventies the numbers dwindled, how the courtship flights that angels coveted became a weary pantomime. About the eggshells that would no longer bear the falcon's weight, and the empty ledges, the unechoed cries, and the cliffs grown barren with loss.

Perhaps you know this, too. It's a sad, shameful story. One they tell to schoolchildren today. One that teaches that nothing done in the world is done with impunity—that when you poke an environment *here* it pushes something off the ledge way over *there*. It's a lesson worth remembering.

So the bird was finished here in the East. *Extirpated* was the word they used. A clean, clinical word that takes the measure of things without feeling. In the West the numbers fell to a vestige. In the Arctic the ranks were sickened and halved. It wasn't until 1962 that the evil thing was found. A chemical substance, called DDT, that, when mixed with human stupidity, was lethal to birds of prey. The chemical was banned by and by (only the stupidity persists), but just as it takes time to poison a world, it takes time to heal one, too.

Their chemical jesses cut, the lesser raptors mended quickly, filling empty niches, shouldering the specter of loss aside with a host of healthy young. But Peregrines lagged in the shadows, right through the seventies, into the eighties, their population still paralyzed by the poison they'd absorbed.

There was a day in 1977 that showed it well—a day that went beyond the DDT-tethered reach of dreams.

The date was October 4, the winds northwest, and in the first light of morning, Sharp-shinned Hawks were already passing through Cape May Point State Park—shadow raptors weaving paths through shadows of trees. By dawn, a river of birds was flowing down the tree line north of the official hawk watch—Sharp-shinneds by the hundreds, kestrels in squadrons. By sunrise, the river had crested, flooding the park. By nine o'clock, the sky over Cape May Point State Park was a great seamless swirl of migrating raptors, a cloud that reached from horizon to horizon. By ten, the sky was black.

There are no words to express such a thing, and no mere number can hope to convey the wonder of it. But still there was a number ascribed to the host of birds that passed through Cape May that day—that number is 21,800. Eleven thousand were Sharp-shinneds, 9,400 Broad-wingeds, and there were hundreds of kestrels, scores of Ospreys, Merlins, Cooper's Hawks. Their sum equals "one cloud"—but a cloud with a cold, dark lining.

Of Peregrine Falcons, those dark-eyed princes of wind, there were none

that day. None at all. During the course of a Cape May autumn, an autumn that saw the passage of 81,000 birds of prey (including 48,000 Sharp-shinned Hawks!), only 61 Peregrines were counted—all the birds the Arctic had to spare in 1977.

Gradually, the Arctic purged itself of the poison. Slowly the falcon blood was cleansed, the eggshells thickened, and from Greenland to the Brooks Range the ledges knew again the tercel's scream, the falcon's weight, and the factiousness of Peregrine young. When these passage princes and princesses returned as haggard birds in another spring, they went out to reclaim lost kingdoms and set about making young of their own, who in turn produced more young, and in this way, after nearly two decades, the poisoned void was filled.

Every autumn, as winter closes its fist around the north, the Peregrine hosts usher from their Arctic fortresses, setting their wings to the wind, and turning their faces toward a tropical sun. The great cold air masses that speed Peregrines on their way sweep them across a continent—over tundra meadows ignited by frost, over forests so vast that their limits defeat even the eyes (if not the wings) of Peregrines.

*Nothing* defeats the wings of a tundra Peregrine, not distance, not darkness, not even seas so vast that the great northern forests would founder within them. When the birds strike the edge of the continent, they put their faith in the wind and put the coast behind.

But this is where the story takes a very special turn. Because commonly (commonly, mind you), when tundra Peregrines chase the wind out over the Atlantic, they spend long hours offshore. The talons of adult males may never feel a perch until they feel the touch of tropical sun upon their wings. But on October 3, 1989, the day the Peregrines flew, the pelagic wind was turned aside, its blow deflected by a dark mantle of clouds lying off the coast of New England. The glancing winds fell back onshore and the birds whose wings are wedded to the wind came with it—right down the Atlantic Coast, right down the Cape May Peninsula, right over the heads of fifty thunderstruck hawk-watchers gathered at Cape May Point, New Jersey.

Tony Leukering, official hawk counter, was at the helm, three metal hand counters in one hand, binoculars in the other. Tony is a professional, and little that passes Cape May Point misses his eyes. The most surreptitious Sharp-shinneds, the highest flying harriers, all find a spot in Tony's ledger.

But any bird that does escape his vigilance must then run a gauntlet of eyes. Mustered on the hawk-watch platform on October 3, 1989, were some of the finest eyes in hawk-watching. Vince Elia was there, flying the hometown colors, and Rosie Widmer, whose morning offerings of jelly doughnuts have kept more than one rat-poor professional hawk counter alive over the years.

Jeff Dodge was down from Braddock Bay, hawk-watching's window on the spring; Jamie Noble, too—Jamie who quits one high-paying job a year (coinciding with the first cold front in September). Paul Kerlinger, director of the Cape May Bird Observatory, shed his desk and joined the assembly, and Louise Zemaitis, a raptor spirit in young mom's clothing, was on hand, drawn to the flight like a fist bird to a lure.

Rounding out the gallery were a visiting host of birders, including an expeditionary force of Danes led by Klaus Malling Olsew. Their faces are still unknown because their eyes never left the ocular lens of their spotting scopes. But their voices are familiar. Lyrical voices whose English seemed limited to a single word and as the day wore on this word assumed the familiarity of a chant.

"Per-Rigreen!" "Per-Rigreen!"

Seven Peregrines passed between 8:00 A.M. and 9:00 A.M., and eight more the following hour. Some were high, some low; some hugged the bay, and some passed well offshore. Most bore right down the middle, drawing a bead on the Cape May Point lighthouse as if it were resting in the notch of their gun sights.

"A good start," the veterans noted sagely. Falcons are afternoon birds at Cape May, and so many Peregrines so early bode well.

"Good looks!" the gallery exclaimed, entranced by the sight of birds so close that binoculars were sometimes more hindrance than help.

Between 10:00 A.M. and 11:00 A.M. *twenty-one Peregrines* bought passage to Delaware, singles and doubles; big, soaring females and scrappy, cut-down males; golden-crowned immatures and dark-helmeted adults.

"Lots of adults," the veterans observed, *invited*, looking to each other

to voice a suspicion that was growing by the minute. "Lots of adults . . . *males?!"* Some of the birds looked tightly proportioned and small. But these pelagic migrants are almost unknown in Cape May, New Jersey; almost unheard of.

By noon, by the time seventeen more Peregrines had passed, suspicion had given way to astonishment. Every third bird that passed looked to be an adult male. More adult male Peregrines in the course of the morning than many present had seen in their lives! Sharp, trim tercels with gleaming white chests, and creamy white faces set off by the crisp, sideburn slash of their kind. Sometimes they flew in tandem with females, offering easy comparison. More often, it seemed they flew alone, lobo birds bound wing and soul to nothing but the wind.

But as the morning drew on, it became more and more difficult for Peregrines to claim even a measure of privacy. The sky is finite, and the birds seemed not to be. Faster and faster they came. More and more in the air all the time. Some soaring. Some sparing. Some racing through Cape May airspace with blind indifference.

"They're coming in flocks!" Vince Elia said, shaking his head.

"I don't believe this," Jamie muttered, voicing the general consensus.

Two immature birds moved down the tree line scattering flickers from their perches and driving a Cooper's Hawk to ground. Two more birds soared out over the town of Cape May, where they were joined by two more and overhead three birds turning lazy circles brought the assembly to their feet. Most were still standing when a pair of sparring adults rocked past the platform so close that people in the front ranks ducked and those behind could smell the ptarmigan on the bird's breath.

"Per-Rigreen," the stalwart Klaus chanted, his spotting scope trained on a bird that was boring a Peregrine-sized hole through the ozone layer. Nobody troubled to look. Klaus was developing a reputation for finding ozone birds.

"Harrier!" Tony, announced, pointing.

"Thank God!" someone from the gallery mumbled. " 'Bout time we had a little variety, here."

Between 1:00 P.M. and 2:00 P.M. Tony was ringing up new Peregrines at the rate of nearly *one a minute*—almost as many Peregrines in one hour as were recorded during the entire 1977 hawk watch—and then, suddenly, just before two o'clock, the river of birds fell to a trickle.

The count stood at 133. The record was 140. Seven birds to tie; eight to break the record.

Now it came down to talent, and it came down to pride. Spotting scopes and binoculars raked the sky. Where earlier it had been a shopping spree, now it came down to an international effort with a focused objective.

Every distant shape was scrutinized, set against the mental image of a crossbow mounted in the sky—the classic cut of a soaring Peregrine. Every distant ripple of motion was studied with care, its pulse measured by calculating eyes to see whether it brushed the Peregrine registry.

Not a person left the platform. Not a wasted word was spent. No one did anything but add their skills to the net cast into the wind. And one by one the birds were snared.

*One adult* s-o-o-o-o high that if the speed of light were factored in, the bird would have gone down in the previous hour. Sing the praises of Danish eyes!

*Another bird*, high and to the northwest, age and sex unknown (probably being recorded simultaneously at Hawk Mountain). This one I can claim.

*One* directly overhead; a stealth Peregrine that had slipped all nets. Credit to the gallery.

*Another* offshore—way to go, Linda! Then *two* to the North (a double for the Danes), closing out the hour with six.

Everyone was standing now. Everyone was at the rail. Fifty ardent hawk-watchers all wanting to be the one to tie the record; all pledging everything to whatever *gods* they worship to be the one to *break* it!

"*Over* Sunset Boulevard," Linda (Peregrine Finder!) Dunne chanted, scoring first.

"*AND ANOTHER BEHIND!*" Tony (Official Counter) Leukering shouted, scoring last!

Seven birds in all were harvested between three and four o'clock. Eleven more found a spot on Tony's field sheet and a place in the record book before he pronounced the flight "over." The greatest one-day movement of Pere-

grine Falcons this side of the DDT era or the other; *the greatest Peregrine flight in history*.

It couldn't have happened a decade earlier, because the birds were too few. It wouldn't have happened if a storm off the New England coast had not bent the wind to its will, sending it and the birds our way.

But this flight *might* not have figured so prominently in my mind, as it did, were it not for one small dark concern, one that offers the greatest Peregrine flight in history both balance and perspective. The thing I hinted at in the beginning of this story. On October 3, 1989, the day 157 Peregrine Falcons passed Cape May, New Jersey, the Sharp-shinned Hawk total was a mere 107—a number that would not have made a respectable hour's tally a short decade ago.

If someone had told me on October 4, 1977, that a day would come when Peregrine Falcons would outnumber Sharp-shinned Hawks in Cape May, New Jersey, I would have called them every kind of fool.

If someone asks me what the future holds, I think I have the answer now. The answer is: change. You can feel it in the wind. You can read it in the ledgers of hawk-watchers.


## REFLECTIONS ON FALLOUTS

*Fallout!*—the great gift of birds deposited by the night sky. It's every birder's dream. It's the reason people come to Cape May in the fall. It is the first thing another birder asks about after you casually let slip that you've "just come from Cape May."

"Cape May!? Did you catch a . . . ?"

*"Fallout!"* The precipitation of wings driven to earth by a northwest wind that makes woodlots dance and fields ripple beneath a blanket of birds. A fallout is to birders what twelve inches of newly fallen powder is to a skier; what summiting is to a climber; what boxes lying beneath the tree are to a child on Christmas morning.

It's a dream.

It's the fusion of hope and fulfillment.

It's a memory that will anchor your thoughts after age and time set your mind adrift.

It might be that you've never been to Cape May and never experienced a fallout. It might be, too, that you *have* been to Cape May, spent a week there, and now don't believe in them. Or worse! That you have been to Cape May, and after a string of birdless mornings woke to a day when warblers bounced in the treetops and binoculars found two as often as one, and now you *think* you've seen a fallout.

That's not a fallout. That's what used to be called a "good flight." The sad fact is that real fallouts are not as common as they used to be—not at Cape May; not elsewhere. Real fallouts occur only once or twice a year. *True* fallouts occur only once or twice a decade—but we're not talking about *true* fallouts. There is no way to discuss *these* and hope to maintain a shred of credibility.

What most people call fallouts today are not even the shadow of a fallout, not a real fallout. The meaning of the word has been thinned to bring it into accord with reduced expectations and a harsh new reality: migratory bird populations are declining; some are crashing. In three short decades, North America's long-distance migrants, the birds that nest in our continent and spend the balance of their lives in another, have declined by 50 percent! Half the number of thrushes that were here when Rachel Carson published *Silent Spring* have disappeared. Half the numbers of vireos. Half the warblers. Half the flycatchers, cuckoos, tanagers, orioles . . . half the wings of autumn torn from the sky during the course of our lives. Nobody understands precisely why. Nobody knows when or where the decline will stop. Nobody knows whether it will stop.

For the sake of those not fortunate enough to have been born in an age to see it; for the benefit of those who *are* fortunate and travel to Cape May while there is still time to see it, I'll take it upon myself to describe a fallout. Maybe this way those who see less will not be deluded, and those whose lives are cheated by the future will believe the old stories, and pass proper judgment upon their ancestors, who let something so incredible slip from the world.

You will know the *possibility* of a fallout if you go to the C-View Inn,

just before seven o'clock in the evening, order a cheese steak and a mug, and watch the weathermen on the Philadelphia evening news stand before a continent branded with a capital H over of the Great Lakes and a saw-toothed line whose teeth reach for the coast. You must seek out the table where a young troop is seated: men and women brandishing Peregrine T-shirts, work-stained jeans, and hands that look as though they have been flayed. These are raptor banders, indentured spirits whose days are spent capturing and banding birds of prey and whose nights are filled with dreams of them.

Now, listen to the meteorologist on the screen for key phrases: "Fast-moving frontal line . . ." "already raining here in the city . . ." "clearing before midnight . . ." "temperatures falling sharply . . ." "winds strong, north to northwest." Then, study the faces of the banders as the words are spoken. If the faces grow bright with anticipation and break into grins; if there are cheers, rebel yells, cries of "Awwwwl right," and "Hot damn," and calls for another round of mugs, you will know that a fallout is possible.

Mind you, hawk banders aren't particularly interested in a "dicky bird" fallout (not *real* hawk banders). But the same conditions that cause hawk flights often cause songbird fallouts, too.

You will know the *promise* of a fallout if you wake, deep in the night, to the clack of shutters that have slipped their mooring on the old Chalfonte Hotel and hear the sound of wind racing through the tree-lined streets of Cape May. As you go for another blanket you should pause at the window and seek assurance from the stars glowing like shards of ice over the town, promising a clear, cold dawn.

You will know the *anticipation* of a fallout when you walk to your car in the morning, while the gaslights still glow, and hear the sound of silver bells ringing in the wind which are the calls of Bobolinks. Note the buzzy yelp of thrushes high overhead. Catch the thin piping calls of warblers. Smile at the rude, raucous squawk of migrating herons. All these things speak of the imminence of a fallout.

You will know the *imminence* of a fallout when you get to Captain's Cove and find a parking space right in front, see that the party boat captains do not rush with their breakfast or wave away another cup of coffee.

The winds, they know, will hold their boats in port and their fishermen clients away.

You will know the *excitement* of a fallout as you drive down New England Road and your headlights capture tiny, darting forms that rise from the roadway, fluttering in confusion. Some make sad, pinging sounds as they strike the sides of your car, and you will slow your speed to a crawl, despite your rising excitement.

Finally, you will know, really *know* a fallout, because when you step out of your car in the parking lot at Higbee Beach, you will not know where to look, where to turn, what to favor with your eyes. Birds will be everywhere.

Everywhere. On the ground and in the air, overhead and at your feet, on every branch and twig. Everywhere. The parking lot will be filled with clusters of birders who stand, staring, with unraised binoculars, shocked into paralysis by the spectacle around them and the fear that by singling out any one thing for scrutiny, a thousand possibilities are lost.

Just the way you are.

The cedar trees in the parking lot will shudder beneath the weight of Cape May Warblers, and around the perimeter, pokeberry will be bent double under the weight of Swainson's and Gray-cheeked Thrush. Rose-breasted Grosbeaks and orioles will crash through the trees, and tanagers will feed on the ground like robins. The tails of American Redstarts will flicker like fireflies from a thousand shadowy places. Packs of Magnolia Warblers, parulas, and Black-and-whites will fight over individual moths while Northern Waterthrush bob and *tic* from fence-post perches. The *yank, yank, yank* of Red-breasted Nuthatches will be so persistent that it approaches torture, and the chiming of Bobolink so incessant that it ceases to be a sound.

Every place you look, everywhere you turn—down any path, through any breach in the wall of trees—there are birds in motion. So many birds that field trip leaders trying to single out individual birds for the scrutiny of their groups are laughed into silence. So many birds that no binocular, no matter how close the focus or how narrow the field, can ever fall on just a single bird. So many birds that there seems no reason even to leave the parking lot—and some birders never do.

If everything is as I have described, but you are still not certain that you are witnessing a real fallout, there is one final test. For just a moment, step away from the flight and take stock. If you don't feel more excited, more privileged, more humbled, and more incredibly alive than you have ever felt before, then it can only mean one of two things.

Either it is not a real fallout. Or you are not a real birder.

## 17 • HAWK MOUNTAIN, PENNSYLVANIA:

## The Endless Mountain

HERE IS A RIDGE THAT LIES IN THE RIDGE-AND-valley province of the Northeast, a rocky spine that marks the eastern flank of the great Appalachian Mountains. The Appalachians are old as mountain systems go—280 million years old by the accounting of geologists—and centuries of ice, wind, and rain have reduced them to a vestige of what was once a mountain chain as majestic as the Alps.

This ridge extends from New York State, where it bears the name Shawangunk, through eastern and central Pennsylvania, where it is called Blue Mountain. In New Jersey, it retains the name given it by earlier stewards of the land, the Lenapi. There it is called the Kittatinny, the "Endless Mountain."

Every fall, perhaps for as long as hawks have migrated, the Endless Mountain has served as a pathway in the sky for thousands of birds of prey—hawks, eagles, vultures. These are soaring birds, able to tease lift out of temperature-troubled air and ride thermals aloft. But when conditions are right, when the northwest winds of autumn vault the Kittatinny, creating updrafts, the birds surrender the open sky and hitch their fortunes to the ridge. There, from September through November, approximately twenty thousand raptors a year coast south on a cushion of air.

This great autumn pageant is monitored from scores of points along the Kittatinny and elsewhere—hallowed locations with esoteric names like Bake Oven, Wachusett, Wagner's Gap, Mendota Fire Tower. Each site boasts its garrison of regular observers. Each site takes the raptorial pulse and uses it to divine the health and stability of the natural world.

But oldest and greatest among them is a site in eastern Pennsylvania that lies near the tiny hamlet of Eckville. Its name is Hawk Mountain.

A sign warned of "new traffic patterns," but every year seems to find new traffic patterns on Hawk Mountain. No matter what sort of navigational wizardry curator Jim Brett concocts, all efforts to improve the flow of Hawk Mountain visitors inevitably fall short—at least on weekends. God help you if you are a late riser and you plan on hawk-watching at The Mountain on a weekend.

But on weekdays, even weekdays in October with northwest winds pushing leaves and juncos around, you can pretty much have any spot in the lot. The hordes of weekend visitors are punching time clocks or sweating deadlines. Hawk Mountain's high ground is held by ardent hawk-watchers (just as it was in the beginning).

How you manage to get yourself to Hawk Mountain on a work day is *your* problem. But as evidenced by the twenty or so cars ahead of me, the problem is not insurmountable. Me? I called in sick—from the pay phone at the convenience store just after you turn off 61 North. "A cold [front]," I explained to my boss, sniffing grandly for effect. "Woke up this morning [to northwest winds] and just felt miserable [at the thought of missing a good hawk flight]. Absolutely miserable." By the time I reached the parking area, I found my condition much improved. By the time I reached the gate guarding the entrance to the trail, I felt splendid. Nothing like a trip to Hawk Mountain to make all things right with the world again.

Sixty thousand visitors pad their way to the North Lookout every autumn, drawn to the vista and vision of the first sanctuary ever established for the protection of birds of prey. But before 1934, the trail knew the tread of different feet, the tread of hawk shooters, and the autumn air reverberated with the report of scatterguns and reeked with the sweet smell of gunpowder. It's hard to recall now that this environmental beacon was once a battlefield and that there was a time when people did not understand the important role birds of prey play in maintaining natural balance. It's difficult to believe that people's ignorance was so complete that they thought of hawks as vermin and shot them on sight. On this rocky promontory above the village of Eckville, they slaughtered them by the thousands.

It was Richard Pough, a Philadelphia conservationist, who came upon the tragic scene in the autumn of 1933. He collected the crumpled bodies, positioned them in moribund ranks, and photographed the lot. The photo set in motion a series of events that culminated in the purchase of the gunners' pulpit and fourteen hundred surrounding acres.

Rosalie Barrow Edge, a tough, sharp crusader from New York, spearheaded the protectionist drive. She searched for and found a caretaker who could make Hawk Mountain Sanctuary live up to its name. His name was Maurice Broun, a young naturalist from New England with a will every bit as strong as that of Mrs. Edge. On September 10, 1934, Maurice Broun and his young bride, Irma, arrived to take on their mountainous task—to stop the killing and to school a reluctant public on the importance of birds of prey.

And the guns fell silent.

And today, even children look back and wonder at the folly of our ancestors.

For more than half a century, raptor conservation and education have been the twin pillars supporting the work of Hawk Mountain Sanctuary. The Mountain is the medium. Well over a million individuals have made the trek to the North Lookout since Irma Broun stood as the "Keeper of the Gate," and Maurice opened his "Classroom in the Clouds," and Rosalie Edge built her vision out of Kittatinny stone. They are gone from The Mountain now. Their vision is shepherded by a staff so committed to their ideals that you'd swear that Rosalie Edge picked them herself. All who visit Hawk Mountain are touched by the magic of the place, and not a few find their lives changed by it. The ranks of North America's field birders and ornithologists are filled with individuals who owe fealty to the "Classroom in the Clouds."

I am one.

The North Lookout was no more crowded than the parking lot. Sprinkled over the stony pulpit were two dozen worshipers, honest birding pilgrims from beyond the ken, here for a day or a week, soulless, lying bastards like myself laid low by a case of west-wind syndrome.

Buffered by a circle of stone, the official counters were calling in their first hour's sightings to the headquarters. Hawk Mountain volunteers Kerry Grim and Doug Wood I recognize as old confederates. The third counter, Robert Hogan, Hawk Mountain's new seasonal research technician, I knew only by name.

With a wave, they ushered me in, offering a spot within the circle (professional courtesy). You sink six thousand hours of your life into scouring the skies for hawks, as I have, you earn the respect of your peers.

"You show up and the birds start," Doug teased, shaking his head, feigning admiration.

"How's the flight?" I asked, ignoring the left-hand jab.

"It just started," they confirmed. "You haven't missed a thing." (*Translation*: You haven't missed anything "good.")

"Any Golden Eagles this year?" I asked, not wanting to sound like every other hawk-watcher who shows his face on the Mountain, and failing badly.

"One," they confirmed. "Early in the month."

"Bird low over Five," a fellow crouched next to the counter's circle advised. "Bird," on the North Lookout, means "hawk."

"Three birds," someone else advised—maybe it's more accurate to say "preempted." If someone else gets on a bird first, one of the ways to score back lost points is to find birds the one with the quick trigger misses. But the way to *really* win points in the old hawk-watching racket, the way to win top-gun awards, is to pin a name on some distant bird before anyone else. (The way to really lose points is to pin a name on a distant bird and discover, along with everyone else, that you are mistaken.)

I brought my binoculars up on the directed point, picked up birds, identified them as probable Sharp-shinneds, and began panning left searching for other, "better" birds. There is a hierarchy in birds of prey directly related to frequency of occurrence. Sharp-shinneds, in mid-October at Hawk

Mountain, are only slightly less common than hex signs in Lancaster County, Pennsylvania. Golden Eagles, on the other hand—well, Golden Eagles are special.

You really want to win great praise and glory on a hawk watch? Go for the gold(en).

My binoculars brushed over features etched in every hawk-watcher's mind. The ripple-backed ridge, with bumps numbered one through five . . . the Donat, a volcano-shaped sandstone cone rising right out of the valley floor . . . then Pinnacle, a Kittatinny spur lying to the south . . . then Owl's Head . . . finally, Hemlock Heights.

The scan produced nothing but a refresher course in the lay of the land. More slowly I brought the glass back along the same path, picking up a small, dark raptor hugging the south side of the ridge, almost invisible against the well-autumned trees. The bird was distant, flapping mostly, gliding intermittently, and something about the bird drew binoculars the way a compass needle holds north. Some intangible message was flashed to discerning eyes that said, "Not a Sharp-shinned Hawk."

Something about the way the wings moved—abrupt, purposeful, downward flicking strokes. (Sharp-shinneds have snappy wing beats.)

Something in the way the bird lost altitude quickly in a glide. (Sharp-shinneds are buoyant. They float.)

Something about the bird being on the south, off-wind side of the ridge. (Sharp-shinneds try to hold an updraft unless it blows them askew.)

Something about the darker-than-Sharp-shinned color. Something about the length of the wings. Something about the bird's direct, no-nonsense approach to getting from point A to point B. Something that said, that *shouted*, "MERLIN!"

And so I did . . . moments before the bird disappeared below the lip of the ridge, out of sight. Merlin isn't as good as Golden Eagle, but it's not a bad bird to kick off your arrival.

"It'll pop up right in front," I promised, hoping it would be true. Almost on cue, a cut-down falcon did pop up in front of all eyes. But to my horror the bird was not a Merlin. Beneath the mantle of the ridge, the bird had been transformed into a classic, card-carrying male American Kestrel.

Every face associated with discerning eyes was halfway to a smirk when a second bird, a Merlin, appeared (saving mine). The feisty falcon took a swipe at the kestrel, then launched itself across the lookout, made several full-throttle passes at the plastic owl decoy, and disappeared.

Merlins are real crowd-pleasers.

"Red-shouldered down below," a visitor shouted. Better directions would have been helpful. But the real shortfall was the identification. The bird was an immature Red-tailed Hawk, not a "shoulder."

Red-tailed Hawks are larger than Red-shouldereds. Immatures are lanky, adults are compact, but at any age Red-shouldered Hawks look more trim and clean-cut than the average Red-tailed—raptorial gentry versus jes' plain folk. Red-shouldereds are also more high-strung than Red-taileds. Shoulders flap more and the wing beat is decidedly Accipiteresque. What the visitor with the fast trigger had done was pick up a buteo that was flapping a great deal and *assume* that it was a shoulder. His failure was in not re-calibrating his estimates to accommodate conditions.

It was still early in the day. Cloud cover was heavy. Thermals hadn't started to perk yet. The bird was low, trying to reach the crest of the ridge where it would find an updraft. That was why it was flapping. That was why the bird suggested a Red-shouldered Hawk.

What made the bird a Red-tailed Hawk? Broad, "muscular" shaped wings; a short, broad tail; lots of white mottling on the back forming a V-shaped pattern. And when the bird turned, it showed nice, white under-parts and a great, big, fat, bellyband—the *classic* Red-tailed field mark. Even "experts" respond to the obvious.

Identifying distant, high-flying birds of prey is fun and challenging, and for those whose minds may have firmed around the principles of "wing bars and tail spots" somewhat mystifying. Many of the birds seen in the course of a day are the kinds of birds only hawk-watchers can love—distant, high-flying raptors whose identifications are more forensic than fact.

But Hawk Mountain Sanctuary would never have gathered the following it has if every raptor that passed flew at altitudes that are barely suborbital. When a northwest wind pins birds to the ridge, the *Ahhh* factor runs high, and under these conditions, a visitor's introduction to raptors is up front and personal.

"Here . . . here," voices shouted, and pointed fingers followed the course of a scrappy little Sharp-shinned Hawk that wove a path *right through the crowd!* Sharpies are crowd-pleasers, too.

More birds appeared. Pulled aloft by sunlight, drawn to the ridge by energy-saving updrafts.

"There's one over the slope of Five."

"Another over Three."

Migrating Sharp-shinneds, Red-taileds, and sinewy Cooper's Hawks, following the serpentine contours of the ridge right to the waiting crowd. Red-shouldered Hawks, true to their Bolshevik natures, favored the off-wind side.

An Osprey suddenly materialized, glaring at the crowd with bright yellow eyes. Half the gasps from the gallery were still being formulated when a second Osprey popped up from below and fell in behind the first.

Another bird started in, hugging the top of the ridge, heading right for the plastic owl decoy perched over the crowd. There is no love lost between hawks and owls, and hawk-watchers capitalize upon this by setting up owl decoys. Sometimes it works and Sharp-shinneds will spin circles around the bogus owl, completely oblivious to the crowds of onlookers. Later in the season, when Sharp-shinned numbers falter and Red-taileds dominate the sky, the allure is not so strong.

But goshawks have been know to take the heads off owl decoys.

Head-on identifications can be tricky, and the fast-approaching bird toed the fine Accipiter line that separates the smaller Sharp-shinned Hawk from Cooper's Hawks. First it was a Sharp-shinned . . . then it was judged to be too big, a Cooper's Hawk. But then it seemed smaller again. Then it wasn't. Then . . .

It was gone, leaving a lookout full of perplexed faces.

"What was that one?" a woman wearing one mitten asked.

"That was a Cooper's Hawk," Kerry pronounced. At Hawk Mountain, as elsewhere, judge's decision is final.

The expression on the woman's face suggested that her money had been on Sharp-shinned Hawk, but that's another thing about hawk-watching. Nobody's identification is ever so absolutely right that someone else must be absolutely wrong.

A soprano din brought heads around, and two sixth-grade classes came into view. Hawk Mountain is visited by over one hundred school groups a year, and today two grammar school classes were attending the "Classroom in the Clouds." At the head of one group was Amy Gaberlein, a tall, brown-haired extrovert, heralding from New Castle, Delaware. Steering the other was Michelle Kovac, a smiling transplant from Somerset, Pennsylvania. Both were recent college graduates working as part of Hawk Mountain's seasonal staff. What they and half a dozen other young people a season give is time, knowledge, and commitment to a cause they believe in—the cause championed by Hawk Mountain. What they gain in return are skills, room, board, a hundred dollars a week, and the memory of the autumn they helped move people and the nature world just a little bit closer to an accommodation.

In December, Amy would be heading for Corkscrew Swamp, where she would assume the position of naturalist. Michelle was heading for West Africa and the Peace Corps. But today, both were emissaries of Hawk Mountain—although, for most of their lesson, they were little better than air traffic controllers of raptors.

"Look at this one coming in low," Amy warned her wide-eyed minions.

"Oh, wowwwww!!!" the troop of students chanted, as the bird floated directly over their heads.

"It's a falcon! It's a falcon!" the tyros in the lot chant, deceived by the swept-back buteo wings narrowing to a falconlike point.

"No, it's not," Amy replied, shaking her head, tossing them a look that said "try again."

"It was a Red-tailed Hawk," one of the students wearing binoculars asserted. "It had a bellyband." He was right, too. Amy had a ringer in the lot.

Amy and Michelle also had their hands full, larding information and facts about the sanctuary between birds that broke into their discourses at two-minute intervals—pop-up raptors that sprouted a sky full of pointed fingers. Get the right ID and score points on the board. That's the game. Name that raptor. It was better than erudition, better than a classroom simulation, even better than a video game.

Because it was real.

Amy and Michelle didn't compete with the flight. They were far too accomplished environmental educators for that. They used the birds to drive home their points—about flight, migration, conservation. They didn't have to fight for anyone's attention, either. Not as long as they used the birds to their best strategic advantage and stood between the students and the birds.

On weekends, the school groups give way to families seduced by near-annual articles in the travel sections of the *Philadelphia Inquirer* or the *Washington Post*. A small army of volunteers helps Hawk Mountain's staff manage what sometimes exceeds six thousand visitors on a peak October weekend —giving lectures, answering questions, offering people from all walks of life the gift of Hawk Mountain's vision. When these weekend visitors leave, with the image of a soaring Red-tailed Hawk fused in their minds and a better understanding of raptors and their role, they too have become emissaries of Hawk Mountain.

Organizations, even conservation organizations, are much like the people who create them. They start off strong and purposeful with a goal worth achieving and the energy to achieve it. Then, sometimes, organizations lose their way. Some achieve their objective and, because they defined their objective too narrowly, serve no higher purpose than self-perpetuation. Others fall into the hands of people whose vision is frozen in time, and then time leaves them and their vision behind.

Hawk Mountain might have become just another hawk-watch site. It could have taken the easy, comfortable course and grown insular—a playground in the clouds for the old guard, the regulars, and the inner circle. Just one more organization that has made a religion of its means and forgotten its ends. But this did not happen.

Maybe the vision of Rosalie Edge was too strong. Maybe the dangers facing birds of prey have never really gone far enough away for Hawk Mountain's purpose to falter. For whatever reasons, Hawk Mountain Sanctuary remains what it has always been, a force working for the protection of birds of prey. Its message was first heard on a rocky outcropping in Pennsylvania. It reaches now across the planet.

The temperature kept dropping, hawk-watchers kept arriving, and the birds kept coming. Between one and two o'clock, with over one hundred observers in attendance, the flight really caught fire. Cooper's Hawks became so numerous they began traveling in pairs, in packs! Small groups of Red-shouldered Hawks turned like leaves in the wind, and a late Broad-winged Hawk hurried by. A high, steady train of Red-tailed Hawks forced eyes skyward, and a goshawk, snaking down the ridge, precipitated a reckless scamper across a boulder-studded track. Sharp-shinneds attacked the plastic owl with such single-minded ferocity that a few deserved to be upgraded to Merlins.

Only one thing marred the perfection of the day. That was the absence of eagles. No bird epitomizes the ridge in autumn more than the Golden Eagle, the bird of kings. Though October 19 was early for an eagle, it wasn't so early that you couldn't *hope*. More and more, it seemed eyes found their way to the slope of Five where the great, dark bird with the golden hackles would appear. A dark, black pinprick set against an ice-blue sky that grows larger . . . and larger.

Two o'clock came and went, wanting. Three and four o'clock came filled with birds, but not the One. Hope, and one of the best flights of the season, held most to the Mountain until four—the witching hour for eagles. When it passed, and an eagle did not, the spell was broken. In ones and twos, parties and small groups, the *ad hoc* assemblage of hawk-watchers departed. Soon, only Kerry, Robert, Doug, and a handful of stalwarts remained.

There is something very special about Hawk Mountain in the late afternoon. The sun lies fully behind, flooding the ridge with yellow light, casting the North Lookout in shadow. Late-flying birds hug the ridge for support and they seem not to be floating on air at all but on sunlight. It makes the backs of Sharp-shinned Hawks shine like gunmetal and sets fire to the wings of Red-shouldered Hawks. Ospreys become frozen in amber light, and Redtileds, their wings stretched full as if to catch the solar winds, glide on gilded feathers.

A large bird appeared off the slope of Five, rising out of the trees, finding lift that had eluded the grasp of lesser wings. The profile was head-on. The flight unwavering. The size . . .

Larger than life.

Its wings were long, curled down at the tips, so brown they edged toward black. Its movements were regal, stately, and its head glowed like honey, like a mirror of the sun. It held our glasses as if it was the only bird in the sky, and for all anyone knew, it was true.

Once, Kerry almost blurted out a name. Twice I nearly did so myself. But that would put the vision to the test, would have forced others to put their skills to the bird and test it for substance and illusion. Through some unspoken pact, for a few moments, hope made all who hoped hold to the illusion.

The fragile zephyrs that held the bird aloft slipped through its slotted feathers. The wings jerked spasmodically and the bird diminished before our eyes, becoming what it had always been. A very large Red-tailed Hawk.

Binoculars fell. Sounds that were halfway to a laugh rose in half a dozen throats, and sheepish, sideways glances were cast all around.

"It almost had us," Doug confessed, not saying what "it" was.

"I could have sworn that one was going to be good," I added, also avoiding the E word. To have said "eagle" would have made the snookering complete—complete by default.

The Red-tailed moved past the lookout with the last rays of an October sun full in its face. Steady as a mountain and fragile as a vision. As we watched, the bird started its descent, heading for some branch below where it would spend the night.

All along the Endless Mountain, other birds were doing the same. Among them, somewhere up-ridge, was the bird with the unspoken name. Soon, maybe tomorrow, someone would buy a look at it with his skill. But only because at Hawk Mountain people had put a down payment on the future with their vision, and their heirs have not squandered the inheritance.

# 18 • SACRAMENTO VALLEY AND TULE LAKE, CALIFORNIA:

## Storms of Wings

### SACRAMENTO NATIONAL WILDLIFE REFUGE

"LOOK AT THEM ALL," A NEARBY VOICE EXCLAIMED, AND the small corner of my mind that was free to contemplate such things thought the words might have come from a child. But it wasn't a child's voice. In timbre and pitch it was a woman's voice, an adult, and this is frightening. For wonder to breach the rubble that lies between adults and their feelings, a thing must be truly wonderful. For excitement and delight to rule expression so completely, the vision that holds a person by the throat must be *so* powerful that it shakes the shackles from souls.

The voice, I realized, was Linda's.

"Look at them all," she said again, staring into the fog, shaking her head, trying to deny what her mind found impossible to accept. But there is no denying such a thing. The great blizzard of birds enfolded in tule fog was all too real.

"Look at them all," she pleaded, seeking support now for what could not be denied. "Look at them all," she chanted. "LOOK AT THEM ALL!" she shouted. *"JUST LOOK AT THEM ALL!"*

But as much as I love her, and as hard as I tried, what Linda asked was impossible. It was patently *impossible* to look at *all* the geese in the air, on the ground, all over Delevan National Wildlife Refuge. Geese rising in clouds. Geese descending in squadrons. Geese flying in chevrons going every way at once. The number of birds was simply too, too vast. But for this same reason it was impossible to look away. The sight and sound of a world where birds have supplanted earth, water, and sky is an incredible thing.

We were standing on the shoulder of Maxwell Road—a narrow strip of asphalt flanked by marshy impoundments that serves as the southern boundary to the Delevan Refuge, one of five refuges that are part of the Sacramento Valley National Wildlife Refuge. We, incidentally, means Linda, myself, and Shawneen Finnegan, a California birder whose enthusiasm for birding is only surpassed by her skills (and her enthusiasm is, clinically speaking, obsessive).

We didn't know *exactly* where we were. It was very early. It was very foggy. And the literature forwarded by refuge personnel wasn't down-to-the-mile precise.

It also didn't matter. The great mass of waterfowl around us proved beyond question or doubt that we were standing in precisely the right spot. In fact, in all of North America, on this morning in late November, there wasn't anyplace finer.

Directly in front of us, beneath its layer of geese, was a large diked impoundment pool. Beyond it, also sheathed in geese, was marsh, and beyond that a sort of goose-fog conglomerate that for all anyone knew might have continued until the fog gave way to geese.

The sky, shining blue above the fog, was a three-dimensional parade ground. Formations of Snow Geese comprised the lower echelons, flocks dropping in to join the other fogbound birds—finding space amid the multitudes or not finding space and having to move somewhere else. Above the Snows were legions of dinky, cut-down Canada Geese ("cacklers"), and here and there, in fact everyplace that wasn't occupied by something else, were wedges of Greater White-fronted Geese, or "speckle bellies." Higher still, above these identifiable birds, were more flocks that were no more than scratches in the sky.

The sight of it was unbelievable, but the sound of it defies description. It wasn't a noise. It wasn't a din. It was a blur of sound wrapping itself around the world like fog. With concentration, it was possible to listen through the harmonic storm and identify flocks by their calls—the single-note yap of the Snow Geese; the tin-horn, two-note toot of the cacklers; the squeaky, petulant nagging of white-fronteds.

With a little more concentration the notes of other marsh birds could be isolated in the fog song. The piped whistle of wigeon . . . the bugled grunt of American Coots . . . the terrier yap of Black-necked Stilts . . . the chirping trill of Green-winged Teal . . . the comical quacks of Mallards.

There was another sound, too. Reaching out across the marshes, muffled in fog, the sound of guns being emptied into the sky. The sharp, one-note bark of doubles and pumps; the deep, resonant, two-note *ka-wumph* of auto-loads. Out in the marshes, staked out in numbered blinds, were waterfowlers, gunners, people whose bonding with waterfowl even surpasses the appreciation of birders, people carrying on a tradition so ancient that it makes birding look like a fad.

When the founding fathers came to the shores of this continent, they discovered a wealth of living things that was scarcely to be believed. Elk bugled in Pennsylvania, sixty million bison roamed the prairies, and forest pigeons were so numerous that for three centuries their flights "darkened the sky" and their numbers vacillated between guesses and estimates. But not *this* century. In this century, there was no need to resort to estimates. The number of Passenger Pigeons left on earth was precisely one in 1900. Her name was Martha. She lived at the Cincinnati Zoo. Died there, too.

Nobody with powder and shot, or sling and bow, went hungry on this great continent. And as ambitious people moved west, they found more and more—more land, more bounty—a limitless wealth of game to whet and satisfy the appetite of a great nation fulfilling its manifest destiny.

The nineteenth century in North America has been called gunning's golden age. It was a wonderful time. An innocent, free-for-all time before conservation, that died, ironically, of success. Waterfowlers who rise hours before dawn in order to bid for one of a limited number of blinds in the morning lottery can only look back upon that age and marvel. Gunners, peering through the slits of their blinds along the Atlantic Coast, hoping to fill their one black duck limit, can only shake their heads.

In that golden age there were professional gunners who made a living shooting game for the market—wagonloads of hides; barrels packed tight with curlew, plover, pigeon. There were sport gunners, too—a class spawned by wealth and leisure who carried their "sport" to tasteless Victorian excess. Both the professional and the sport hunter approached the killing of "game" with zeal and the conviction that North America's wildlife was infinite. The faith was ill-founded. Not only is a continent's wildlife finite, but, to the shock of many, by the turn of the century much of it was gone and a lot more was going fast.

Gunning with no holds barred was not the only reason wildlife declined in the last century. Greed had a partner: habitat loss. Manifest destiny levied a toll upon the land and many living things were stripped of the very habitat they depended upon to sustain them.

The Passenger Pigeon might have been spared extinction if the slaughter had been stopped in time. But the bird would have declined in equal measure with the loss of the great eastern forests that sustained it. True, waterfowl populations were decimated by unregulated shooting. But the loss of prairie wetlands to agriculture—wetlands essential to nesting waterfowl —was devastating. The slaughter of sixty million bison is a moral outrage. But the creature would never have adapted to a prairie parceled to homesteaders in forty-acre plots. If not killed for pleasure and their hides, the buffalo would have been killed as vermin.

Habitat loss and the killing binge brought hunting's golden age to an end and helped usher in the age of wildlife protection. States took their own initiative, enacting laws that regulated hunting. In 1916, the governments of the United States and Great Britain forged a migratory bird treaty, offering continent-wide protection to many beleaguered species. In 1918, the passage of the Migratory Bird Act brought a merciful end to spring shooting and prescribed bag limits for migratory birds.

The new regulations dealt with the problem of overhunting, but the problem caused by habitat loss was more difficult to combat. It went head to head with another American totem even more cherished than the myth of America's infinite wealth: the right of individuals to manage their property as they see fit, even when these activities destroy habitat other creatures need to survive.

The partial solution was for the United States government to purchase property of its own—to manage it for the benefit of wildlife, to offset the loss of habitat that threatened the existence of North America's wildlife. The first refuge, at Pelican Island, Florida, was purchased in 1903. Today, there are over 450; they form a network called the National Wildlife Refuge System, administered by the U.S. Fish and Wildlife Service.

Under the double-barreled protection plan—regulated hunting and active management—much of what had been lost during the golden age was restored. Although the continent will never again know the riches it had, there are places you can go and still catch a glimpse of the incredible wealth that should have been ours.

The fog began to lift, disclosing more and more birds by the minute. We tried to count the number of Snow Geese spread out before us, but we might just as well have tried to quantify icing on a cake. We tried to estimate the number of geese flying overhead and discovered that none of our estimates could come within a standard deviation of each other. "Overhead" is a big and ill-defined place, and on this November morning, it was also very, very crowded.

Suddenly, for reasons beyond our grasp, the great host of Snow Geese began to rise. It started as a ripple that swelled to a wave that became an ascending avalanche of birds and sound that spread, wing tip to wing tip, cry to cry, from one end of our world to another.

It wasn't a flock. It was a living storm, and we were enveloped by it, humbled by it, lashed by a vortex of wings and sound, until all the senses we know (and maybe some that we do not) were fused in, and fused to, a white hot core of wonder.

Linda was trying to say something, but the storm tore the words from her mouth and fed them to the vortex. I am not certain and I did not ask. But if I had to guess, if someone wanted to know, I think the words might have been:

"Oh my God."

Greg Mensik is a U.S. Fish and Wildlife Service biologist working out of the Sacramento Valley NWR. He is thirty-six, with brown hair, blue eyes, and the build of a light heavyweight, yet he looks as if he could have played Hamlet. The cowboy boots beneath his desk are muddy, but this is what you would expect from a man whose job is to ride herd on fifty percent of the waterfowl funneling down the Pacific Flyway.

"Why do so many birds come here?" I asked.

"Tradition," he responds unhesitant. For thousands of years, the marshes of the Sacramento Valley served the needs of ducks, geese, swans. "Over a million acres," Greg relates, recalling a historic fact.

Then, beginning in the late 1800s, the marshes gave way to agriculture, the industry that would come to dominate California's economy. "Ninety-five percent" according to Greg. Over much of the Sacramento Valley this meant conversion from wetlands to rice fields. Wintering waterfowl responded to the usurpation of their historic wintering grounds in much the same way Native Americans did to the loss of their land: they raided the crops, inflicting considerable damage. And . . . they declined.

Beginning in 1937, the year the Pittman-Robertson Federal Aid in Wildlife Restoration Act was passed, the first of five federal wildlife refuges was established ninety miles north of Sacramento. The Sacramento NWR was paid for by congressional appropriation. The others—Delevan, Colusa, Sutter, and Butte Sink—were paid for with money generated from the purchase of Duck Stamps. The dual purpose of these refuges was to provide habitat for waterfowl and reduce crop damage.

Note, I did not say "restore" habitat. That might imply a return to the natural marshes of the past. The truth is that the marshes are anything but natural. Water levels are carefully monitored and manipulated by refuge personnel—drawn down in the spring to encourage plant growth, reflooded in the fall when birds arrive. This pattern mimics the natural cycle but sidesteps nature's capriciousness.

What's more, the refuge system encourages unnatural crowding of birds. Where waterfowl wintering in the Sacramento Valley once spread out over a million acres of wetlands, now they must wedge themselves into 23,780 acres.

How did the birds respond?

Instead of replying, Greg dipped into the pile of paper on his desk and brought out the balance sheet. They contained the results of the most recent aerial surveys—very impressive results. Snow Geese in the complex in late November numbered 479,805; "Cackling Canada Geese," one of the smaller races, tallied 591,142. White-fronteds weighed in at 92,222.

I whistled to indicate my appreciation of such wealth.

Pintails were the most numerous puddle duck, with 194,030 on the board. Mallards numbered 167,565; Northern Shoveler 129,295; Green-winged Teal close behind with 128,865. Another dozen species of waterfowl were tallied on the form, with numbers ranging from over 100,000 (American Wigeon) to 10 (Redhead).

The bottom line, as of November 22, 1989, was 842,715 ducks and geese.

"Impressive," I said, and meant it. But the survey was just a frozen snapshot; it lacked the perspective of time.

"How are duck populations doing in general?" I asked. "Weren't they beat up pretty badly by drought?"

"Yeah," Greg confirmed, "waterfowl were down in the eighties." In the Bean Patch, a productive little corner of Butte Sink Refuge, wintering pintail used to number a million birds in the seventies. "Now," Greg advised, "the surveys are only coming up with a third of a million."

But the thing that worries biologists like Greg are not the short term "oscillations," the rises and falls in populations that occur in response to natural conditions. What troubles waterfowl biologists are long-term trends—and the trend in waterfowl is decidedly down.

"The peaks [in the oscillations] never approach the old peaks," Greg explained. "Each low in the cycle is lower than the one before."

Greg shrugged and sighed. It was a gesture that said, "You know how it is."

Yes, I knew how it was.

I also wanted to get out, find Linda and Shawneen, and enjoy some more of the refuge. But before I did I asked Greg whether he knew anything about waterfowl up at Tule Lake NWR, a major stopover point for migrating waterfowl and our next stop.

Greg seemed surprised to hear that our plans called for Tule. This late in the season, as the surveys indicated, most of the geese had already moved down to Sacramento—those that troubled to stop at Tule all. The recent trend has been for birds just to overfly Tule and shoot straight for Sacramento.

"How come?" I asked.

"Not enough habitat around Tule," he replied.

## TULE NATIONAL WILDLIFE REFUGE

Tulelake, California, population 1,000 more or less, lies in the Klamath Basin, and this is about as far north as you can go in California before you start sending your state tax dollars to Oregon. The streets are wide enough to turn a pickup around in without difficulty. The local constabulary is accommodating enough to let you get away with it, particularly if you are local and he knows you (which in Tulelake pretty much comes to the same thing). The town's two traffic lights are set perpetually on "blink," and when the Christmas decorations go up, just after Thanksgiving, evergreen trees get plopped in the center of major intersections. They don't really interfere with anything, and this way, the town figures, everyone gets to see them.

Tulelake is a small town, an American town. The kind of town that when kids graduate from high school, they can hardly wait to leave and find their fortune in the real world. It's also the kind of town that five, ten, or maybe twenty years later, they return to. Because the real world, most discover, may be many things. But it isn't Tulelake.

Coffee in one hand, doughnut in the other, I coaxed our van out of its parking spot and executed a wide, sweeping arch that put us heading south out of town.

"Want me to hold your cup?" Linda encouraged.

"Nnnnuh," I said, which is "no" spoken through a cinnamon doughnut. If you get to Tulelake, you *must* try the bakery. No joke. Best little sinker doughnuts in the Klamath Basin (although I can't really claim to have tried them all).

"Turn here," Shawneen suggested, just a little bit after the fact, I must add in my own defense. We did, eventually, get onto the East-West Road heading in the right direction, turned left past the Visitor Center, and got our first look at Tule, the lake.

There are many places in North America that may rival the Klamath Basin in wheat production, in waterfowl, maybe even in the number of eagles that gather here each winter. But very few can rival it for pure, dramatic beauty.

The protective ring of peaks, dominated by stately Mount Shasta, holds the wind at bay and sheds a Shangri-La air of magic upon the basin. Sculptured stone, wrought by a violent volcanic past, puts a surreal edge to the south end. The marshes, spreading outward from the centerpiece of a lake, are tawny and lush and at odds with the hard, contrary horizon. Then there is the lake itself. Tule Lake. A great blue mirror filled with sky that serves the vanity of mountains and the needs of tens upon tens of thousands of wintering ducks, geese, and swans.

Established in 1928, Tule Lake National Wildlife Refuge contains 38,908 acres of lake, marsh, and cropland. During the peak of the autumn migration, most of the waterfowl using the Pacific Flyway, approximately one million birds, use Tule and adjacent refuges. This seems like a lot until you realize that historically the Klamath Basin used to boast 185,000 wetland acres, and waterfowl concentrations once numbered *six million*.

There weren't six million birds sitting out on the lake when we pulled up on Hill Road to do a scan. There weren't even a million. Winter was closing in on the Klamath Valley and many of the namby-pamby geese and wimpy *Anas* waterfowl had already bolted south. What was left were tough ducks—greenheads and goldeneye—big, burly, full-sized Canada Geese (none of those tin-horn subcompact cacklers), and . . .

"Tundra Swans," Shawneen intoned, setting up her scope, getting down to the serious business of searching through the mass and ferreting out the nuggets. "Let's see what we can do with these guys," she said.

Half a hundred Tundra Swans were within immediate range of our scopes, segregated by family groups. Perhaps a thousand more of the great birds were concentrated in a distant mound. But Shawneen was setting her sights on bigger game, a bigger swan. Tundra Swans are nice birds. Trumpeter Swan, in California, would be a *real* prize.

The roadway offered an elevated view of the lake and basin. The shoreline was rimmed by a dark band of waterfowl, puddle ducks whose limited reach bound them to the shallows. Mallards were by far the most common duck afloat. But shovelers were common and wigeon and pintail well represented. Farther out were divers—goldeneye, Ruddy Ducks, and a sprinkling of Bufflehead. Beyond them, pale-back rafts—Canvasback—and charcoal-backed Ring-necks.

The only white in sight was being flown by the swans. They stood out like coral island clusters—dusky young and ice-colored adults. Around each bird was a fawning entourage of coots and wigeon. These attendant lackeys snuggled up to the great-necked birds, snatching aquatic plants from the bills of their lords and providers. The swans looked on the petty pilfering with equanimity.

The clank of metal on metal announced that Shawneen had worked her patch of lake to the limit.

"Anything?" she asked.

"No," I replied. "Nothing special." (Nothing but about a heptabillion ducks!) "If this is off-season, I can't imagine what this place looks like at prime time."

"Ohhh," Shawneen observed. "That's easy. It looks white!" she assured, feigning a simplicity she has never known. "Just like Snow Geese."

It was just about this moment that the near-shore waters came very close to turning chocolate brown. A large, dark raptor made its very deliberate way along the edge of the lake, sending a wave of waterfowl to either side. Only the swans ignored the interloper, and the young Bald Eagle, for its part, ignored the swans.

The eagle wasn't really serious, didn't have any particular targets in mind. It was just checking out the buffet table, seeing whether crippled duck was on the menu today. Chances were excellent that it was. Duck Impaired is a specialty of the house.

"There's a *bunch* of eagles around," Linda confirmed, offering us the benefits of her several scans of the horizon. "Lots of other raptors too."

Waterfowl have long had a historic lock on Tule's popularity. "Duck and Goose spoken here" was the legend inscribed on the notice board of the motel where we were staying. But since the advent of the raptorially conscious seventies, Tule's fame has broadened to include raptors. Hundreds of birds of prey winter in the basin—drawn to rodents and the waterfowl that are drawn to the surfeit of grain. Among them are Red-taileds, Rough-leggeds, Northern Harriers, Prairie Falcons, and Short-eared Owls.

But the bird whose winter appearance has come to dominate public interest is the Bald Eagle, and not without reason. The bird is large. Not as large as a swan, but larger than any other North American bird of prey (except one). It is handsome, regal—a dark-mantled bird with a snow-colored crown and an intelligent yellow eye. And, it is powerful—a powerful flyer, a powerful hunter.

Since Benjamin Franklin's eloquent bad-mouthing of the bird when the time came to select a national emblem, the Bald Eagle has been an unjust target for abuse. Its taste for winter-killed fish has made it a "carrion eater." Its talent for close-range aerial pursuit has made it a "thief." Its penchant for sitting for long periods and not expending energy without need has made it "lazy," and this is not fair. Only humans seem to equate frenetic activity with success. Eagles can and do sit for extended periods precisely because they are successful predators who can find food at need. Energy wasted is just that. A waste.

As for the charge of thief, outmaneuvering an Osprey—a smaller, more agile bird—takes a measure of doing. If an eagle relieving an Osprey of its fish is so bad, perhaps somebody can explain why a successful leveraged buy-out wins so much admiration.

As for the charge of "carrion eater," well, it's a pretty glass-enclosed house if you ask me. Eagles, at least, pick their carrion up fresh out of the stream. A creature that gets its carrion cut into slabs, plastic wrapped, and chemically enhanced would do well not to cast stones.

The Bald Eagle is a skilled fisherman able to capture fish as adroitly as an Osprey. It is also a consummate hunter. I knew one adult male that wintered at Brigantine NWR in New Jersey and whose specialty was Black duck. Bald Eagles selectively kill weak or injured birds, but only because it is more energy efficient than going after intact birds, not because they lack for skill. The Brigantine bird would approach the impoundments every morning, gain altitude, and maneuver itself above and downwind of the very unhappy flock. Then he would make his move, using gravity and long pushing wing beats to close the distance. The flock, which never did learn any defensive maneuver more imaginative than flying straight away, would flush in panic. And although ducks are fast flyers, and although they had a good lead on the eagle, the predator always caught the flock with ease, *reached down somewhere in the middle*, and scooped up a duck.

I cannot say that the targets were not chosen in advance or that the ducks taken by the eagle did not show some infirmity beyond the grasp of human apprehension. My impression was that this eagle was able to have any bird it wanted. Well, almost any bird. Usually the eagle lost its first catch of the morning to an adult female forcing him to go get another.

Criticisms and merits notwithstanding, when the chips are down it is part of the national character to rally around the flag, and several short decades ago, the chips were decidedly down for the Bald Eagle. Like the Peregrine, it was a victim of pesticides. Also like the Peregrine, its numbers became so depleted that the national emblem of the most powerful nation on earth became a federally endangered species—a distinction it still holds.

The bird's recovery has been slow and painful. But during the late seventies, the decline was checked. Through the eighties, nest productivity increased and the population began to rebound. And in the Klamath Basin, the number of wintering eagles began to increase and win attention. Arriving in November, remaining until late March or early April, birds from northern Canada augment resident eagles whose lives are bound to the basin. At dawn, the eagles spread out to forage. By midafternoon, the successful ones are already returning to one of five major roosts located around the area. Three hundred eagles may occupy a single roost.

Akimi Shono, a graduate of Humboldt State University and a refuge manager trainee, was on duty at the refuge when later in the morning we stopped by to check up on any recent sightings. Shawneen was particularly interested in a Gyrfalcon that was being seen periodically.

Ms. Shono was politely conversant, explained without unnecessary detail about the eagles, their ecology, and the importance of keeping disruption to a minimum (a dictate called Eagle Etiquette). Only once did her enthusiasm breach the upper limits of professionalism. This was when she told of the day the previous winter when she had counted six hundred eagles all sitting around a single hole in the ice.

"Why are so many eagles suddenly wintering here?" I asked. Before DDT, when eagle numbers were high, the Klamath Basin wasn't known as an eagle hot spot. Something must have changed.

"Because the numbers of waterfowl wintering in the basin has been increasing in the last fifteen years," she explained.

"Why's that?" I asked.

"Because there is less waterfowl habitat farther south," she replied.

I came close to telling her that Greg Mensik, down at Sacramento, had said almost this exact same thing about Tule. But then I realized, with a start, that there was nothing contradictory in their statements. In fact, there was nothing but sad accord.

We were poised on the road again, watching evening creep into the basin, watching harriers, and Red-taileds, and Rough-leggeds, and eagles, listening to the mindless babble of waterfowl as they prepared to meet the night. Only the swans seemed unmoved. As evening leached the color out of the world, the swans, if anything, seemed more luminous than ever— bright clusters resting on a dark lake. It was still, and the air ferried the swan sounds to our ears. It's a strange sound, eerie and sad, plaintive and soulful. It's a sound that makes the call of geese appear harsh and uncouth, and one that claims blood kinship to feelings that run deeper than understanding.

It is a wild sound. If you do not know it, I hope some day you do.

Overhead, a dozen Red-tailed Hawks were wheeling over the escarpment, jockeying for position. Six others and a Prairie Falcon had already claimed their roost sites and settled in for the night. Northern Harriers were patrolling fields that had already lost all color, and the Short-eared Owls would soon replace them.

"Do you hear the owl?" Linda whispered.

I waited, listening . . . and heard it. The resonant call to darkness heard all across North America, familiar to birders and nonbirders alike. The bird called again. Another answered.

"Do you remember the Great Horned Owls in the Pawnee Grasslands?" Linda wondered.

"Yes," I said. And I did. Two young birds huddled in the shadows of Pawnee Butte. I recalled them, and without much effort could bring to mind a dozen more that we had heard or seen in our travels.

"What made you think of the grasslands?" I probed.

"Oh," she said, "I guess this place just reminds of the grasslands. The escarpment," she explained, "the raptors . . . the open space. It's a great place," she added.

I didn't know whether she was speaking of Tule or the Pawnee Grasslands—not that it mattered. They were both great places. Treasures. Like all the places Linda and I had sought out, key pieces in a mosaic whose sum is a continent of riches.

"It is a great place," I affirmed, discriminating even less than Linda.

The great mass of waterfowl were hardly more than a darker band of shadow now. Even the swans had lost their luster, though their sound reached out across the distance. Across the basin, the lights of Tulelake shimmered, beckoned.

"I guess we missed the evening lineup of Gyrfalcons," I shouted down to Shawneen.

"It sure looks that way," she agreed.

"Does anybody want dinner?" I asked. "I mean, besides me?"

There were no dissenting votes.

We started back to the van, drawn by a sudden hunger, pursued by the sound of swans and the babble of half a million waterfowl.

# 19 • LOS PADRES NATIONAL FOREST, CALIFORNIA:

## Ghost Dancing on Mount Pinos

HE ROAD TURNED UGLY JUST BELOW THE CREST. So we parked, climbed like penitents the last quarter-mile or so, were jeered at every step by Mountain Chickadees and Pygmy Nuthatches. The air at 8,800 feet is clear but thin, and by the time we reached the top of Mount Pinos, we were breathing hard.

Two columns of stone and a parking lot mark the spot. Both were empty, and I would have been surprised if it were otherwise. The pillars once supported a sign that described the California Condor, North America's greatest soaring bird. The lot once served the needs of those who hoped to catch a glimpse of the creature. But the condor is gone now. So is the sign and the people and their cars. All that remains is the significance of the place, because significance, like energy, cannot be destroyed. It only assumes new meaning.

"It's OK if I wander, isn't it?" Linda asked. Linda wasn't at all sure why we'd traveled here, and I wasn't sure I could explain it.

"Sure," I said, looking at my watch. "It's almost noon. What say we meet back at the van around three?"

There was no reason for her to stay, actually. Linda had already seen a free-flying California Condor. There was little enough reason for *me* to stay. As I said, the bird was gone. Chances of seeing a free-flying condor that had somehow escaped the Condor Recovery Team's last roundup were all but nonexistent—stood, maybe, the ghost of a chance.

Still . . . I felt compelled to see this place—driven partly by curiosity and partly, believe it or not, by hope. Unlike Linda, I had never seen California Condors while their nine-foot wingspan cast shadows upon the earth.

It's a powerful thing, hope. More powerful, certainly, than reason. There have even been instances—yes a few—when hope has even proven itself to be more powerful than loss.

There was one other reason why this pilgrimage was made. Maybe *the* reason. But a part of me still wanted to believe that this wasn't the reason. That, after all, is what hope is all about.

The sun doesn't waste much energy on the Sierra Madres in December. The air is dry cold, the light frail. Below the crest of the ridge is a bony hillside whose principal features are rock and thorny growth. At the bottom of the sloping plain was a tree; more accurately, the remains of a tree—a stripped and wind-tortured stump. Judging by its girth, it must have been a giant in its day. Now . . .

Now, it's a lifeless corpse hanging over a bony hillside.

Reaching outward from the base of Mount Pinos were a series of pus-colored hills. What wasn't rock was shadow and what wasn't shadow was a bristly sort of pine, sticking up along the ridgetops like the hair on a pig's back. Pig pine. Mangy pig pine. Beyond were more hills, and behind these more hills again, until finally the Los Angeles smog closed in and claimed all that was left of the world.

I looked at the tree again, the stump. Something about it seemed familiar, recalled something. A discarded memory? A photo maybe. In some book or magazine! A photo of a tree with a condor perched in it?

I could picture it. Could superimpose the memory over the arms of the stump and *almost* believe that the great bird was there. Wings spread benediction-wide to absorb the rays of the sun, waiting for the thermals that would bear it aloft.

I could do everything but make the vision real.

*You should have come sooner,* an evil and all too familiar voice inside  my head chided.

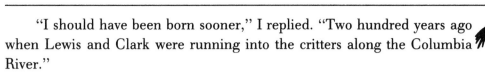

"I should have been born sooner," I replied. "Two hundred years ago when Lewis and Clark were running into the critters along the Columbia River."

*You haven't got a chance of seeing this bird*, the voice said, sidestepping the metaphysical dodge. *Not a ghost of a chance.*

Ignoring the failed vote of confidence, I brought my binoculars up, starting left, working right, moving them along the horizon. Why left to right? I don't know. Maybe it's vestigial—a throwback to my Hawk Mountain days. Six thousand hours of hawk-watching brought to bear on a California sky. Six thousand hours, good optics, and all the hope there is in the world against nothing worse than bad odds.

Remember Pandora and her box?

Remember that song about the goat and the dam, the ant and the rubber tree plant? The one the junior senator from Massachusetts used in his bid for the American presidency back in 1960?

Remember Mary Martin, shepherding a fragile, poisoned light, asking you, and all the children on earth, to clap your hands and restore the light?

Hey, I'm an American baby boomer. I was raised on hope.

Through the binoculars, the hills looked no more friendly, but they took on definition. The Los Padres National Forest is a big place—plenty big enough for even a condor to get lost in. Back in the Pleistocene era, condors used to range all up and down the Pacific Coast and across the Southwest all the way to the Gulf of Mexico. There were even populations in Florida and New York State—maybe elsewhere!

Who was to say that just one truant bird hadn't taken a sojourn down into Mexico and given the whole recovery program the slip? Who's to say that a single living, breathing, free-flying California Condor had not cheated fate? We weren't talking decades after all. We were talking 1987—less than three years since the last condor was corralled.

Wasn't there some Greek hero who cheated the fates?

Prometheus? No, he was the klepto-pyro whose liver was ruined by vultures.

Icarus? No, he flew too high.

*He fell!* my inner voice corrected.

Yes. He fell. My binoculars all the while were falling on empty sky. Not even a Red-tailed Hawk was aloft to break up the blue monotony. Not even a raven.

The California Condor was an inspired creation—great in size, great in primal origin. It heralded from an age that knew the likes of mastodons and saber-toothed cats, but when that world lapsed, ten thousand years ago, the bird showed a resourcefulness its contemporaries lacked. Condors tightened their range, stabilized their populations, and settled in, by all appearances, to wait out the millennia.

Then the white man arrived. And Icarus fell.

Many condors were simply shot. No, they weren't edible. No, their feathers weren't prized adornments for ladies' headgear. Despite their size, they posed no threat to humans or livestock. Yet there are nearly two hundred *documented* cases of condors that were killed for no better reason than to satisfy somebody's perverted vanity.

Shooting had another impact on condors—one less direct but perhaps even more devastating. As carrion-eaters, condors fed frequently upon deer and other animals shot and lost by hunters. Bullet fragments ingested by condors caused uncounted numbers of the birds to die slow, lingering deaths due to lead poisoning.

The demise of the creature did not come unheralded. A hundred years before the fact, California ornithologist James Cooper predicted that "unless protected our great vulture is doomed to rapid extinction." In the 1940s, there were approximately sixty California Condors left in the wild, ranging in the hills north of Los Angeles. By the 1960s that number had dropped to forty. By 1981–1984, condors were down to four or five breeding pairs, with a total of fifteen birds surviving in the wild. Then disaster.

Between November 1984 and April 1985, nine condors, more than half the birds in the wild, were lost. In a desperate effort to save the species from extinction, biologists intervened. A decision was made to take all living California Condors out of the wild and gamble that an artificial propagation program would offer the species some kind of future. On April 19, 1987, the last free-flying California Condor on earth joined the twenty-six others in captivity. The wings that had spanned evolutionary eras were folded. The bird became a ward of science.

The condor isn't the only bird to have reached biological bankruptcy in this century. This was the century that closed the books on the Passenger Pigeon, the Heath Hen, the Carolina Parakeet, and the Dusky Seaside Sparrow.

Some might argue that the sparrow doesn't belong in this list. Technically, the bird was a subspecies, one split hair down the phylogenic ladder. Most would probably argue that the condor doesn't belong in the same class as the pigeon and the parakeet, either. The bird isn't dead! It's just indoors and due for restocking once the numbers get fleshed out a bit. There are other birds vying for the distinction of being the last bird to be declared extinct in the twentieth century—the Ivory-billed Woodpecker, the Bachman's Warbler. Both might make it. It would be nice to clean up the books before entering the next century. Help keep the body count straight for future ornithohistorians.

I brought the binoculars back across the horizon, one more time—a long, careful, futile sweep that coasted over a hundred empty square miles. People sometimes ask a very funny question when they see you peering through binoculars. They want to know, "How far you can see with those things?" Well, you can see forever, all the way to Alpha Centauri if you want. Left at the Milky Way and straight on 'til morning. The one thing you can't do with binoculars is look back.

When the Passenger Pigeon—the bird that "darkened the skies"—collapsed a very interesting thing happened. People refused to believe it. A popular notion, at the turn of the century, was that the great host of birds had simply migrated. To South America, said some; Australia, said others. Those not gifted enough to fantasize the loss away attributed the bird's demise to some natural disaster—to epidemics, tornadoes, snowstorms, mass drowning . . . everything, *anything*, but the real cause.

It is funny and it would be funnier if it were not so desperately sad, but people's reaction to the loss of the California Condor is just a contemporary remake of the Passenger Pigeon play. When the demise of the condor was imminent, many individuals and a surprisingly number of conservation organizations advanced the old natural disaster rubric, insisting that extinction is a natural process and that the condor had been on the way out since it ran out of mastodons to eat. We in the twentieth century had just gotten stuck burying the corpse.

There is no evidence for this. No evidence that the birds were not doing perfectly fine in their Pacific Coast stronghold until the white man came along. Frankly, the idea insults my sense of rightness. I don't believe it. But the resort to laissez-faire Darwinism served several important ends. It paid lip service to science (the prerequisite for any decision reached in the twentieth century). It explained (publicly) why more effort and resources were not being directed toward trying to save the creature. Most of all, it assuaged guilt.

But the way most people have dealt with the loss of the California Condor is simple, convenient denial. The bird isn't gone. It's safe and somewhere else. No, not Australia. The San Diego Wild Animal Park and Los Angeles Zoo. We've saved it with science.

At the end of the last century, just about the time that the Passenger Pigeon and the Eskimo curlew were collapsing, a religious movement swept the ranks of Indians of North America's Great Plains (a wonderful people whose civilization was collapsing for reasons not unlike those that were devastating the curlew and the pigeon). The movement was called the Ghost Dance. Practitioners donned magic shirts, which, they were told, would turn away bullets. And they danced—to turn back the clock, to resurrect the glory of their culture and their past.

The Condor Recovery Project, though I hope it succeeds and averts one more biological tragedy, is just the latest brand of denial—the Ghost Dance of our time. We, who are the products of this age, are donning a magic shirt called technology, hoping that it will protect the past, while we just forge ahead with the future.

It's a great shirt, this Ghost Dance coverall, tailored to fit an age that worships science. There is just enough fact woven into the fabric to make it defensible. It deflects the guilt that comes of letting a species collapse during

our lifetime. And it keeps us from having to come to grips with a cold, hard reality. The same reality that brought down the Passenger Pigeon. The same reality that is killing the planet we live on.

A tiny, dark pinpoint brought my binoculars to a stop. A soaring bird so far away that when it turned wing on, it was invisible, so far away that it owed half its existence to the force of my will.

"It's Big," I knew, from the way it moved, from its ability to project its image across the terrible distance that separated us.

"*It's impossible*," a cold, dark corner of my mind hissed.

Impossible or not, the bird was there, a dark, dark bird soaring on broad steady wings, immune from denial or fact. The strain made my shoulders ache, made my arms shake, made the fragile image dance and disappear. Very slowly, very deliberately, I brought my elbows down until they rested on my knees, holding the glass steady, hoping that I had not lost its place in the sky.

And the bird was there.

Now, it came down to distance and time. Now it came down to all the skills I had gathered during a lifetime of birding. And to hope.

Sometimes the bird seemed to be drifting my way. Sometimes it disappeared, in the heat, in the haze . . . for seconds that lasted for epochs. Sometimes I thought that I could *almost* see white, somewhere on the bird, somewhere on the underwings. Sometimes I could *almost* convince myself that the upper wings had the look of tarnished silver. Once I felt certain! Almost certain.

I held the bird for five minutes or more as it soared at the limit of conjecture, where reality and hope battle for conviction. Held it as though it were the last California Condor on earth and its survival depended upon the strength of my will. Held it, in fact, until long after the point I knew it was just a subadult Golden Eagle pinned against an American sky.

I held it because this was as close as I would ever get to seeing the bird whose unfolded wings stretch all the way back to another age of this world, and I wanted to savor it.

*"Impossible,"* a voice pronounced from a cold, dark corner in my mind. This time, I knew it was so. Hope is many things, but it throws itself against fact and shatters.

I brought my binoculars down, leaned back on my elbows, and stared out at the great empty span of hill. It was time to take off the Ghost Dance shirt and confront the real reason why I'd come here. That was to come to terms with loss. Because "loss" is something that people in general, and birders in particular, are going to know intimately in the next century. Bird populations are declining. Ranges will retract. Species will disappear or, at best, become closeted in carefully monitored environments, keeping their genetic blueprints on file. Throughout North America, and South America, and Europe and Africa, Asia, and Australia, the incredible wealth of plants and animals, the earth's critical habitat, is being lost.

As "the Environmental President" said about something else, "That is not a threat, that is not a promise, that is just the way it is going to be."

It has been estimated that some life form expires on this planet every twenty minutes. It is projected that at its current rate of depletion, the tropical rain forest, the place where many of our nesting birds spend most of their lives, will be gone by the middle of the next century. Very likely, so will most of those birds.

Michigan's jack pine country, home of the Kirtland's Warbler, is slated to disappear because of global warming. The expiration date is 2010. Barring a condor-scale bailout, the warblers go with it.

In the water-starved Everglades, the number of wading birds—herons, egrets, ibis, storks—has fallen to less than 10 percent of the numbers that existed when the refuge was established.

Shorebird populations are in decline. The incidence of the Sanderling, the common sandpiper of the beach, fell 80 percent between 1978 and 1987. Whimbrel declined 60 percent; Black-bellied Plover and dowitcher 40 percent. The hosts of migratory songbirds have been shattered. Between 1947 and 1989, half of North America's cross-Gulf migrants disappeared.

Despite extensive management, widespread popular support from organizations like Ducks Unlimited, and virtually an entire government agency committed to their maintenance, waterfowl numbers keep slipping. And the

ranks of raptors, who recovered the ground they had lost to DDT, have been breached, again. At Hawk Mountain, the Red-shouldered Hawk never pulled out of its decline, and at Cape May, New Jersey, the "Accipiter Capital of North America," Sharp-shinned Hawk numbers have crashed.

This is what is happening in North America—with its resources and history of environmental concern. In many parts of the world the picture of loss is far, far worse.

*Why?* There is a long answer and a short one. The long answer enumerates all of the human activities that reduce bird populations—a list that would fill a book in itself. The short answer takes them in sum: birds are declining, in North America and elsewhere, because our species is waging a war of attrition against the other living things on this planet—and we are winning. We are altering the face of the planet to serve our ambitions. They are losing—habitat, numbers, any future in this world of our making. The California Condor is not an exception. The condor is a bellwether.

The shadow cast by the nub of a tree was longer now. It fell across the bony hillside like some broad-winged bird in flight, like Icarus after the state-of-the-art technology on which he had pinned his hopes failed.

The ambition of the Condor Recovery Program is to return condors to the wild. The birds are not expected to survive without tending and feeding. By closeting the birds in a controlled environment, here, in Los Padres National Forest, or perhaps in a place like the Grand Canyon, a historic stronghold, the recovery team hopes that the things that drove the bird to the brink of extinction can be reduced.

Not eliminated. That would require humans to adopt a whole new approach to this world. That is something we are clearly not prepared to do yet. It is far easier to don the Ghost Dance shirt, hope that it can protect something of our heritage, and dance, while all the living things on this planet get backed into manageable little corners, placed on reservations or in cages.

Just like the condor—the bird whose unfolded wings once reached back in time; and whose pinions have been trimmed to fit our future.

*Pilgrimage*

A LIGHT RAIN WAS FALLING, THE KIND THAT IS TOO steady for the intermittent wiper setting but not heavy enough for a steady sweep of the blades. The rain gave the battered surface of the New Jersey Turnpike an oily sheen. It softened the outlines of the New York skyline, but it could not wash it away.

In the passenger seat, her forehead pressed against the glass, Linda stared out the window. I couldn't tell whether she was seeing the mosaic of waste and wetlands or whether her eyes were turned inward, focused on some patch of western sky. I guessed the latter.

"Not much traffic," I said to break the silence, to divine something of the wifely mood.

Her answer was a nod that tugged against the glass, making her eyes widen like a frightened child.

"We're going to get killed going home," I added, apologizing in advance. "Sunday afternoons are bad westbound."

Linda didn't even nod this time. Her western soul recoils at an urban touch, and the view from the north end of the turnpike is a sensory truncheon even to those inured to it.

"How far is Old Lyme?" she asked, without turning.

"Only a couple of hours," I said, trying to sound cheerful. "That's without traffic," I added, losing any ground I may have gained.

She accepted this with silence and another nod, never shifting her gaze from the remnants of the Hackensack Meadowlands—a wetlands too tough to die.

"Rough-legged!" she announced suddenly.

Sure enough, hovering over a landscape that looked like a cross between Attu and Mordor was a light-phase Rough-legged Hawk. Hackensack Meadowlands rats or tundra lemmings—it's all the same to this Arctic buteo. The Meadowlands supports an astonishing number of wintering birds. One hundred twenty-two species and 409,170 individual birds on the 1989 Christmas Bird Count—totals that birders in Colorado only dream of! Accounted in the 1989 tally were 4 Turkey Vultures, 37 Northern Harriers, 2 Sharp-shinned Hawks, 2 Cooper's Hawks, 1 Northern Goshawk, 1 Red-shouldered Hawk, 54 Red-tailed Hawks, 33 Rough-legged Hawks, 45 American Kestrel, 1 Merlin, 3 Barn Owls, 1 Eastern Screech-Owl, 1 Great Horned Owl, 1 Snowy Owl, 4 Short-eared Owls, 1 Northern Saw-whet Owl.

Birds, like estuaries, can be amazingly resilient.

As our van drew abreast of the Meadowlands Sports Complex (home of the New Jersey Giants), a Belted Kingfisher flashed across six lanes of traffic, nimbly avoiding a tractor trailer. The bird brought to mind the first time I had enjoyed the company of the man we were journeying to see—although, in a very real and very special way, I guess I have known him all my life. The man's name is Roger Tory Peterson. As you may recall, he more or less invented birding in America.

When I was young, ten, and lived at 57 Washington Avenue, I used to sit by the mailbox—waiting for the postman to deliver the manila envelope bearing the Audubon Society brand. Inside were leaflets. Junior Audubon leaflets. All about birds!

Orioles like the ones that nested in our yard. Wood Thrushes like the one that piped the shadows out of hiding. Grosbeaks, tanagers, Red-winged Blackbirds, even birds like the Indigo Bunting—a bird that was plainly too, too beautiful ever to see.

I read those leaflets, and reread them, and reread them again, until there was no reason to read them anymore—because I'd memorized them. The leaflets were written by a man named Roger T. Peterson.

When I was twelve, I received a wonderful present: a two-volume set of books printed by the National Geographic Society. The books were about North America's birds and they were filled with information and photos. In Volume I there was an essay entitled "What Bird Is That?" It described a careful eight-step process for bird identification, a process called the Peterson system.

Know what? I'll bet you do. The Peterson of the process and the Peterson of the leaflets were the same.

Later, much later (several years in fact), a favorite uncle died—one who loved hunting and fishing and whose name I bear. Among the personal effects entrusted to the nephew who promised to keep the outdoor tradition alive was a shotgun with a stock that was too short, a jacket with shoulders too wide, and a book. The book was titled *A Field Guide to the Birds*. And do you know what?

Yes, somehow I feel confident you do.

For as long as I have been a birder, and this is a very long time, there has been a man named Peterson whose guidance has figured every step of the way. I am not alone in this regard. Everyone who has picked up a pair of binoculars and trained them on birds since 1934, the year his first field guide was published, has felt the hand of the Master, either directly or indirectly—the hand that has gripped "birding's" tiller since before the name was coined.

So when the idea of a birding competition was first discussed in 1983, one that would pit teams of birders against each other, it was automatic that minds inclined to hear the thoughts of Roger Tory Peterson. Would he favor the idea?

"Whose team can *I* be on?" said the premier birder of our age to a thunderstruck director of the Cape May Bird Observatory. "Can I be on yours? We should start in Troy Meadows, don't you think? Then head for the hills around Boonton at dawn."

So on May 19, 1984, at the age of seventy-six, Roger Tory Peterson became a member of the Guerrilla Birding Team in the first World Series of Birding. His eyes and ears and marshalling skills brought us the championship and a state record—brought us almost everything, in fact, but a kingfisher. The day after the event, as we left Cape May en route to Old Lyme, Connecticut, the first bird that flashed in front of our car was a kingfisher.

Since the first World Series of Birding, the old master-pupil bond that was the basis for our long relationship has been overlaid with friendship. Our meetings and exchanges have been as many as fortune allowed. Birding has been our bond. But now, I needed the wisdom of the Master again. A question had been growing in my mind. One whose answer was beyond me—maybe beyond anyone, but plainly beyond me.

We had traveled far, Linda and I. We had seen many special places, witnessed many remarkable things, and shared incredible moments with a host of exceptional people. We had delved deep into birding's heritage and basked in the sun of its golden age. We had had a wonderful time.

But almost from the beginning of our adventure, even before, our path had been dogged by an air of disquiet. Out of the corner of our eyes, we could glimpse a shadow, and it fell upon birding's future. At places like the Gulf Coast, on the World Series of Birding and at Cape May, the shadow had brushed us. From Mount Pinos, you could plainly see it.

What I hoped was that the man who had given birding so much of its past could look down the long tunnel of his experience and disclose to us, and birders everywhere, something of its future. That's why Linda and I were heading to Old Lyme.

We crossed the George Washington Bridge, picking up the Cross Bronx Expressway—a trench cut through a broken landscape filled with anger, failure, and despair. It made Linda retreat deeper into her seat and made our mission seem shallow and small.

Then familiar names began to appear on highway overpasses. Signs to Van Cortland Park . . . Hunts Point . . . Bronx Park . . . Pelham Bay Park —places I have never seen but whose names I know as well as a student of the Bible recognizes the names of ancient Hebrew cities. These were the haunts of the Bronx County Bird Club, the places where Roger Peterson, the young bird student, had polished his skills.

Along the New England Thruway, the urban crucible gave way to cluttered sprawl. Trees began to intrude, concrete began to falter, then patches of woodland appeared. Parks! By the time we reached Connecticut, we had outrun the rain, and concrete was clearly on the defensive. Beyond New Haven, the metropolitan area's last stronghold, woodlands claimed the land, with oaks in winter dress standing above freshly fallen leaves. Once, not many years ago, there had been farms here. Now forests have reclaimed the land—young forests, which some day would be old.

By the time we crossed the Connecticut River, there were Red-tailed Hawks soaring. By the time we reached "The Cedars," it was a perfect winter day—cold and clear and bluer than its tempera namesake on Roger Peterson's palette.

We sat in an airy, enclosed porch, Roger and Ginny, Linda and I, drinking tea, munching cookies, making the small talk that people who have not seen each other for several months make—talk of places, talk of mutual friends, and, of course, talk of birds. You can hardly have a discussion with Roger Tory Peterson and not discuss birds.

Ginny is tall, willowy, and golden-haired. There is a part of her that skips across adversity like a stone across water—and this must be the Irish in her. There is a part that sees too deep, takes the world's hurts the way elms find lightning—and this is the Irish in her, too. Tempered by both natures is a wonderful, intelligent woman whose strengths can balance the gravitational pull of a star.

Roger? It is dangerous to look too closely at the gods, because if a flaw is found it may prove their undoing. Luckily, Roger is not a god, yet. Future generations may elevate him to that level, but for now, in this age of this world, he is merely a great, great man, and therefore approachable by mortals.

He is tall and handsome and healthy as Thor. He has the discipline of a general, the spirit of a lifelong truant, and the presence of a man whose accomplishments have moved the axis of the world, just a little. His hair is unruly and white, his forehead prominent, and he is armed with a set of eyes that can nail a misstatement in flight and pin it to the wall in one minute. The next . . . they can seem so deep and so far away that you want to draw close, just to see if they will ever reach bottom.

If you have ever wondered who the role model was for cartoonist Gary Trudeau's ardent birder, the one who searched tirelessly for the Bachman's Warbler, well, look at the similarities in profile, look at the patrician forehead, look at the man whose North American Life List includes every North American warbler . . . except one. In other words, look no farther.

"Well," Roger said, reining in the chitchat with a word, drawing back on the bowstrings behind both eyes. "You said you had a question you wanted to ask?"

Yes, that was the fact of it. That was our reason for coming. But now that it came right down to it, I wasn't so certain I wanted to ask the question at all. What if the question were posed and Roger Tory Peterson didn't have an answer?

So I hedged. Started to discuss the decline in North American birds in a general way. Discussed it as if it were common knowledge, a *fait accompli*, and was surprised when Roger said, "I'm not so certain that all bird populations are that bad off."

I guess it's fair to say that I was surprised. Maybe startled would be closer to the truth. I had accepted the inevitability of declining numbers for so long that I'd never considered any other possibility. I confess, too, that a small, dark corner of my mind found Roger's statement evasively naïve. Of course birds were declining! How could Roger even suggest otherwise?

Something of my confusion must have communicated itself to the Master. The crossbow strings were loosed and the eyes turned deep and earnest, opening back along the tunnel of his experience.

"You know," he said, in the fervent way older men recall the past, "I saw the first Least Terns return to the New York beaches in the 1920s, after the end of the millinery slaughter. The Laughing Gull, too."

These things are matters of lore, I thought. What was Roger getting at?

"In the 1960s," he continued, "there were only a dozen Osprey nesting on the Connecticut River—down from 150 a decade earlier. Now, the population is healthy again because . . ."

Because DDT was outlawed, I thought, jumping ahead in a lesson plan

I knew by heart. This isn't what I had expected. The man who went halfway back to John James Audubon was recounting stories about bird populations that had suffered because of human stupidity and recovered because concerned people put an end to it. But, hell, I was talking about the whole sky falling. Didn't Roger understand that?

Of course, what Roger was saying was true. Birds have faced threats before. In every generation, it seems, concerned and clear-thinking individuals have had to take an environmental stand, do battle in the name of preservation. In the last century, it was the millinery trade, and a group of Boston matrons reared out of their overstuffed chairs, organized, and shut down the slaughter.

In the 1930s, it was hawk-shooting, and a minority who believed that birds of prey were important went head to head with a majority who thought that hawks were vermin. And the shooting stopped.

In the 1960s the battle was more difficult because the enemy was a hidden gun that fired a smoking cloud of chemicals. Experts in lab coats went toe to toe with other experts in white lab coats. And DDT was banned.

But I wasn't talking about just a battle, I was talking about Armageddon. I was talking about the 1990s and the whole damn sky falling and how do you stop th . . .

I suddenly realized that Roger had stopped speaking and that he was watching, waiting. Maybe appraising. Suddenly, I *thought* I understood what it was that Roger was trying to tell me. *Not* that there wasn't a problem. But that when the sky falls on a generation the only thing to do is stop it.

*Every* environmental challenge seems insurmountable at first because it must confront formidable opponents—convention, ignorance, greed. No crisis comes complete with the blueprint to a solution. These must be found. The problem that birds are facing today, the environmental challenge of our time, is actually very obvious. Birds are losing habitat. Nesting habitat in the Northern Hemisphere, wintering habitat in the Southern Hemisphere, and the habitats that are the critical migratory links that permit migratory birds to reach the poles that anchor their lives. Protecting birds is no more complicated (but no easier) than protecting their habitat, *and* habitat protected for birds is habitat protected for all living things, *including us.*

I was beginning to realize another thing. When I had taken off the Ghost Shirt on Pinos, the one woven of technology, all I had done was replace it with another woven of resignation. If technology wasn't going to save us, then nothing was going to save us. And if nothing was going to save us, then that absolved me from having to do anything, to safeguard birds and their habitat, didn't it? I could still feel bad about it. But I didn't have to feel guilty, and I didn't have to do anything to stop it.

What the man who goes halfway back to Audubon had done was to look back along the tunnel of his experience. He had given me not the answer to the environmental crisis of our time, but the key to its solution. People cause environmental problems; people solve them. He had also placed the responsibility for meeting the challenge right back where it belonged. On me . . . on us—on all who live in this age of this world. If we fail, we will render all the environmental victories of the past pyrrhic. We will earn and deserve the enmity of those who will inherit the world's empty shell.

Roger had given me more than I had come for, much more. But I still had my original question, the one I had hesitated to ask. It was getting late. All of us were eager to put this part of our discussion aside, and get to lunch and an afternoon together.

"Roger," I said, "you've watched bird-watching, as we know it, develop all your life—seen it go from a toddling infancy to adolescent exuberance to tempered maturity. More than any other person in history you have paced it every step of the way. Roger," I asked, "where is birding going?"

He didn't answer right away. It might have been that the question took him off-guard. It might be that when you are a man like Roger, mobilizing a lifetime of experience and bringing it to bear on the future takes a bit of doing. Then, slowly, more like a student reciting a lesson than the instructor who taught the world to bird, Roger formulated a reply.

"Birding, you know, can be so many things," he said, pausing, looking down at the hands that had painted the illustrations that made the world come alive for millions. "It can be a science, an art, a sport, a game, an ethic, a challenge . . ."

This, I thought without much enthusiasm, was fine as far as it went, but it fell short of what I had in mind. It was textbook Peterson, and writers don't like to think of their books as retreads of the old. This wouldn't do.

"Yes . . . yes, right, Roger," I said, interrupting, hoping to deflect him onto a fresh track. "But," I prompted, laying down my challenge again, "where is birding going?"

Roger sat there a moment, stumped it seemed. Maybe vexed. Maybe just searching for the words to bridge the distance that lies between one life filled with experience and another.

"Birding," he began again, striving to make his vision mine, "can be *so many things.*" And as he spoke, his eyes grew wide and deep in the contemplation of them all.

"It can be," he said, in thoughtfully measured tones, "a science!"

*Like the shotgun ornithologists of years past; like the Cape May Bird Observatory crew on the dike above Higbee Beach.*

"It can be a challenge!"

*Like the one that faced Rosalie Edge at Hawk Mountain, like the gauntlet thrown at the teams competing in the World Series of Birding.*

"It can be an art!"

*Like the art of John James Audubon; like the brush of Roger Tory Peterson.*

"It can be a sport . . . or a game!"

*Like the listers on Attu; like the mockingbird in my parents' backyard that had ushered in the New Year, and our travels so many adventures ago, now.*

All that Roger was saying was true. But I still couldn't see where it answered my question. For the first time I faced the possibility that maybe Roger Tory Peterson didn't have the answer, that Thor had dropped his hammer.

"Yes, of course," I said, interrupting again, cutting off the flow of words. "But Roger," I pleaded, calling upon the ceiling for support, "what I really need to know is *where is birding going?*"

My eyes stopped communing with the ceiling to discover, with a start, that beneath a shock of snow-white hair, a pair of steel-blue eyes had drawn down to about the dimensions of crossbows and that the line of their sights crossed right where I was seated. The hands that had crafted the illustrations that brought people and birds together were face-down on the table and the knuckles were the color of canvas.

It wasn't Roger Peterson, friend and teacher, who had half-risen from his chair. It was North American Birding *Himself* who was looking across the table, barely masking his exasperation with a prize pupil who had not learned his lesson.

"*That*," he said, and the word cracked like the report of Audubon's fowling piece, "is *precisely* what I have been telling you. *Birding* is going in *many* directions. Birding is going EVERYWHERE! Everywhere," he repeated, dropping back in his chair, blue eyes blazing, wondering, no doubt, whether this dolt of a student was ever going to get the point.

"Everywhere," I said silently, thinking back to all the places Linda and I had been, all the many facets of birding we'd seen and experienced. "Everywhere," I thought, feeling the catalytic word open up doors beyond doors beyond doors.

"Of course! Birding is going *everywhere!* From your own backyard to wherever fancy or ambition takes you. To people and places and a world of discovery . . . for as long as people and birds last."

What a simple thing and what a dolt of a student! To have traveled so far in search of an answer and to have had it in his keeping all along.

"Thank you, Roger," I said.

"*Everywhere*," I thought.

## Little Count on the Prairies

"E VERYWHERE" INCLUDES MANY PLACES, AND ONE OF THEM is Baldwin City, Kansas, a town that looks as if it's right out of the Currier and Ives portfolio. The houses are sturdy and trim; the streets tree-lined and shaded. Together they impart a New England air to this prairie community—and not without basis or reason. Baldwin lies astride the old Santa Fe Trail, and many a New England family with gumption passed this way, taking their belongings and heritage with them. Some plainly stayed.

If you head north out of town you come to Baker University, a small liberal arts college with cut-stone buildings and Methodist inclinations. In the summer the campus is grassy, busy, and pretty as a Monet. But in December, after the students have gone home for the holidays, it is snow-covered and silent and stark as Wyeth.

Between the arboretum and the science building, you'll find a snow-capped boulder fitted with a plaque—a tribute to Ivan Boyd, Dean of Science and a founder of the Kansas Ornithological Society. I learned, later, that it was his son, Roger Boyd, who levered the stone into place and chiseled the face to receive the plaque. Roger Boyd, who succeeded to his father's chair on the faculty, is the compiler of the Baldwin Christmas Bird Count. It was Roger that we were coming to see.

"Roger and . . . Jan?" I whispered.

"Jan," Linda affirmed. The sound of the doorbell faded and the tread of footsteps grew louder. In the meantime, we tried to compose ourselves—doing our best to appear congenial and friendly and anything but what we were. Two total strangers arriving as burdensome houseguests to a busy family on the weekend before Christmas.

But it wasn't Roger *or* Jan who greeted us. The open door framed a young boy, eleven, maybe twelve, who gave us quick appraisal, conditional approval, and invited us into his home.

How had this unlikely episode come about?

Well, like most things, it didn't just happen. The story begins in Arizona in July, when Linda and I met a birding couple in Cave Creek Canyon, a couple from Kansas. We had thought to anchor the chapter treating Christmas Bird Counts somewhere in America's heartland. During one of our several conversations we asked our newfound acquaintances about possibilities. They promised to look into the matter, and, in time, a letter arrived that offered a town, the name of the compiler, and a telephone number. I called. Explained who I was. Described what I was doing. Asked whether we might participate in the count.

And here we were.

Maybe this doesn't sound very unusual to you, and if this is the case, it means that you are a birder. Just for fun, just for perspective, try shifting avocations and replaying this scenario. Imagine, for a moment, that you are a housewife in Livingston, New Jersey, and somebody calls right in the middle of *Wheel of Fortune*, introduces herself as a housewife from Lawrence, Kansas, who would love to do some Christmas shopping in the Livingston Mall, and would it be OK if she went with you?

"OH, YeeAhh [accent over the a]," Livingston housewife replies. "I love to shop with strangers. How about the third Saturday in December? Just come out and stay at our place. Do people from Kansas eat pizza?"

Sounds plausible, doesn't it?

Or imagine that you are a football fan from Oakland, California, and some guy calls just as you get in from work, introduces himself as a football fan from East Rutherford, New Jersey, who would love to sit around with the guys at your place and watch the 49ers in the Superbowl. He promises to bring pretzels.

"Oh, sure," the Oakland Raiders fan replies, "anyone who loves watching football on TV is a friend of mine. Come and stay the night before the game. That way you won't miss any of the pregame show."

Fat chance.

Roger Boyd, in addition to being a generous and trusting individual, is an energetic man with serious eyes and a face that hasn't quite caught up with a life poised at midspan. Jan, who works at the university library, is gracious, congenial, and has that bolt-upright way of standing that women from America's heartland do. Roger was born in Baldwin. Jan is a Kansas City native. They met as students at Baker University and have been married twenty years. Both are what you might call "good stock."

Jon Boyd? Jon is intelligent and mature in a way that wins instant favor with adults. His room is festooned with posters of Ferraris and Lamborghinis, Batman, and a Baker University pennant. The house, he has been told, will be his. While his parents and their out-of-town guests were engaged in a crash course of getting to know each other, he was watching TV.

"How was your flight?"

"Fine. Uneventful."

"Your house is wonderful! How long have you been in it?"

"Oh, about a year. Come on. I'll show you around."

Question by question, posture by probe, we inched our way toward friendship across the footing afforded by common ground, a mutual interest in birds. Facilitating the bonding procedure was the conviction, supported by experience, that a member of the birding community is as good as a friend you haven't met.

"Oh, we *love* the Pawnee Grasslands. When were you there?"

"What was your thesis on? Horned Larks? Oh, Linda got some great shots of Horned Larks."

There were favorite places held in common, acquaintances shared, opinions that met with nothing but accord . . . and so on and so forth until suddenly and too soon it dawned on everyone that it was late. The morning would be an early one.

"There are towels in the bathroom."

"Thank you! You've gone to so much trouble."

"No trouble. If the room gets cold there are two quilts hanging near the bed. The one in front is warmer."

"I'm sure we'll be fine. Thank you. Good night."

"Good night."

The moon held the stars at bay, and the glow of it fell through the south-facing window and across the bed. Sleep did not come easily. It never does the night before a count. Tomorrow, there would be excitement and feathered treasure beneath the trees. Tomorrow, there would be challenges and discoveries and maybe, with fortune, some very special gift of the season. Only tomorrow. Only a night away.

But now the room was *so* quiet. The bed beneath the quilt so warm and comfortable. The clock ticking in some distant part of the house grows faint and familiar and indistinguishable from the breathing of the person next to you. When the timepiece reached the triumph of the hour, there was no one awake to appreciate the milestone . . . unless some foraging house mouse paused in its hurry to listen.

It clouded over and snowed during the night. When we rose at five, the dusting was almost complete and the air was quiet and still—so still that you could almost hear the silent laughter of stars. So still, you could hear an owl sneeze all the way in Colorado.

"See if you can get a rise out of the screech owl," Roger encouraged. "I'll start the car." I don't know which of us faced the greater challenge. On snowy mornings with the mercury hovering near zero, both owls and autos can be slow starters.

In homes across Baldwin, Kansas, and all over North America, birders were mobilizing for the ninetieth Christmas Bird Count, one of birding's most cherished traditions. Orchestrated by the National Audubon Society, the espoused purpose of the event is to monitor winter bird populations. Most participants freely admit that they do it for the fun. Even Frank M. Chapman, who initiated the grand tradition, did so with an ulterior motive—to offer a bloodless substitute for the Christmas Day shoots that were a holiday tradition among sportsmen of the day. On December 25, 1900, the editor of *Bird Lore* and twenty-six other participants at twenty-five locations across the continent went out to *count* instead of kill the birds they saw. Ninety years later, 42,671 participants at 1,563 locations keep the tradition alive.

Some counts, like Edmonton, Alberta, involve over one thousand participants, braving the winds of the Siberian Express or monitoring their feeders from the warm side of windows. Then there is Izembek NWR, Alaska, a count involving one compiler and one counter—both of them the same man, Christian P. Dau.

Some, like the count in Santa Barbara, California, tally in excess of two hundred species, and its participants approach the event the way Sherman approached Atlanta. At the near polar extreme is Prudhoe Bay, Alaska, whose three participants spent a total of eight party hours in the field on January 2, 1990, and recorded fourteen birds for their effort—all of them Common Ravens.

Each count is conducted in a circle fifteen miles in diameter on the two weekends before and the one following Christmas. It is not uncommon for birders to participate in multiple counts—some may do as many as six! But the count that CBC participants take to heart is *their* count, the hometown count. Other counts may have better habitat and more birds. But other counts don't include your own backyard.

Linda, Jan, and I stepped onto the Boyds' back porch and faced the woodlot. The owl, if he was about, would probably be there. Puckering up, I loosed a whinny his way. The bird must have been roosting in a set of starting blocks, because in something under ten seconds, one very angry gray-phase Eastern Screech-Owl was perched directly above our heads whinnying pointed epithets in our direction.

*Check* screech owl. An auspicious beginning to the forty-seventh Baldwin CBC. Roger's success with the car was just as good, and five minutes later we were standing at the edge of the Baker University Arboretum, trying to call up another owl. But five minutes of coaxing produced nothing.

"I was afraid of that," Roger confessed. "We couldn't get a response last year, either."

That's the difference between a Christmas Bird Count and a Big Day. A Big Day is only interested in species. "They all count as one," as Linda had so succinctly observed back in May. CBCs are a census. On a CBC *every* individual bird counts; so every bird is counted.

Our next stop was several blocks away in the middle of a suburban street. Two Great Horned Owls traded hoots, and from one of the darkened houses, a dog did its duty and informed the world that there were strangers about. A police cruiser edged down Main Street but turned around in the IGA parking lot before reaching us. Suspicious cops are a perennial hazard of CBCs. I have had to offer a good account of myself to police from at least a dozen municipalities.

"Ever have any trouble with the members of the force?" I asked Roger.

"No," he replied. "Not usually. It used to be that they all knew me. But now there are a few strangers in the department," he added thoughtfully.

"What a town!" I thought. "Where the residents are so long-standing that members of the police force bear the stigma of outsiders."

The clock on the Baldwin City Bank read 6:27. The temperature was 8 degrees Farenheit. Two screech owls later, we were en route to the Baldwin train depot and a scheduled rendezvous with the rest of the count's participants. Most were already assembled—seasoned veterans, cocky and confident, knowing the routine and what was ·expected of them, first-timers, standing at the edge of the tribe, waiting eagerly for their assignments. Chatter was lively, greetings and season's cheer exchanged all around. In the corner, Roger was making frantic last-minute adjustments—shifting territory lines, shuffling parties to get the most out of the talent on hand. Several key participants were absent—one felled by a cold that promised to get worse; another attending to a death in the family. Roger's mother, age eighty-two, was also going to miss the count—only the second time since its inception.

"I'm giving you two territories," Captain Boyd said to one trusted lieutenant. "Both small," he added to soften the blow. The fellow raised his eyebrows but accepted the burden of his charge bravely.

A territory is a personal thing. Knowing the turf, knowing the thickets where berries thrive, knowing the places where open water is likely to be found, offers a real advantage on a CBC. A good observer on his home turf is a formidable sword in the hands of a good CBC field commander . . . and sometimes a blade that cuts two ways. Yes, there is rivalry on CBCs, too. Roger's prime challenger was Cal Cink, another professor at Baker University.

Cal is a big man with eyes that are both mocking and shy and have a direct way of looking at a person. On the Lawrence CBC, Roger and Cal are partners. But on the Baldwin count, they direct their talents on different territories. Cal's turf was the key Douglas County Lake area, a critical corner and a productive one, too.

"Is the crossbill still coming to the feeder?" Roger asked one feisty count elder, a woman who would have been uncommonly tall for a Munchkin but whose bright, birdlike eyes barely crested Cal's midsection.

"Yes," she said, with an animated nod. "Seen yesterday," she assured him.

Red Crossbill would be a coup for the count. Although a CBC is a census, part of the fun of a CBC comes from trying to tally as many different species in the count circle as you can. Every year, the hope is that the old count record will be broken—that more species will be tallied than in any previous year.

Competition extends to intercount rivalries, too. The Lawrence CBC, organized by the Jayhawk Audubon Society, is Baldwin's unofficial rival. With almost twice the participants of Baldwin and the advantage of a large reservoir within their count circle, Lawrence is a perennial powerhouse among Kansas CBCs. Their count, conducted the previous day in temperatures that barely reached double digits, started at 11 below zero. Seventy-seven species were accepted at the evening roundup—a very respectable total for an inland count given the harsh conditions and the absence of open water. Waterfowl, a Lawrence CBC trump, were almost nonexistent.

But it's an ill wind that blows nobody some good. The frozen conditions evened up the odds. Without a duck-rich reservoir boosting Lawrence's total, this year, Roger thought, Baldwin stood a chance of closing in on their archrival. Maybe even besting them! Yes, the species game is taken very seriously on CBCs.

Among all the little games and challenges and tests of skill, there is no greater honor to be won than finding a bird that has never been recorded on the count before. On fledgling counts, this is an every-year matter. But on older, more established counts, the possibilities have been drawn fine by success. On a count with the lineage of the Baldwin count, finding a new bird is a heralded event, something that doesn't happen every year.

Finally, all the territories were assigned, the troops dispatched. We left, too, heading southwest toward Roger's territory. It was still dark enough that a particularly mean cop might pull you over for not having your headlights on (not that any did). The bank clock read 7:44. The temperature hadn't budged.

We hit some of the more productive feeders in town first. Pulling halfway up driveways or drawing to a halt up front—whichever offered the better view of the feeder. The night had been a cold one. The birds were hungry. Perches were never left vacant for long.

"Two cardinals," Roger announced. "Two Blue Jays . . . twenty starlings . . . three chickadees . . ."

Jan jotted the numbers down on the field form as Roger spoke. "Whose house is this?" I asked.

"Jane Chubb," he replied. I was to discover as the day progressed that Roger Boyd was privy to the name of just about every owner of every driveway we navigated—and there were many. Such is life in a small midwestern community.

We drove to the edge of town, to a river woodland filled with oaks and rich in promise. It was, I realized with some surprise, a very comfortable and familiar setting—filled with trees I could name at a glance, trees I had known as a boy. It was an eastern woodland, here at the limit of its range. Many of the birds it promised were eastern birds, too.

The game plan called for Roger, Linda, and me to walk the woodland corridor. Jan would pick us up a half-mile downstream.

*Braking with our heels, half-falling anyway, we careened down the embankment and thrashed our way through a wall of branches. Leaves crunched beneath the frosted surface. Snow squeaked with cold. Branches stung our ears like hot whips and toes ached and went numb.*

"Don't you believe in trails?" I chided.

"It opens up pretty soon," our guide assured.

*A band of Black-capped Chickadees and Tufted Titmice moved through the canopy like a hungry cloud—poking into crevices, searching branches for insect larvae. I tried the screech owl call again, flooding the glen with the warbled challenge, and the feathered frenzy swarmed around us, scolding, fretting, some closing to an arm's length. A Downy Woodpecker flew in, rattling a challenge, and a squadron of Blue Jays hit the clearing with the coordination of a SWAT team, making the winter woodlands ring.*

There were other birds, too—"good birds." Borderline expected species; birds that could be missed on a CBC. The tidy little streamside corridor produced a whole troop of Brown Creepers, a pair of Golden-crowned Kinglets, and three Carolina Wrens. Roger's search of a streamside tangle produced a real prize—a Winter Wren—a bird, he noted with satisfaction, that had been *missed* on the Lawrence count. When we got to the car, there was another bonus: a Belted Kingfisher bolted into view—a bird that the frozen conditions should have put out of our reach. Then a Barred Owl sounded off!

"Great!" said Roger.

"Wonderful!" said Jan.

"Awwwl right!" said Linda.

We have chased the Woosel. And he is ours.

We celebrated by dipping into Jan's larder of cookies. To the victors belong the spoils.

Everywhere we went that cold December morning, fortune smiled. Judicious screening of a flock of juncos produced two Oregon-type. Spirited pishing at a pine grove made it erupt with robins and Cedar Waxwings. A two-cookie celebration for sure.

Tree sparrows poured out of hiding at every beckon and pish. Burly Harris's Sparrows hitched themselves up on weedy stalks, and secretive

Swamp Sparrows betrayed themselves time and time again. Even an elusive Fox Sparrow *chaffed* to be recognized. Every bird found was one bird closer to the Baldwin all-time record of seventy-four (not to mention Lawrence's tally-up total of seventy-seven).

A large raptor perched in an open field turned out to be an adult Cooper's Hawk—a tough one! A two-cookie bird all by itself. At a weedy patch that Roger assessed to be "promising," a stream of pishes roused a balanced swarm of birds including . . .

"Towhee," Linda shouted. "Rufous-sided Towhee." A *real* gift. A prize! One of the key half-hardy species that the bitter temperatures might have claimed (and another bird, Roger noted with a smile, that Lawrence missed).

The cookie tin suffered visibly this time, and nobody kept count.

We stopped at a frozen lake. A thin trickle of water below the spillway was all the open water to be found. We still needed snipe, and this place held promise . . . that as events turned out couldn't be met. But along the icy edge were large bird tracks plainly visible in the snow. Their size and shape made them unmistakably the tracks of Great Blue Heron. Now, the moral dilemma. Should we count it? *Could* we count it? We hadn't actually seen the bird, but the identification was hardly in question. The tracks had to have been made during the count day because snow had fallen until morning.

Still, the fact remained, we hadn't actually *seen* the bird.

"Maybe someone else will get one," Roger said hopefully.

On our way back to town, Jan ran a halftime tally. "Forty-nine," she noted. Forty-nine species of birds in six hours, in the middle of the continent, during one of the coldest Decembers on record.

"Not too bad," Roger said, summing it up nicely.

By the time we arrived at the depot, toes that had ached all morning had fallen to sting levels. Jaws began to move freely again.

The room was hot, conversation ran high, and plates were piled higher—with chicken and dumplings, stewed fruit, peach pie—good, wholesome fare and lots of it. It is the tradition of the Baldwin Bird Club for all parties to meet for a potluck lunch, orchestrated, this year, by Roger's mother.

At eighty-two she is the count's grande dame, her position on the count having shifted from active to emeritus.

While the troops fed, Roger ran a quick tally and exhorted his troops with a halftime pep talk.

"How we doing on waterfowl?" he demanded. "Any ducks?"

The silence spoke volumes.

"How about sparrows? Anybody find a Field Sparrow yet?"

Silence.

"Lincoln's?"

More silence.

"We'll have to hit those thickets a little harder," he encouraged.

In the corner, Cal seemed uncommonly quiet—a point that wasn't lost on any of those assembled. "Cal's got something good he's holding back," someone accused. But the shy, mocking eyes refused to confirm or deny the suspicion.

"You know," Roger's mother whispered, "Roger was birding before he was born." I studied this energetic octogenarian, guardian of so much tradition. Once, she had watched her husband direct this count. Now, she watched her son.

"Well, small wonder he's so good," I said. She accepted the compliment with a proud smile. Maybe a mother's smile.

Jon Boyd was also on hand—sticking close to Mom, casting worshiping glances at Dad, and making his presence known at the dessert table. Would there be a third generation of Boyds chairing the Baldwin CBC?

"Jon," I said, figuring I'd phrase my query in a multiple-choice fashion, "if you had to rate your interest in birding between football, TV, and going to school, where would you put it?"

"Just ahead of school," he answered immediately.

I guess the answer is, maybe.

"OK," the man who had participated in his first Christmas Bird Count during his first trimester of life demanded. "How much more time do we need here?"

Considering the temperatures outside, all day would have sounded like a reasonable reply. But they are hardy folks, those Baldwin Bird Club members. Hardy and proud. Dishes were stacked. Boots and heavy outer gear donned. Last-minute cookies palmed and stuffed into pockets. Fully provisioned, the troops moved out.

"THE TALLY IS AT OUR HOUSE AT 7:00," Roger shouted to the backs of his command. "If you can't make it, drop your sheets off beforehand."

Roger was tardy getting to the car. His jaw set, his eyes turned in upon some matter of urgency or concern.

"Cal found three Ruffed Grouse," he allowed, smiling ruefully. "That's why he was being so quiet in there. He wants to surprise everyone at the final tally."

Ruffed Grouse is a tough bird in New Jersey. They are relatively uncommon, and a bugger to find. Clearly, here at the edge of the hardwood forests, the significance was even greater.

"How good *is* grouse on this count?" I asked.

"It's a first," Roger admitted. In the spirit of CBC rivalry, Cal had just drawn a hand that was going to be hard to beat. It looked like Cal was going to take home the coonskin at the tally unless fortune threw our side a mighty big bone.

If fortune held some great prize, she kept it hidden, though clearly we were much in her favor. Afternoons can be desperate times on CBCs. The morning grab bag is over. The easy birds have all been accounted for. Birds that proved elusive in the morning are no easier to find in the afternoon.

But as the sun arched across the Kansas sky on that winter afternoon, we hopped, skipped, and sometimes jumped up and down upon a veritable yellow brick road of treasure. At one spot it was a flock of Lapland Longspurs trying to pass themselves off as just another group of Horned Larks. At another, five Rusty Blackbirds were coaxed out of hiding.

Linda, fighting a heroic battle against sleep, pulled a Sharp-shinned Hawk right out of thin air and then . . . by golly, we found another one! Everywhere we went on that charmed, windless afternoon, birds stood up to be recognized. Another towhee . . . another Fox Sparrow . . . our second kingfisher . . . five Pine Siskin that led the charge from a stand of cedars where robins, waxwings, kinglets, and Purple Finch had settled in to roost.

If the day had simply wound itself down in this gentle and productive fashion, it would have been a proud and satisfied foursome that showed up at the tally. But fortune still held one card face-down on the table. One she had chosen not to play until the very end of the day.

"What do you think of this perched raptor?" Roger asked.

I focused my binoculars on the bird Roger was studying. A dark silhouette keyed up in a tree some four hundred yards away. At 7x, there was little to see. But I *did* see the things that had drawn Roger's eye—the large head, slim build, long wings; things that distinguished this bird from the many Red-tailed Hawks we had seen all day. The bird looked for all the world like a large falcon, and *any* large falcon would constitute an outlandish find on a Kansas Christmas Count.

"I think its worth scoping," I replied, moving for the trunk, trying to keep any excitement out of my voice.

At 30x, what had been just a possibility was transformed into a perfectly beautiful Prairie Falcon. Fortune was kind enough to let each member of our party get a look at the bird before it tired of scrutiny and fled—an elegant gray shadow lining out for the horizon. A gift of the season.

"How good is Prairie Falcon?" I asked, although I felt certain I already had the answer.

"First for the count!" Roger affirmed with no small measure of satisfaction (and if he was thinking of Cal's Ruffed Grouse—well, no one can fault him for that).

The day was fading fast, but our fortune was not. Just up the road, atop a gentle knoll, overlooking eighty acres of tallgrass prairie, four Northern Harriers were patrolling. As we watched, two Short-eared Owls lofted into sight and disappeared into a sky that was quickly running out of color—only the third time in forty-seven years that Short-eareds have turned up for the Baldwin count. Cal was going to have his work cut out for him to beat Prairie Falcon *and* Short-eared Owl.

Not that he wasn't capable of it.

On our way back to the Boyds', Roger stopped at Spring Creek Lake, whose ice-strangled spillway had held the tantalizing tracks earlier in the day. Sure enough, an indignant Great Blue Heron lifted off, lumbering into the trees.

Not only would we be going to the tally with a good hand to play, we'd have a clean one, too.

All across North America, in every state, in every province, cars filled with birders were drawing together—heading for brightly lit households, church halls, and traditional old bars. In hundreds of locations, tired but happy figures were shaking off their heavy garments, shouting greetings across crowded rooms—to friends and fellow birders who had shared the challenge and adventure of the day.

The rooms are warm and glowing, kindled by the heat thrown from a merry blaze and from friendships that run the length of lifetimes. Hot mugs of wine take the chill out of limbs that have not been warm all day, and excitement sweeps tiredness aside.

There is food. There is drink. There is brightness and gaiety enough to rival even the stars that flood the winter sky. There is excitement and hushed disclosures. There is jealousy and nervousness and pique and wonder and pride and chagrin and boasting, and laughter that is long and loud and wholehearted. There is everything that is when good people meet in the name of fun and friendship. Most of all, there is a shared sense of belonging, of being one with the tribe, as it assembles in the great halls for the solstice celebration, just as people and tribes have done for centuries.

This is the scene enacted all across North America. No different in Boonton, New Jersey, than in Anchorage, Alaska. The same in Freeport, Texas, and likewise in Ashtabula, Ohio; White Rock, British Columbia; Washington, D.C.; Zuni, New Mexico; and Errol-Umbagog, New Hampshire. The tribe comes together to join and share.

"Welcome."

"Did you see any good birds today?"

Soon the great moment arrives. The compilers call the rooms to order. Chairs are drawn up, forming a ring around the chieftains that are, themselves, just links in the greater ring forming all around the continent. Conversations wind down. A log is thrown on the fire. The participants hold their tally sheets like poker players, like choral singers, like bindle stiffs sitting around a fire looking to add their offering to the communal stew. The only sound to be heard is the greedy sound of flames tasting the fresh offering.

"OK," the compilers say, "let's begin." And all around the circle heads bow, and the compiler calls the roll.

"Loons? Anybody see any loons out there today?"

"Grebes? How about grebes?"

Sometimes the answers are yes, and everyone swells with relief and pride.

"Pied-billed Grebe, yes!"

"Oh, terrific! Where was it? On the reservoir?"

Sometimes the questions evoke silence, and the loss is felt by all.

"Grebes? No grebes! Oh, that's bad. That's real bad, folks. How about herons? Anybody find any herons out there today?"

Linda and I were in the circle, but had been spared any clerical duties. We could sit back, listen, and enjoy the excitement, the fire, and our thoughts. Linda's eyes were filled with coals, and since coals have a way of drawing the memories out of a person, I guessed that she was thinking back on our travels and all the places we'd been. It was an easy guess to make. I was doing the same.

She must have felt my gaze, because her eyes left the fire and found mine.

"It's been fun," I whispered.

"It's been great," she corrected.

"What do you want to do next year?"

"Go birding," she replied, putting a finger to her lips.

Yes, go birding. We had been to many places, seen most of the birds that the continent has to offer, and done little else but don binoculars for the better part of a year. If there was a way to do it all over, we'd both be on the road tomorrow—seeking out the birds that eluded us, visiting the many places we'd missed, and getting to know more of those whose ranks are drawn from the finest people on the planet.

I realized suddenly that the room had grown very quiet. The log was gone. The flames had receded. Around the circle, heads were raised, tally sheets were flush upon laps. All eyes were on the compiler, and his eyes were upon them. It was plain that the great moment had arrived.

"All right," the compiler announced, pausing, savoring the moment, giving those who were about to be tested time to prepare themselves.

A chair creaked.

The fire hissed.

A man, in his nervousness, coughed.

In circles all around the continent, the Christmas Count compilers laid down their great challenge.

"Is there anyone in this room," they said, looking at those assembled, "who has seen any bird whose name I have not called out?"

And in Baldwin City, Kansas; in Aiken, South Carolina; in Yarmouth, Nova Scotia; and in a half a thousand other places there is silence.

Then a person stands. A name is named.

And some new star will shine.

## APPENDIX:

## Binoculars

BINOCULARS ARE THE PRIMARY TOOL OF BIRD-watching. They are like the woodsman's ax, the infantryman's rifle, the first baseman's glove. No "user group," as the marketing jargon goes, *uses* binoculars more than birders, and nobody demands more from them. Some binoculars meet birding's peculiar demands; most do not.

After years of teaching bird identification and leading field trips, I have realized that the greatest obstacle beginning birders face is not inexperience. It is ill-suited binoculars—binoculars that do not offer a wide enough field of view, that are not the proper magnification, that have poor-quality optics, that do not provide eyeglass wearers with sufficient eye relief, that do not focus close enough . . . in short, binoculars that are *not suited for birding*.

Unfortunately, beginning birders often do not recognize the source of their frustration. All they know is that they can't seem to see what everyone else is seeing. They wrongfully attribute it to some personal failing.

And then they get frustrated. And then they stop birding.

Some birders do realize that the binoculars they are using—the ones Grandpa brought home from the war, or the pair their ex bought on sale and left in the closet—are inadequate. They go through a money-wasting pattern that is almost ritual.

They go to a department store and replace their 7x binocular with a cheap, high-powered binocular, seduced by the impression that bigger is better. They find, after they buy them, that the field of view offered by a pair of 15x binoculars wouldn't do justice to a medium-length soda straw. After several weeks, they go back to the department store and this time walk away with a pair of zoom binoculars, which let you change magnification with the throw of a lever. As the painfully young salesperson explains, "You can find the bird with low power, then just zooooom right in for a close-up look."

What he doesn't explain is that the things weigh a ton, that the optics are junk, and that the field of view, even at low power, is none too generous. The makers of quality binoculars eschew zoom binoculars. This should send a message to discerning consumers.

The next chapter in the saga (if there is a next chapter) finds the frustrated birder in a camera store, expecting to pay more money but anticipating birder-worthy binoculars. Only one of these expectations is usually realized. Most camera store salespeople know little about binoculars and less about the needs of birders. They sell binoculars because the camera lines they carry make it easy, and occasionally somebody even buys a pair. Optically, the binoculars made by camera companies are fine, some are excellent. But from a birding standpoint, many if not most of these camera brands have design flaws. The focus is stiff and critical. A sharp image is often not possible at distances under twenty feet because nobody thought to design them for close focus. The eye relief afforded eyeglass wearers is poor. Most camera brand models also tend to be delicate. Bang them, and they go out of alignment.

There are many binoculars on the market that will serve, but few that excel. After a couple of years, it's a wiser birder who finally buys the pair of binoculars he should have had all along. A pair of binoculars manufactured with birders in mind. Binoculars that offer the following qualities.

Good resolution. This means a sharp, clear image right across the binocular field. There should be no distortion, no colored rings, and no eye fatigue when you use them. Resolution is directly related to the quality of the optics, and this is directly related to price. High-quality optics cost from $250 and up.

- Adequate brightness. Colors should be distinguishable in poor morning light or in dark woodlands. Brightness relates in part to the size of the "objective lens," the big lens in the front. The size of this lens, in millimeters, is given as the second number in the formula found on all binoculars (7x35; 7x50; 8x40; 10x42). A 7x35 binocular has an objective lens that is 35mm wide—plenty big enough for a 7x binocular.

  Brightness also relates to the quality of the coating used on the lens. All lenses, inside and out, should be coated by a substance that prevents light from being lost (reflected away) each time it strikes a glass surface. These binoculars bear the label "fully coated lenses." Better still are "multicoated lenses," created by an expensive process that reduces light loss to mere fractions of a percent.

- Magnification between 7x (seven power) and 10x. Eastern birders, who do a lot of woodland birding, find that 7x binoculars are good in the clinches. Seven-power binoculars also excel for offshore birding by boat, where the birds are not the *only* thing in motion. Western birders prefer 10x binoculars, to cut the distance on those wide open spaces. Never buy a zoom-focus binocular. I repeat: *Never buy a zoom.*

- An adequate field of view. A field of no less than 250 feet at 1,000 yards is essential. A wide field makes finding birds easier. Lower magnifications offer wider fields.

- Proper eye relief for eyeglass wearers. Binoculars should be designed so that with the rubber eyecups rolled down, a birder who wears eyeglasses while looking through binocular will enjoy the same wide field of view afforded non-eyeglass wearers.

- Close-focus capability. Birds are not always far away. Birds in dense woodlands or on a bird feeder may be hardly more than arm's reach. Good, all-around birding binoculars should be able to focus down to *at least* 15 feet. Some exceptional models focus down to 8 feet.

- Proper weight, size, and shape. Birding binoculars should be large enough to be gripped or cradled easily. They should be light enough to be suspended from your neck comfortably. They should be designed so that your index finger falls directly upon the focus wheel without having to shift your grip.

Rugged construction. Birders *use* binoculars, and use entails risks. Good binoculars should be able to absorb the occasional bump. Superior binoculars can walk away from a fall, can be brought out in the rain without fear of internal fogging, can even be loaned to friends who, unconstrained by the burden of ownership, will cheerfully abuse them.

This is the bottom line. Birding is an activity that offers fun and pleasure. Good binoculars reduce frustration and increase enjoyment. The rule of thumb is: *Buy the best pair of binoculars you can afford and buy them as soon as you can.* If you cannot afford the ones you want, tolerate the ones you are using or borrow a pair for the interim. Save for the ones you want. You are going to buy them eventually, anyway. Any money spent on half-step optics along the way is money wasted.

If you don't know what binoculars to buy, ask an accomplished birder. *Don't* ask your average salesperson. *Don't* ask Uncle Mike who took your wedding photos. Ask a birder—in fact, ask several. Expect differences of opinion. Binoculars, like cars, are matters of taste and opinion. But count on the brands and models birders endorse to be at least fundamentally birder-worthy.

# BIBLIOGRAPHY

American Ornithologists Union. *Check-list of North American Birds*. 6th ed. Lawrence, Kans.: Allen Press, 1983.

*Arctic National Wildlife Refuge*. United States Department of the Interior, Fish and Wildlife Service, 1982.

Baily, William L. *Our Own Birds of the United States*. Philadelphia: J.B. Lippincott, 1869.

Balch, Lawrence G. "Attu Information." Highland Park, Ill.: Attour, 1989.

———. "1989 List Report," *Winging It* 2(1990), pp. 3–39.

Bent, Arthur Cleveland. *Life Histories of North American Birds of Prey*. 2 vols. National Museum Bulletins nos. 167 and 170. Washington, D.C.: Smithsonian Institution, 1937 and 1938.

———. *Life Histories of North American Cuckoos, Goatsuckers, Hummingbirds and Their Allies*. National Museum Bulletin no. 176. Washington, D.C.: Smithsonian Institution, 1940.

———. *Life Histories of North American Wild Fowl*. 2 vols. National Museum Bulletins nos. 126 and 130. Washington, D.C.: Smithsonian Institution, 1923 and 1925.

———. *Life Histories of North American Wood Warblers*. National Museum Bulletin no. 203. Washington, D.C.: Smithsonian Institution, 1953.

Blanchan, Neltje. *Bird Neighbors*. New York: Doubleday & McClure, 1897.

Brett, James J. *The Mountain & the Migration*. (New and Expanded Second Edition) Ithaca, NY: Cornell University Press, 1991.

Brown, Lauren. *Grasslands*. National Audubon Society. New York: Alfred A. Knopf, 1985.

Bull, John. *Birds of the New York Area*. New York: Harper & Row, 1964.

Butler, James R., and Gregory D. Fenton. "Bird Watchers of Point Pelee National Park, Canada: Their Characteristics and Activities, with Special Consideration to their Social and Resource Impacts." Paper presented at First National Symposium on Social Science in Resource Management, May 12–16, 1986, at Oregon State University, Corvallis, Oregon.

Butler, James R., and Glen T. Hvengaard. "The Economic Values of Bird Watching Associated with Point Pelee National Park, Canada, and Their Contribution to Adjacent Communities." Paper presented at the Second Symposium on Social Sciences in Resource Management, June 6–9, 1988, at the University of Illinois, Urbana, Illinois.

Butler, James R., Glen T. Hvengaard, and Douglas K. Krystofiak. *The Bird-watchers of Point Pelee—Interim Progress Report*. Edmonton: University of Alberta, 1988.

Carson, Rachel. *Silent Spring*. Boston: Houghton Mifflin, 1962.

Casidy, James, ed. *Book of North American Birds*. Pleasantville, N.Y.: Reader's Digest Association, 1990.

Chapman, Frank M. *Birds of Eastern North America*. New York: D. Appleton, 1895.

Devlin, John C., and Grace Naismith. *The World of Roger Tory Peterson*. New York: New York Times Books, 1977.

Dunn, Jon L., and Eirik A. T. Blom. *A Field Guide to the Birds of North America*. 2nd ed. Washington, D.C.: National Geographic Society, 1987.

Elman, Robert. *The Atlantic Flyway*. New York: Winchester Press, 1970.

Eynon, A. E. "Origins of the Big Day," *Urner Field Observer* 5, no. 2 (1962).

*Fort Jefferson*. United States Department of the Interior, National Park Service, 1984.

Garfield, Brian. *The Thousand-Mile War*. New York: Doubleday, 1969.

Gautreaux, Sidney A. "Long-term Patterns of Trans-gulf Migration in Spring: A Weather Radar Analysis." Paper presented at New Jersey at the Crossroads of Migration Conference, October 5, 1990, at Cape May, New Jersey.

Gibbons, Felton, and Deborah Strom. *Neighbors to the Birds*. New York: W.W. Norton, 1988.

Grafel, Bev, ed. *Fish & Wildlife Resources of the Arctic Coastal Plain*. United States Department of the Interior, Fish and Wildlife Service, October 1986.

*Guide to Churchill, Manitoba*. 5th ed. Churchill, Manitoba: Chamber of Commerce, 1988.

Hince, Tom G. "Point Pelee National Park—Ontario, Canada," *American Birds* 40 (1986), pp. 26–31.

Hvenegaard, Glen T., James R. Butler, and Doug K. Krystofiak. "Economic Values of Bird Watching at Point Pelee National Park, Canada," *Wildlife Society Bulletin* 17 (1989), pp. 526–31.

*J.N. Ding Darling National Wildlife Refuge*. United States Department of the Interior, Fish and Wildlife Service, January 1989.

Kastner, Joseph. *A World of Watchers*. New York: Alfred A. Knopf, 1986.

Kiff, Lloyd. "To the Brink and Back," *Terra* 28 (1990), pp. 7–18.

Krider, John. *Forty Years Notes of a Field Ornithologist*. Philadelphia: Academy of Natural Sciences, 1879.

Lane, James A. *A Birder's Guide to Churchill, Manitoba*. Denver: L & P Press, 1971.

Lane, James A., and Harold R. Holt. *A Birder's Guide to Denver and Eastern Colorado*. Denver: L & P Press, 1979.

———. *A Birder's Guide to Florida*. Denver: L & P Press, 1981.

———. *A Birder's Guide to the Rio Grande Valley of Texas*. Denver: L & P Press, 1971.

———. *A Birder's Guide to Southeastern Arizona*. Denver: L & P Press, 1984.

———. *A Birder's Guide to Southern California*. Denver: L & P Press, 1968.

LeBaron, Geoffrey S., ed. "The 89th Christmas Bird Count." *American Birds* 43 (1989), pp. 551–59.

———. "The 90th Christmas Bird Count," *American Birds* 44 (1990), pp. 516–23.

MacMohon, James A. *Deserts*. National Audubon Society. New York: Alfred A. Knopf, 1985.

Matthiessen, Peter. *Wildlife in America*. New York: Viking Press, 1964.

Miliotis, Paul, and P. A. Buckley. "The Massachusetts Ross' Gull," *American Birds* 29 (1975), pp. 643–46.

Moon, William Least Heat. *Blue Highways*. New York: Ballantine Books, 1982.

Morse, Robert J. "Mystery Bird of the Chiricahuas: The Status of Eared Trogon," *Birding* 19, no. 5, pp. 16–20.

Myers, J. P. "Phone Freebies," *American Birds* 43 (1989), pp. 389–91.

Peterson, Roger Tory. *A Field Guide to the Birds*. Boston: Houghton Mifflin, 1934.

Pettingill, Olin Sewall, Jr. *A Guide to Bird Finding West of the Mississippi*. 2nd ed. New York: Oxford University Press, 1981.

"Point Pelee Changes the Rules," *Winging It* 2 (1990), p. 14.

Plate, Robert. *Alexander Wilson—Wanderer in the Wilderness*. New York: David McKay, 1966.

Reed, Charles K. *Bird Guide—Land Birds East of the Rockies*. Worcester, Mass., 1906.

Rhoads, Lee, and Dorothy Rhodes. *History of the Pawnee National Grassland*. Briggs-dale, Colo., 1986.

Robbins, Chandler S., Bertel Bruun, and Herbert S. Zim. *Birds of North America*. New York: Golden Press, 1983.

Blanchan, Neltje. *Bird Neighbors*. New York: Doubleday & McClure, 1897.

*Sacramento Valley National Wildlife Refuges*. Washington, D.C.: U.S. Government Printing Office, 1988.

Spencer, David L., Claus M. Naske, and John Carnahan. *National Wildlife Refuges of Alaska—A Historical Perspective*. Part 1. Fairbanks, Alaska: Department of History, University of Alaska, January 1979.

*Spring Migration [at] Point Pelee National Park*. Canadian Park Service.

Stallcup, Rich. "Taking a Pelagic Trip," *Winging It* 2 (1990), pp. 1–5.

Steinbeck, John. *Cannery Row*. New York: Bantam Books, 1947.

Toups, Judith A., and Jerome A. Jackson. *Birds and Birding on the Mississippi Coast*. Jackson, Miss.: University Press of Mississippi, 1987.

Tyrrell, Esther Quesada. *Hummingbirds—Their Life and Behavior*. New York: Crown, 1984.

United States Department of the Interior. "The 1980 National Survey of Fishing, Hunting and Wildlife Associated Recreation." Washington, D.C.: Fish and Wildlife Service, 1982.

———. "The 1985 National Survey of Fishing, Hunting and Wildlife Associated Recreation." Washington, D.C.: Fish and Wildlife Service, 1989.

Walton, Richard K. *Bird Finding in New England*. Boston: Godine, 1988.

*Water, Prey and Game Birds of North America*. Washington, D.C.: National Geographic Society, 1965.

Wetmore, Alexander. *Song and Garden Birds of North America.* Washington, D.C.: National Geographic Society, 1964.

Wiedner, David, and Paul Kerlinger. "Economics of Birding: A National Survey of Active Birders," *American Birds* 44 (1990), pp. 209–13.

*Wood Storks.* New York: National Audubon Society.

Zim, Herbert S. *Birds.* New York: Simon and Schuster, 1949.

# INDEX

# A

Ademec, Otto, 190, 198, 199
Aguila-Rancho, 230–233
Albatross, Laysan, 153, 248
Allen, Susan, 191
American Birding Association, 56, 121, 191
*American Birds*, 30
American Ornithologists' Union, 19, 20
Amerman, Ed, 190
Anhinga, 40
Ani, Smooth-billed, 41
Ann's Diner, 15–21
Arctic National Wildlife Refuge, Alaska, 169–185
Arizona, 223–236
Attu, Alaska, 143–167
Audubon, John James, 17–18, 23, 313, 315, 316
*Audubon Magazine*, 20
Audubon societies, 21
Augustine, Bob, 84

Auklet, Rhinoceros, 241
Axtell, Dr. Harold, 108

# B

Bacinski, Pete, 30, 120, 122–141
Back River Sewage Treatment Facility, 79–87
Baker University, 317, 319
Balch, Larry, 147, 148–149, 150, 164
Baldwin City, Kansas, 327–332
Baltimore, Maryland, 75–87
Bananaquit, 51
Banders, raptor, 267
Banker, Louis, 41–42, 151–156
Becard, Rose-throated, 56, 58, 59, 242
Bee Tree, 93–94
Bentsen State Park, Texas, 56–60, 171
"Big Day, The," 119–141, 322
Binoculars, 23–24, 35, 37–38, 39–40, 333–336
*Birder's Guides* (Lane), 57, 68–69
Bird fallouts, 103, 107–108, 115, 252, 265–269

Izembek National Wildlife Refuge,
    Alaska, 321

# J

Jacquemot, A., 111
Jaeger, Long-tailed, 177, 247
    Parasitic, 177, 204
    Pomarine, 205, 249
Jay, Blue, 4, 10, 129, 324, 325
    Green, 58, 89, 171
Jayhawk Audubon Society, 323
Junco, Dark-eyed, 4, 7, 325
    Oregon, 325

# K

Karlson, Kevin, 136
Kerlinger, Dr. Paul, 76, 109, 110, 262
Kern, Mary Ann, 190
Kestrel, American, 308
Killdeer, 126, 218, 219
Kingbird, Cassin's, 51
    Couch's, 56, 58
    Eastern, 131
    Thick-billed, 224
    Western, 215
Kingfisher, Belted, 36, 131, 308, 310, 325,
    328
    Green, 59
Kinglet, Golden-crowned, 10, 11, 325
    Ruby-crowned, 10–11
Kiskadee, Great, 56, 58, 60
Kite, Hook-billed, 59
    Snail, 171
Kittiwake, Black-legged, 153
Klamath Basin, California, 290–296
Knot, Red, 138

Komito, Sandy, 148, 151, 152–153, 154,
    155, 157, 162
Kovac, Michelle, 278–279
Kreuper, Dave, 235
Krider, John, 25
Kuerzi, R. J., 121
Kuethe, Jim, 162
Kutac, Ed, 239

# L

Lane, James A., 16, 56, 57, 68–69, 171
Langridge, Howard, 46–51
Lark, Horned, 179, 216, 219, 220, 221,
    320
LaVia, John, 83–84, 86, 87
Lawrence Christmas Bird Count, 323–
    324, 325, 326
Leukering, Tony, 261–262, 264
Linnaean Ornithological Society, 24
Longspur, Chestnut-collared, 217
    Lapland, 152, 177, 328
    McCown's, 216–217, 221
    Smith's, 174, 204
Loon, Common, 25
    Pacific, 203, 205
    Red-throated, 201, 203, 204
    Yellow-billed, 178
Los Padres National Forest, California,
    297–305

# M

McDowell, Donna Jean, xxiii–xxiv
McLane, Tito, 84, 86
Madison, Sam, 152, 163, 164, 165
Maisel, Dr. Gerald, 148, 161–162
Manitoba, Canada, 187–207
Martin, Purple, 96

# P

Pacific Flyway, 288–296
Pangburn, C. H., 121
Parakeet, Carolina, 301
Partridge, Gray, 191
Parula, Northern, 114, 131, 254, 257, 268
  Tropical, 58, 59, 60
Patterson, Flora, 190
Pauraque, Common, 56
Pawnee National Grasslands, Colorado,
  209–222, 296
Pelagic birding, 237–249
Pelican, White, 197
Peterson, Ginny, 311
Peterson, Roger Tory, 25–27, 30, 72, 122,
  308–316
Pettingill, Olin Sewall, 69
Pewee, Eastern Wood, 129
Phalarope, Red, 204, 247–248
Phoebe, Eastern, 129
Picelli, Father Tom, 71
Pigeon, Passenger, 285, 286, 301, 302,
  303
  Red-billed, 65, 67
  White-crowned, 44
Pintail, Northern, 38, 220, 289, 292
Pipit, American, 132, 177, 179
  Olive Tree, 149
  Sprague's, 193
Pishing, 10–11
Pittman-Robertson Federal Aid in Wild-
  life Restoration Act, 288
Plover, Black-bellied, 304
  Mountain, 215, 218–219, 221
  Semipalmated, 48, 177
  Wilson's, 48
Point Pelee National Park, Ontario, 105–
  118, 171
Pough, Richard, 121, 273
Prairie dogs, 220

Price, Connie, 190
Proctor, Noble, 153, 154, 155–156, 157
Prudhoe Bay, Alaska, 321
Ptarmigan, Rock, 177
  Willow, 206

# R

Radis, Rick, 120–141
Rail, King, 126, 127
  Virginia, 126, 191
  Yellow, 193–196
Raven, Common, 321
  White-necked, 67, 73
Redpoll, Hoary, 178, 204, 206
Redstart, American, 114, 253, 254, 256,
  257, 268
Ricketts, Ed, 239
Rio Grande Valley Birding Hotline, 71, 72
Rio Grande Valley, Texas, 55–73, 92
Robbins, Chandler and Helen, 84
Robin, American, 26, 170–171, 173–174,
  325
  Clay-colored, 58–59, 61, 72
Roosevelt, Franklin Delano, 100, 109
Roosevelt, Teddy, 20, 109
Rosefinch, Common, 161, 163
Rosenband, Jerry, 148, 153, 156, 157,
  158–159
Rosenberg, Gary, 191
Rowlett, John, 188
Rowlett, Rose Ann, 188
Roy, Kayo, 162
Russell, Will, 191

# S

Sacramento National Wildlife Refuge,
  California, 283–290
Sanderling, 71, 304